Obser\
at G

Observing Hancock at Gettysburg

The General's Leadership through Eyewitness Accounts

PAUL E. BRETZGER

McFarland & Company, Inc., Publishers

Jefferson, North Carolina

LIBRARY OF CONGRESS CATALOGUING-IN-PUBLICATION DATA

Names: Bretzger, Paul E., 1965– author.
Title: Observing Hancock at Gettysburg : the general's leadership through
    eyewitness accounts / Paul E. Bretzger.
Description: Jefferson, North Carolina : McFarland & Company, Inc.,
    Publishers, 2016. | Includes bibliographical references and index.
Identifiers: LCCN 2015048995 | ISBN 9780786499786 (softcover : acid
    free paper) ∞
Subjects: LCSH: Gettysburg, Battle of, Gettysburg, Pa., 1863. | Hancock,
    Winfield Scott, 1824–1886—Military leadership. | Generals—United
    States—Biography.
Classification: LCC E475.53 .B847 2016 | DDC 973.7/349—dc23
LC record available at http://lccn.loc.gov/2015048995

BRITISH LIBRARY CATALOGUING DATA ARE AVAILABLE

On the cover: Major General Winfield S. Hancock, Washington, D.C.
Campbell Photo Service, between 1861 and 1865 (Library of Congress);
background image Gettysburg National Park (© 2016 Bill Dowling/iStock)

Printed in the United States of America

*McFarland & Company, Inc., Publishers
    Box 611, Jefferson, North Carolina 28640
    www.mcfarlandpub.com*

To my parents, Judy and Don

Table of Contents

Acknowledgments

First thanks must go to my parents, Judy and Don, for taking me to Gettysburg and inspiring my childhood imagination. Then the department of Historical Studies at Stockton University, as it was when I graduated in 1987 (then "Stockton State College"), has my highest gratitude for fostering in me the discipline of historical method. Professors Richard Elmore and William Lubenow were of particularly positive influence and encouragement.

The seemingly endless collection at the New York Public Library put an enormous array of diverse sources within walking distance. Other institutions that were particularly essential before the proliferation of the internet include the Civil War Library and Museum of Philadelphia and, of course, the library at Gettysburg National Military Park. The Historical Society of Montgomery County in Norristown, Pennsylvania, Hancock's home town, was both an early and last minute resource. The staffs at all these and other institutions were helpful and courteous without fail. Groups such as the Civil War Round Table of New York and the Gettysburg Discussion Group provided company when it seemed I was alone with my interest in the Civil War and Gettysburg in particular. I will not forget the kind encouragement Al Gambone, author of *Hancock at Gettysburg ... and beyond,* provided me despite knowing we would be, in some sense, competitors. I met another biographer of Hancock, David Jordan (*Winfield Scott Hancock: A Soldier's Life*), at a book signing. He will not remember me, but his clear and detailed depiction of the general's life has served as a reference and guide to me for twenty years.

By far the most essential acquaintance to me in the creation of this book is my brother Bill. An accomplished professional photographer, he not only created some of the illustrations herein, but encouraged and advised me throughout the process, keeping me abreast of current events in the Civil War community and making me aware of new sources and similar research as they emerged.

Introduction:
Who Was Winfield Scott Hancock?

... children will recite at school the story of Hancock at Gettysburg....[1]
— Brevet Colonel Basil Norris, 1886.

On the afternoon of 2 July 1863, the Union's Army of the Potomac was fighting for its life, and losing. Outside Gettysburg Pennsylvania, northern territory, the army was being pushed back and broken down. A determined Confederate assault had ruined the Union Third Corps, leaving a gap one half mile wide in its place. Robert E. Lee's Army of Northern Virginia smelled victory as it raced into the breach.

Meanwhile, Union Major General Winfield Scott Hancock rode about the jeopardized ground, desperately searching for troops to stop the surging Confederates. Amid the dense smoke and the din of artillery, musketry, and the anguished cries of men, Hancock scampered out to address an approaching line of soldiers. He assumed they were retreating Federals until, when he got within very short range, they fired at him, twice hitting his one remaining aide.[2]

Hancock had always exuded calm and confidence during crises, but now the situation was grave. After fleeing the advancing Confederates, he frantically sought a friendly force to counter them. He found but one regiment, the First Minnesota Volunteers, numbering less than three hundred. The charging Confederates were several times that number, but Hancock did not hesitate. He galloped to the regiment's commander and shouted, "Advance, Colonel, and take those colors!"[3] Despite the inevitability of great loss, Colonel William Colvill, Jr., led the Minnesotans ahead on the double-quick

Their audacious charge staggered the Confederate advance for a few short minutes. But the delay was just enough time for the Federals to gather scattered units and mend the vast broken section of battle line. Hancock had ordered

1

the Minnesotans to a ghastly sacrifice. Some accounts place the casualty rate of that charge as high as 82 percent.[4] But Hancock did not regret his order:

> I had no alternative but to order the regiment in. We had no force on hand to meet the sudden emergency. Troops had been ordered up and were coming on the run, but I saw that in some way five minutes must be gained or we were lost. It was fortunate that I found there so grand a body of men as the First Minnesota. I knew they must lose heavily and it caused me pain to give the order for them to advance, but I would have done it if I had known that every man would be killed. It was a sacrifice that must be made. The superb gallantry of those men saved our line from being broken. No soldiers, on any field, in this or any other country, ever displayed grander heroism.[5]

Hancock had shown several great qualities in this one brief but critical episode. He was alert, courageous, and decisive. He was desperate, yet poised. He realized the gravity of the situation. The First Minnesota was clearly a brave group, but few soldiers ever hesitated in the face of Hancock's quick, determined manner.

The confluence of Hancock and the First Minnesota at that moment was critical to the Union cause. General Abner Doubleday, who was on the field at Gettysburg, would later note:

> On the second day, when Anderson's division pierced our centre, Hancock checked them by ordering a desperate charge in which the First Minnesota sacrificed itself for the common good ... he thus saved the army from being cut in two.[6]

But this was just one of countless moments at Gettysburg when Hancock's presence had proven so fruitful. Said Brevet Brigadier General William Burns "...to General Hancock the Nation owes the victory of the battle of Gettys-

Hancock the Superb at the height of his physical virtue (Library of Congress reproduction number LC-DIG-cwpb–05825).

burg ... but for him it would have been lost!"[7] He received widespread accolades for his work. Winfield Scott Hancock was a household name in his day. His national reputation was so great that the press and the public called him "Hancock the Superb." The flattering alias, and the fact that Hancock became the Democratic party's nominee for President in 1880, illustrate the extent of his fame.

Ulysses S. Grant, commander of all Union armies and two-term President of the United States, remembered near the end of his life "Hancock stands the most conspicuous figure of all the generals who did not exercise a separate command."[8] When Grant died in 1885, the parade carrying his body from New York's City Hall to the burial site featured President Grover Cleveland and his cabinet, the Supreme Court, senators, congressmen and other dignitaries, but it was Hancock who led the contingent. When Hancock died in 1886, the *New York Evening Post* declared "No soldier on either side of the late great conflict of arms commanded more fully the admiration and love of his fellow-countrymen."[9] The *New York Herald* observed "No soldier known to this country ever approached in popularity, in wide-horizoned public favor, [Hancock]."[10]

While Hancock's fame arose from several great battles of the Civil War, and continued to solidify after the war in both the military and political arenas, Gettysburg remained the centerpiece of his career. There are several reasons for this. First, Hancock had greater authority and discretion at Gettysburg than he had on any other field of the Civil War. On the battle's first day, Major General George Gordon Meade, commanding the Army of the Potomac from his headquarters at Taneytown, Maryland, sent Hancock to Gettysburg, in effect, to command all Union forces present. Hancock's temporary responsibility for the entire field was therefore more like an army commander than his regular position as commander of a single corps. The following day and arguably on the battle's third day as well, Meade gave Hancock similar authority over units beyond Hancock's regular command.

Furthermore, Hancock did more than just *hold* special authority at Gettysburg, he *exercised* it to make decisions critical to Union victory. On the first day of battle, Hancock transformed the fleeing and defeated troops into a solid, organized body and placed them in a strong position. On the second day, he repeatedly met dire crises with fast, appropriate, and perhaps brilliant tactical dispositions. Then, the third day saw Hancock repulse the grand Confederate assault known as Pickett's Charge, a surge considered "the high water mark of the Rebellion." There Hancock paid for his bravery by receiving a wound that almost proved fatal.

Finally, the battle of Gettysburg was the centerpiece of his career because it was the centerpiece of the Civil War. It was the largest and deadliest. The public on both sides immediately recognized its importance. Historians today still view it as a seminal moment in American history, if not the turning point of our Civil War. Hancock is a player who rendered his greatest performance at the biggest moment.

Many eyewitnesses and other Hancock contemporaries testified to the importance of him at Gettysburg. Hancock's friend and once fellow member of the Army of the Potomac Major General William B. Franklin said of him "I think he was distinctly the hero of that battle."[11] Hancock subordinate and intrepid brigade commander Samuel S. Carroll stated quite simply "He was, next to the commanding general, the prominent man at Gettysburg."[12]

Some commentators predicted increasing fame and legendary status for Hancock. Major General Daniel Sickles wrote "…his renown is associated with events in the annals of the American Republic which history will make imperishable."[13] One of Hancock's political supporters and contemporary biographer, G. B. Herbert, went so far as to say "His name and fame are as inseparably interwoven with the history of this great Republic as are those of the immortal George Washington."[14]

However, Hancock's fame eventually eroded and essentially dissipated. As the Civil War became more distant, and other conflicts occurred, the national psyche turned to other soldiers for legend: Teddy Roosevelt, Pershing, Patton, Eisenhower, and MacArthur. Even George Armstrong Custer, who never attained a level of accomplishment approaching Hancock's, would supersede Hancock in legend with his blunderous death.

While historians and Civil War buffs remember the likes of Hancock, Stuart, Cleburne, Sheridan, Forrest and many others, popular consciousness has reduced the pantheon of Civil War generalship to the quartet of Lee, Jackson, Grant, and Sherman. This is not to say that the national collective memory is unjust or inconsistent in its selectivity. The mere rank of Grant and Lee as top soldiers for their respective countries earns them their status. Their accomplishments further justify their legend. Meanwhile, Jackson and Sherman each had unparalleled impact as confidants to the supreme commanders.

Hancock was never as close to the supreme commander as Sherman and Jackson were. He never had independent command of an army. He came close, but lost his presidential bid in 1880. He was, in many ways, always a bridesmaid but never a bride; or, as Hancock biographer Glenn Tucker put it "Second in War, Second in Peace."[15] Yet, Hancock's absence from the modern public consciousness does not make his deeds less important to the course of history. This book seeks to reclaim Hancock's true historical importance and explain the qualities he had that enabled him to be so important.

This study of Hancock at Gettysburg renders other benefits. For instance, it makes conclusions about many of Gettysburg's lingering controversies, including Confederate General Ewell's alleged missed opportunity, the Hancock-Howard controversy, the Sickles question, the Hancock-Hunt debate, and more. Also, this discussion gives a new view of the battle that might provide some clarity to the complex myriad of events. Finally, the story itself is a drama so compelling as to be worthy of legend.

1

Prologue

I am disposed to believe that this period of Hancock's life was passed to even better advantage than if it had comprised active operations, on the large scale, against a powerful enemy.[1]
—Francis Amasa Walker

A brief look at Hancock's background is a way to begin understanding the abilities that made Hancock so well suited for Gettysburg. First, it is worthy to recognize what Hancock's story is *not*. Unlikely biographies fill the pages of history. Napoleon's Corsican accent and early difficulty with the French language, make his ultimate rise seem especially astonishing. Abe Lincoln's physical awkwardness and lack of a formal education belie his historical stature, as do FDR's infirmity and Churchill's early failures. The list of historical figures who overcame seemingly disqualifying conditions is endless.

Winfield Scott Hancock is not one such figure. His story is noticeably void of irony and unlikelihood. All indications are that his parents were of what Americans considered solid middle class stock and appropriately Christian virtue. Winfield's youth was apparently as wholesome as anyone would have desired. Even as a youngster, Hancock drew admiration and respect for his intelligence, morality, and leadership. It is important to note the breadth of his aptitude. Young Winfield was successful in a myriad of arenas and disciplines, not just a few that one would expect from a career soldier and fiery combat leader. Hancock was a very complete young man.

Besides a strong grasp of Christianity, Hancock succeeded in the study of many of the physical sciences, including chemistry, geology, and electricity.[2] He was creative, even artistic, and skilled in the art of rhetoric. He followed contemporary political discussion. He was honest, personable, and popular. Although his unusual neatness and penchant for leadership seem to, in hindsight, point toward a military career, it is important to note that he intended to follow his father's footsteps and become a lawyer.[3]

The depth of Hancock's virtue contributed greatly to his battlefield success. So to better understand the diversity of character that helped make Hancock so successful at Gettysburg, one should understand the origins of that diversity.

A Cadet Is Born

On 14 February 1824, Elizabeth Hancock, wife of Benjamin Franklin Hancock, gave birth to identical twin boys. The place was Montgomery Square, Pennsylvania, some twenty miles outside Philadelphia. The couple named one boy Hilary Baker and the other Winfield Scott. The family moved to another Montgomery Square home a year later and then, when the boys were at age four, to the Montgomery County seat of Norristown, Pennsylvania.[4] Benjamin

Undated photograph of the birthplace of Winfield Scott Hancock and his identical twin brother, Hilary Baker Hancock (from the collection of the Historical Society of Montgomery County).

The Hancock family home in Norristown, Pennsylvania (from the collection of the Historical Society of Montgomery County).

Franklin Hancock had been a school teacher but was seeking a career in law, and gained admittance to the bar in 1828.[5] This probably explains the second move.

Squire Hancock wore many hats. Besides being a deacon in the Baptist church in Norristown and the Superintendent at the Baptist Sunday School, he soon became a Trustee of the Norristown Academy, a member of the Norristown School Board, and in 1841, won election as town Burgess.[6]

Elizabeth, whose maiden name was Hoxworth, was a farmer's daughter. She opened a milliner's shop in the Norristown home to supplement the family income.[7] She gave birth to a third son, John, when the twins were six.[8]

The twins attended school regularly through high school, joining the Norristown Academy when it was founded.[9] While the two seemed inseparable, Winfield began to develop more as a leader. Sometime between age seven and twelve, he began leading the local boys in a militia marching company.[10] He became a central figure in the Youth's Improvement Society of Norristown.[11] The local adults appreciated Winfield's presence as much as his peers. They chose him, at age fifteen, to read aloud the Declaration of Independence for Norristown's Independence Day celebration.[12] In the following February 1840, Benjamin Franklin Hancock submitted an application for Winfield to attend West Point. That 31 March, Winfield accepted a conditional appointment to the Academy.[13] Winfield Scott Hancock officially began his military career when he entered West Point as a cadet on 1 July 1840, exactly twenty-three years before he rode onto the field at Gettysburg as a Major General.

Cadet Becomes a Soldier

He was sixteen years old, five feet five inches tall, and separated from his family (most notably his twin brother) for the first time.[14] His academic accomplishments were modest as he graduated eighteenth out of a class of twenty-five on 30 June 1844. But by then he had become a six foot two inch model of a man, and very popular among his classmates. He joined the Sixth United States Regular Infantry, becoming a brevet second lieutenant. He became a full second lieutenant in 1846.[15] His initial posts were Fort Towson and then Fort Washita in present day Oklahoma. Despite being on the Indian Frontier, however, they were relatively quiet stations, not visited by significant events during Hancock's stay.

When the Mexican War began in spring 1846, he began an anxious, frustrating, year-long campaign to join the action. But he had been assigned to recruiting activities, and apparently his own success in these tasks helped cause the army to deny his repeated applications for transfer to the front. His recruiting duties led him on various trips through Kentucky, Ohio, Missouri, and likely other western posts, but they left him estranged from the Sixth United States Regular Infantry, which had gone off to Mexico.[16] It was not until 31 May 1847, that the army ordered Winfield to lead a group of recruits to Mexico, where he was to rejoin the Sixth.[17]

His departure from Cincinnati for the front on 21 June began a flurry of activity that would go largely uninterrupted until the end of the war. He arrived at Vera Cruz, a coastal city held by the Americans, on 13 July.[18] The next day he left with a detachment under Brigadier General Franklin Pierce to join the main army at Puebla.[19] Upon reaching there on 6 August he reunited with the Sixth Infantry.[20]

He had seen some small skirmishes on the road to Puebla, but it was not until rejoining the Sixth that Hancock encountered the first sharp fighting of his spectacular military career. On 20 August, Hancock was part of a group that pursued a Mexican contingent to a strong defensive position at Churubusco.[21] There the Sixth Infantry took part in an impetuous, and ultimately successful, assault. He received a slight wound below the knee, but pressed on. All indications are that he took to the fight with a seemingly natural vigor, and thereafter received a brevet promotion to first lieutenant for distinguished conduct.[22]

On 7 September Hancock led a company in a successful fight for a fortified building called Casa Mata. The command had devolved on him when the previous commander fell seriously wounded. That wounding was one of many that attest to the severity of the fight that day as half the officers and almost a third of the men in Hancock's brigade were lost.

Still, the army pressed on.[23] The next day Hancock took part in the taking of a neighboring fortress, the Molino del Rey.[24]

Hancock was ill when the army took nearby Chapultepec castle.[25] This did not seem to detract from the seemingly unanimous contention that Hancock performed splendidly throughout the campaign, and that combat leadership appeared natural for him.[26] He recovered in time for the march into Mexico City itself, an event that effectively ended the shooting war. He took full advantage of the ensuing period of peaceful occupation. As a soldier the young lieutenant became regimental quartermaster.[27] As a tourist he savored the pleasures of Mexico's food, landscape, and ladies. He shared much of this happy time with a couple buddies, First Lieutenant Lewis A. Armistead and Second Lieutenant Henry Heth, both of Virginia.[28]

A Soldier in Peacetime

The period between the Mexican and Civil Wars, although relatively peaceful, was full of activity for the young, but by then experienced soldier. Even in a time of such crude transportation, a military career demanded constant relocation to and from distant corners of the still unsettled country. Despite the arduous demands of this lifestyle, Winfield would find time to take a bride and start a family. The Sixth Infantry returned to the St. Louis area but quickly received orders to move to Fort Crawford at Prairie du Chien, Wisconsin. Before leaving St. Louis, however, Heth and Hancock made quite a play for the local ladies. On the eve of their departure they procured the services of the regimental band to serenade their various love interests. As the band finished a number in front of one particular home, the young lady inside dropped a glove to the street to show her appreciation.[29]

Hancock was not at Fort Crawford long before he volunteered to accompany Heth, who had become gravely ill, back to Heth's home in Richmond. On the way, Heth made an unexpected recovery. So upon reaching Washington, D.C., Hancock headed back to Ft. Crawford as his comrade made toward home on his own.[30] Hancock became regimental adjutant and aide-de-camp to Sixth Infantry commander General Newman S. Clarke on October 1, 1849. Shortly thereafter the unit moved back to the Jefferson Barracks, outside of St. Louis.[31]

The Soldier Starts a Family

It was then that Major Don Carlos Buell introduced Hancock to Almira Russell, one of the most desirable ladies in St. Louis. She was the one who had earlier shown her approval of the tactically sophisticated serenade that Hancock helped organize. A storybook romance fast developed and came to full fruition when Winfield and Almira married on 24 January 1850. The lieutenant was twenty-five, she was eighteen.[32]

On October 29, 1850, Allie gave birth to a son, who the couple named "Russell" in honor of the young mother's lineage.[33] The demands of Hancock's military career did not ease for the added charge of supporting a family, as the army continued to relocate the Hancocks time and again. In 1851, they followed as General Clarke moved his station from St. Louis proper back to the nearby Jefferson Barracks.[34] In 1855 they followed the general back to the town as Winfield became assistant adjutant-general for the Department of the West.[35] In November of that year Hancock became a captain in the Quartermaster's

The career of West Point graduate Winfield Scott Hancock (top left) was slow in developing, owing greatly to his mediocre academic rank. He posed with his son, Russell (top right), born in 1850. Daughter Ada (bottom left) was born in 1857 at Fort Myers, Florida. His marriage to Almira (bottom right) lasted from 1850 to the end of his life (all images from *Reminiscences of Winfield Scott Hancock*, 1887, courtesy Digital Scanning).

Department. A new assignment to Fort Myers, Florida ensued in February of 1856.[36]

The stint in Florida was dangerous. Not only was the area a swampy wilderness, but the army was in hostilities against the Seminole Indians.[37] Still, Almira gave birth on 24 February 1857. "In this forsaken country, prodigal only in the number and variety of venomous snakes and insects of every kind," Almira later wrote, "our sweet child Ada was born."[38] The fact that Ada was said to be the first white child born at Fort Myers illustrates the depth of frontier isolation at the fort.[39]

As quartermaster Hancock kept the base well supplied despite its isolation. So General William Harney, one of the most prominent officers of the antebellum army, procured Hancock's services for his new assignment at Fort Leavenworth, Kansas. It was a relief to leave the unpleasant surroundings of Fort Myers, but relocating his growing family must not have been easy.[40] He was only at Fort Leavenworth some nine months before he was on the move again. But this time, Hancock's family got to stay put. Hancock helped plan an expedition under General Harney to reinforce the contingent sent to settle the Mormon crisis in Utah. He left with the column of 1,500 men in May 1858.[41]

Authorities reached a peaceful settlement, so the army had little to do when it reached Salt Lake City on 26 June.[42] Hancock found shortly thereafter that he would be rejoining the Sixth Infantry at Fort Bridger in what is now Wyoming. From there, he served as quartermaster on a march to Benicia, California that took from 21 August to 15 November. Then, he quickly obtained leave to meet his family back on the east coast and bring them to his new post in California.[43] They had a particularly difficult trip from New York to San Francisco, where they arrived on 23 May 1859, only to find they were to head south to Los Angeles instead of nearby Benicia.[44] In Los Angeles Winfield served as quartermaster for the southern district of California.[45]

Duty Trumps Friendship

The next two years were the lull before the storm for Captain Hancock. In Los Angeles, he found himself amidst a predominantly civilian population. However, the election of 1860 precipitated rancorous debate between federal and states rights sympathizers. Many of Hancock's military pals were with him then, and many of them were southern, including George Pickett, Richard Garnett, and Lewis Armistead.[46] Lincoln's victory and the firing on Fort Sumter precipitated the resignation of these friends and a teary farewell party at the Hancock household. Hancock was a Democrat, and held some sympathy for southern grievances, but was a steadfast unionist. In the spring of 1861 he was critical in holding together the federal garrison and maintaining California's loyalty to the union, which was in serious question.[47] One of his staffers and biographers, Francis Amasa Walker, later wrote the young soldier had made the most of the relative peacetime between the Mexican and Civil Wars:

> I am disposed to believe that this period of Hancock's life was passed to even better advantage than if it had comprised active operations, on the large scale, against a powerful enemy.[48]

Winfield was anxious to be where the action was. So he, as he had in the early days of the Mexican War, issued a barrage of requests to be transferred there. Relief came on 3 August when he received orders to proceed to Washington, D.C.[49]

Hancock Gets a Command

By the time he arrived there his friend George B. McClellan had obtained command of the army. The General-in-Chief recognized Hancock's skills and on 23 September 1861, Hancock became a brigadier-general of volunteers. He got command of the Third Brigade of General William Farrar (Baldy) Smith's Third Division in what would become the Fourth Corps.[50]

Hancock had prepared himself for war well in the first part of his career, a topic to be discussed in greater detail shortly. For now, let it be known that he quickly, tirelessly, and effectively endeavored to manifest that preparedness on his green brigade. His unit, camped just south of Washington, spent the ensuing fall and winter training for the campaign that was surely coming in the spring.[51]

The Fourth Corps made its departure on what would be known as the Army of the Potomac's "Peninsula Campaign" on 23 March 1862. While McClellan over-cautiously laid siege to lightly defended works at Yorktown, Hancock's brigade took part in just a few skirmishes. It was not until the battle of Williamsburg that Hancock's brilliance became apparent. On 5 May, east of Williamsburg, Hancock was to advance on the Confederate left as Union General Joseph Hooker struggled to take Fort Magruder. The brigadier found little to no resistance on his expedition until he realized he had flanked the fort and the Confederate army itself. Stiff resistance came only from his own superiors, however, as General Edwin Sumner, unaware of the opportunity Hancock had found, ordered him to withdraw. Hancock was in a dilemma between his military discipline and his realization that to withdraw would be to waste a grand opportunity for the whole army.

A tense period where Hancock flirted with insubordination ensued. He refused to move and sent several dispatches to his superiors futilely pleading his case. Then, relief came in the form of an attack against Hancock's force by Confederate General Jubal Early's brigade.[52] Withdrawal became impossible, but Hancock still had to win the fight, or his preceding obstinacy might have ruined his career.

Win the fight he did, and he did so with tactical brilliance. Not only did he execute a repositioning that the enemy mistook for a withdrawal, he then led a beautifully timed counterattack that sent Early's men fleeing.[53]

McClellan praised Hancock both for understanding the importance of his flanking position and conducting a highly successful engagement. The next day McClellan wired to Mrs. McClellan that "Hancock was superb yesterday."[54] The press seized on this and thus was born the title "Hancock the Superb."[55]

As McClellan famously lost the initiative of the campaign to the newly installed Confederate commander, Robert E. Lee, Hancock's brigade had a relatively few, relatively light engagements. All were successful, however. Hancock maintained the excellent repute he had gained at Williamsburg.[56] Following McClellan's aborted Peninsula Campaign was the even starker failure of General Pope's Army of Virginia at Second Bull Run. Hancock had little to do with that engagement, but the role he did play is indicative of his character. He selflessly accepted a late night plea by railroad man Colonel Herman Haupt to lead his unit in escort of a supply train headed for General Pope. Once again, the brigadier had demonstrated his enthusiasm and intuitive ability to be a military asset.[57] It was the end of August 1862.

At Antietam, 17 September, McClellan supported his words about Hancock with action. The commander of the Second Corps' First Division, Israel Richardson, fell mortally wounded. Despite the fact that the unit was in the center of the battle, and Hancock was a brigadier from a different corps, McClellan personally placed Hancock in command of Richardson's division.[58] The new division commander seemed to take naturally to his new and expanded responsibility. He had neither experience as a division commander nor familiarity with the men he now led. Yet, his confidence and bearing gained him immediate recognition as the man in charge.[59] It would not be the last time he exerted such influence so quickly and positively in a new command.

To make his rank appropriate to his command, Hancock became a major general of volunteers on 29 November.[60] He remained with the Second Corps until very nearly the end of the war, and it was that unit with which his name would become indelibly associated. It was also under Hancock that the First Division would perform some of the most tragically courageous fighting with which it became associated. Among the most famous of such deeds was the charge Hancock's division made on 13 December 1862 against the stone wall on Marye's Heights. The new commander of the Army of the Potomac, Ambrose Burnside, had stumbled into a nearly hopeless assault at the battle of Fredericksburg.

Although the First Division was a key participant in the futile effort of Fredericksburg, Hancock had actually protested against the planned attack to Burnside himself.[61] Hancock's resistance was as futile as the assault itself, though not as valiant.

Hancock arranged his three brigades, those of Generals Samuel K. Zook, Thomas F. "Meagher of the Sword" Meagher, and John C. Caldwell outside the town of Fredericksburg. Facing an impregnable position, they moved one after the other and lost over 2,000 of the 5,000 they carried into the fight.[62]

After Fredericksburg the First Division went into winter quarters. Its commander took leave to spend some time with Almira and the kids in St. Louis.[63] He returned to the army and, in the months preceding the 1863 spring campaign, went to work restoring the material and spirit of his beleaguered division.[64] For St. Patrick's Day, Meagher's "Irish Brigade" held a steeplechase race followed by a boisterous party.[65] Perhaps this is evidence that Hancock's restoration effort had been successful.

The last major engagement before the Gettysburg campaign was the battle of Chancellorsville. Chancellorsville, fought on the first three days of May 1863, will always elicit interest in the daring of Lee and the inexplicable paralysis of Joseph Hooker, the Army of the Potomac's latest commander. But for the First Division of the Second Corps, it was a heroic, if not brilliant, rear guard action. On 2 May, Hancock's men performed successful defensive actions along with their neighbors on the Union line.[66] By morning of 3 May, however, they found themselves alone, the last division covering the retreat of the army. Despite having to split his division to fight opposite directions simultaneously, Hancock held until the army was safe and he was able to extricate the division.[67]

The Stage Is Set for Gettysburg

Darius Couch, who replaced Sumner as Second Corps commander after Antietam, was so disgusted with General Hooker that he gained reassignment from the Army of the Potomac.[68] Hancock was the obvious replacement. He took command of the Second Corps on 10 June 1863.[69]

Shortly after Chancellorsville, General Lee decided to take advantage of his startling string of victories by invading the north. On 28 June, as the opposing armies maneuvered for position while moving into Maryland and Pennsylvania, Major General George Gordon Meade received an order from President Lincoln placing him in command of the Army of the Potomac.[70] Meade was a fellow Pennsylvanian and a friend of Hancock. Meade clearly admired, and perhaps revered, the corps commander he now commanded. In December 1862 Meade's son, who was on the general's staff, observed his father and Hancock in a brief meeting. After Hancock left, the son asked his father who was the man with whom his father had been speaking. He later recalled "I well remember the hearty intonation of voice with which General Meade replied to my question- 'Why, don't you know who that is? why, that's Hancock.' These were truly brothers-in-arms."[71]

The effect of their relationship on the campaign took a dramatic turn on 1 July 1863. General Meade appeared at Hancock's headquarters with dire news and extraordinary orders. He related that the left wing of the army was heavily engaged at Gettysburg and that its commander, General John Reynolds, had been either killed or mortally wounded. He ordered Hancock, who barely had three weeks experience leading a corps, to proceed to the front and take command of the field. Hancock was thirty-nine. He had over two decades of military training and experience from West Point to Mexico and from Florida to California. Now he returned to his native state as a major general and corps commander for what became the greatest battle of the American Civil War.

With a battle imminent, the appointments of Meade and Hancock to new levels of responsibility may have seemed ill-timed. But when the armies did collide at Gettysburg on Wednesday, 1 July, the placement of those men in their respective positions proved utterly serendipitous to the Union cause.

2

Harmonious Systems

... the opening of battle operates with very different results on different organizations. In General Hancock I should say that the nervous, the moral, and the mental systems were all harmoniously stimulated, and that he was therefore at his very best on the field of battle.[1]

—William Farrar (Baldy) Smith. 1886.

It is easy to understand why Meade saw Hancock as a good soldier. Almost everyone did. But reviewing Hancock's qualities in more detail, we can understand why Meade realized that Hancock was extraordinary. The enormously successful service Hancock rendered on each day of the battle of Gettysburg was an event waiting to happen. Hancock was not just at the right place at the right time, he was the right man. In fact, he had been preparing for such an occasion for most of his career. Francis A. Walker, a member of his staff during the Civil War and eventually a chronicler of both Hancock's career and the history of the Second Corps, testified to this:

I doubt if there was an officer in the United States Army who, during that period while political, social, and industrial forces were preparing the war of secession, learned so much that was to become of use when that great occasion came.[2]

Another member of Hancock's staff, Henry Bingham, echoed Walker:

He seemed, however, to have developed traits of character, detail and method during the years 1850 to 1861, specially qualifying him for that larger field of usefulness which at the commencement of the War of the Rebellion he was immediately called upon to enter as a commanding officer.[3]

Bingham continued and reiterated that Hancock's antebellum development was not just substantial but deliberate:

His years since the Mexican War were full of observation, thoughtful reflection and training; all in the direction of his profession and developing his mental powers in a marked degree.[4]

Walker also noted:

> To a man who is trying to do everything in the best possible way, who is study-
> ing his profession, and accumulating experience against the day of larger things,
> nothing is more instructive, enlarging, and strengthening ... than such prelimi-
> nary practice.
> It followed that the outbreak of the war found Hancock singularly well endowed
> and equipped for the responsibilities and duties that were to devolve upon him.[5]

Finally, Walker drove the point home by referring to the period between
the Mexican and Civil Wars as Hancock's "one long term of military education."[6]

That education continued through the Civil War as well. To have developed military skill in such a conflagration is not remarkable. What is remarkable
is that he did it to the exclusion of all political jockeying that was so rampant
in the army at that time. General Franklin later noted:

> ... the secret of his success was, that he, above all professional soldiers of the war,
> from the time that he commanded a brigade until the war was ended, when he
> commanded a corps, realized the fact that the time had arrived when the profes-
> sional soldier had his opportunity and that such an opportunity, if improved,
> would bring distinction. That it was necessary, therefore, to keep an eye single
> to the acquirement of military experience from what he saw going on around
> him- to make no effort to unduly push himself forward,- not to be jealous or dis-
> contented if less worthy men were preferred before him- to be diverted by no
> side issue, but to await events,- in short, to press forward toward the mark of his
> high calling. He felt assured that the day would come, as it did come, when his
> dearly bought experience would serve him, and when his merit would be acknowl-
> edged. His action just before and during the battle of Gettysburg was the looked-
> for opportunity.[7]

The Army of the Potomac was particularly rife with competing political
alliances and personal intrigue. General McClellan had a large and devoted
following within the Army; and Hancock was a personal friend of his. But when
heavy disillusionment with McClellan's removal was in the air (which happened
twice), Hancock expressed his loyalty to the appropriate cause:

> The Army are not satisfied with the change, and consider the treatment of McClel-
> lan most ungracious and inopportune. Yet I do not sympathize in the movement
> going on to resist the order. "It is useless," I tell the gentlemen around me. "We
> are serving no one man: we are serving our country."[8]

He had such revulsion for the internecine scheming in the Army of the
Potomac, that he even expressed, to his wife, objection to being its commander:

> I am told that some of the New York papers recommend General—and Gen-
> eral—for command of the Army. I should ask to be relieved at once.... I have

been approached again in connection with the command of the Army of the Potomac. Give yourself no uneasiness-under no conditions would I accept the command. I do not belong to that class of generals whom the Republicans care to bolster up. I should be sacrificed.[9]

He had developed a wide variety of talents and virtues that contributed to his array of battlefield achievements. Among them were extraordinary *tactical skill*, exemplary military *discipline*, strong *decisiveness* in judgment, and finally, he wrapped all these traits into a persona of great *charisma*.

The Tactician

Military teaching holds that *tactics* are the means through which one achieves the goals of *strategy*. For instance, the intent to capture Richmond is a strategy. The intent to do so by flanking the fortifications outside Williamsburg is a tactic. An example of Hancock's tactical prowess was his conduct at the battle of Williamsburg. First, he recognized that the flanking position of his brigade was such a tactical advantage for the army that he refused to abandon it, even under pressure from his superiors. He then further demonstrated his tactical facilities by maneuvering his unit with such deftness that it threw the oncoming Confederates into a full retreat.

His tactical skill consisted of talent shaped by military training and experience. It is notable that while he finished a lackluster eighteenth out of twenty-five in his West Point class, infantry and artillery tactics were among the subjects at which Hancock proved adept.[10] He seemed to have continued his deliberate study of tactics well after graduation. He obtained several books on military history and on military tactics itself, including Caesar's *Commentaries*, the four volume *History of the War on the Peninsula and in the South of France* by W.F.P Napier, *Life of Wallenstein* and *Thoughts on Tactics, and Military Organization*, both by British Lieutenant Colonel J. Mitchell.[11]

All of the great campaigns he studied required logistical feats, and this was not lost on the young soldier. Logistics is an essential part of military tactics, and logistics is an area where Hancock demonstrated exceptional ability early in his career. In fact, he became a highly valued and commended quartermaster despite a distaste for such duties.[12] Recent biographer David N. Jordan put it well: "Though Winfield Hancock did not want to be a quartermaster, the Quartermaster's Department wanted him."[13] He honed his skills as a provider of supplies to the garrison in St. Louis, which was a relatively easy task because the unit was stationary and St. Louis had become adequately accessible. But in 1856, when he followed his boss, General William Harney, to Fort Myers,

Florida, the location was extremely remote and the troops were engaged in the field. Almira wrote that, despite the great difficulty of the job, her husband succeeded "with apparent ease, and entire satisfaction to each and everyone in authority."[14]

He continued performing quartermaster service as he relocated again and again from the remote southeast in 1856 eventually to California in late 1858.[15] The initial move, being from Fort Myers to Fort Leavenworth in "Bleeding Kansas" came, once again, at the request of General William Harney, who was not about to leave such a master of supply procurement behind.[16] From Kansas to Utah, and then from Fort Bridger (in what is now Wyoming) to California, the young quartermaster did an exemplary job.[17] These were long journeys through rugged country by large parties. One should not underestimate how the ability to prepare and maintain supplies and equipment on such journeys, with great success, demonstrates the man's ability to make proper tactical decisions in and around a battlefield. Walker echoed this sentiment:

> the future commander of the Second Army Corps, of the left wing at Gettysburg and in the Wilderness, was being trained for his high duties by conducting the orders and correspondence of a military department, or by fitting out expeditions of a company or squadron, supplying outlying posts, making long marches ... or conducting the business of a quartermaster's depot on the plains or on the Pacific coast.[18]

Another essential to being a master tactician is a sharp eye. Lieutenant Frank A. Haskell, on General John Gibbon's staff at Gettysburg, recalls that during Pickett's Charge, Hancock's "quick eye, in a flash, saw what was to be done."[19] General John Hartranft, a fellow Montgomery County man and eventual governor of Pennsylvania recalled "his quick, alert, mind."[20] The aforementioned events at Williamsburg and Hancock's handling of the First Minnesota at Gettysburg are further illustrations of the commander's *coupes d'oeil* (quick eye).

He had an aptitude for drawing, which points to an ability to make a fast and accurate assessment of terrain. Drawing was a major part of the West Point curriculum, due in part to the school's focus on engineering.[21] Yet, it is also likely that the academy understood that the act of drawing develops critical observational skills. For instance, drawing promotes the facility to understand space, volume, distance and other elements essential to tactics. Drawing was another area of study where Winfield thrived as a student, thus helping to offset the mediocrity of his overall grades.[22] He had displayed a penchant for drawing since he was a boy. Perhaps he inherited it from his mother, who demonstrated an artistic facility by running a milliner shop out of their house.

At West Point, he crafted many depictions of the academy's picturesque natural and architectural landscapes.[23] He also produced humorous cartoons that would dissuade any misconceptions that the future war hero was just a martinet.[24] Like many of his endeavors, his artwork falls short of genius but demonstrates an unusual aptitude and diligence. It was that diligence which, over time, helped develop his raw facilities for observation into highly accomplished tactical skills. However, it was also diligence which helped earn him a reputation for rigorous discipline.

The Disciplinarian

The hallmark of military discipline is the well-drilled line of soldiers. Hancock's units would be no exception to this. He knew that only the repetition of drill can give large groups of men the ability to maneuver as a single organism. Walker explained:

> In fact, it was with infinite labor that he forged the weapon his hand was to wield with such effect … it was with great care and pains inexpressible that he shaped and tempered it for the conflict.[25]

Walker surmised "No commander ever more carefully prepared in camp for success in the field than did Hancock…."[26]

There was much more to his discipline than standard army drill, however. It was of Hancock's nature and experience as a quartermaster to be extremely meticulous in details such as clerical matters. There is an abundance of testimony by his staff and other acquaintances to his rigorous, even tenacious attention to detail. Staff member E. W. Clark remembered:

> If I recall one trait of Hancock's more than another, I would name his conscientious devotion to details and his thoroughness in the minutiae of affairs. Nothing seemed too trivial to claim his consideration, and yet he did not magnify the minor things to the exclusion of weightier matters. His mind seemed happily formed to take the lesser with the greater; his eye to be equipped with a wonderful sweep for the particulars of a business.[27]

Walker points out that Hancock's emphasis on clerical matters, despite their tedium, was actually essential to his military success:

> … the union of martial and civic functions need not be ludicrous…. Hancock was, perhaps, the greatest hand at "papers" that the army ever knew. Even now my head aches from the long night vigils, when, after some weary march or fight, we pored for hours over reports and returns, and discussed minute points of the regulations apropos of the correspondence appertaining to seventy or ninety regiments and batteries.
>
> It is usual to make flings at this sort of work, and express contempt for "papers" and regulations and red-tape…. [*But Hancock*] deemed it no less important a

part of his duty to study the state of his command through the morning reports and the monthly returns than on parade or review; and he knew that he could administer a tonic to a sickly regiment through the order-book and the letter-book not less effectually than at Sunday-morning inspection.[28]

Elsewhere, Walker observed that:

> In a somewhat protracted experience, I never but once knew the Second Corps, while under his command, no matter how extreme the distance or severe the conditions, by day or by night, arrive at its destination in bad form, straggling and broken; and its marches were often very long and trying....
>
> In the supply of troops, Hancock, as the result of thorough training and down-right hard work ... achieved almost the highest possible success.[29]

W. D. W. Miller, one of Hancock's aides-de-camp, remarked:

> He was a man of great industry, marvelous in his attention to detail, and always, as far as possible, exercised a personal supervision over his own orders.[30]

Even William Tecumseh Sherman, himself not one to be unprepared, echoed Miller's sentiments about Hancock's "personal supervision":

> I sometimes joked him about attending to little details which could have been devolved on his staff, but he insisted on seeing everything to himself.[31]

Lieutenant Colonel Franklin Sawyer commanded the Eighth Ohio Regiment in the Second Corps, and he shows that the general's attention went at least as low as the regimental level:

> Gen. Hancock ... was frequently present at our drills, and had a way of winning the esteem of the men, who believed "our corps" all right in his hands.[32]

The general's thoroughness may or may not have originated in his childhood. Whether the West Point regimen and ensuing military life began or only encouraged it is not obvious. However, that young Winfield had known rigorous personal discipline well before entering the academy is very likely. His family was of the upstanding, dignified and Christian background that was especially respectable in his time. His father's name, Benjamin Franklin Hancock, recalled the local yet world-renowned and enlightened patriot. B.F. Hancock was a figure of local repute for his participation in a myriad of community affairs. The father of twin boys (as well as a third, later) gained admission to the bar when the twins were four. He was a Baptist church deacon, superintendent of the Sunday School, town burgess, trustee of the Norristown Academy, school board member and Collector of Internal Revenue.[33]

The boys' mother, Elizabeth Hoxworth Hancock, had military roots. She had at least one grandfather who fought in both the French and Indian and Revolutionary Wars. Her father also fought in the latter under George Washington.[34] When Winfield received an offer to be nominated for West Point, she agreed to it before her husband.[35]

Upon revisiting his hometown during his later years, Hancock noticed some boys sitting on a fence outside church during a service. He, who had attended church regularly as a boy, concluded that they looked "like so many crows" who, unlike himself, did not have "strong-minded mothers and fathers."[36]

Benjamin Franklin Hancock did not just influence Winfield in a passive, general way. A lawyer, he impressed upon his son the philosophy and values of the law. That Winfield's twin, Hilary, actually became a lawyer is evidence of this. Jordan asserts in his 1988 biography "Winfield the lawyer's son had instilled in him from an early age respect and reverence for the law, for Blackstone and Coke, for the concept of due process, for the Almighty, and for the principles and tenets of the Democratic party."[37] Elsewhere Jordan notes "His father, he knew, had intended that he become a lawyer; at Benjamin's request, the young cadet took Chitty's *Blackstone* to West Point and read it through six times."[38]

Historian Glenn Tucker, who published his Hancock biography in 1960, differs from Jordan only slightly: "As Winfield departed for the Military Academy, his attentive father put two volumes into his valise.... The books were the *Constitution of the United States of America* and Blackstone's *Commentaries*."[39] Tucker later continues "Blackstone whetted his interest in his father's profession. Throughout his life he was continually captivated by the logic of the law."[40]

Years later the general himself indicated how his father's values affected him: "I never knew a man whom I respected as much as my father.... It was due to his character, his appearance, and the method of his life."[41] The point here is that Hancock had a highly disciplined character that derived from his upbringing. However, Tucker notes that this personal philosophy also derives from a pragmatic logic: "The father emphasized this point: since the young man was about to become a soldier, he should know his government. He should understand the principles of civil law and respect them because, said the father, when republics have fallen, generally it has been by soldiers' swords."[42]

It is likely that young Winfield not only received admonitions from "strong minded" parents but that he listened as well. A teacher at the Norristown academy would later recall "I never found a knife-mark on his section of the long, old fashioned, white pine desk, nor was I ever obliged to speak to him about its condition."[43] His deeply rooted habit of discipline greatly influenced the performance of his men on the march, in drill, on the battlefield, and even on paper. But discipline was not the only essential command trait he had displayed as a child. It seems that young Winfield also had a clarity of judgment and confidence that distinguished him from other lads.[44]

The Decisive Leader

His decisiveness not only made him stand by his judgments, they contributed to the personal magnetism and leadership ability that also dated back to his childhood. Denison and Herbert, who published their Hancock biography in 1880, related that:

> It was in this spirit that he obtained that control over other boys, some of them older than himself, that distinguished his boyhood. Very frequently, when juvenile difficulties occurred, and it seemed impossible to adjust them amicably, the general cry would arise:
> "Oh, leave it to Winfield; he'll settle it."[45]

There are several stories to indicate that this courage and confidence in his own judgment dates back to his childhood. For instance, he is said to have steadfastly defended a smaller boy from town bullies who, when confronted by the future war hero's bold intervention, inquired "What business is it to you, Winfield Hancock?" "I will make it my business," he replied. "If you want to take hold of a boy, why don't you find one of my size? Let little Johnny alone!"[46]

In a separate instance, a tumult outside the office of his father caught the attention of the lawyer and his visitor. Winfield had gotten into a brawl. His father managed to call him away from the tumult and ask him what was going on. "Why, that big boy out there, tried to whip me; and *I wasn't going to let him!*" His father reasoned "But he is a great deal larger than you are, my son." "I know he is father, but he shan't whip me, for all that!" Mr. Hancock finally convinced him to cease hostilities, perhaps with the use of some hard-learned legal reasoning.[47]

Another anecdote has Winfield intervening on behalf of a fellow singing-school student who received a soiled songbook. Winfield, whose father ran the session, felt this was unfair. "Leave this matter to me," he told his colleague "I'll see what can be done. You shall have a good book in the place of this." Shortly thereafter, Winfield volunteered to his father that he had erased his colleague's name from the damaged book because he felt the boy deserved better.[48]

Sometimes the boy's resolute decisiveness determined that higher authorities were more apt to settle issues. As the one who emerged leader of the local play militia, he would sometimes turn over a disobedient soldier to the offender's mother.[49] Denison and Herbert reasoned "It not only enabled him to avoid the vexations of a court-martial, but it gave satisfaction to all concerned; for if a good mother cannot bring a soldier to terms, who can?"[50]

His personal convictions were not always in favor of the prevailing authority. Just as he would resolutely stand by his own judgment against his superiors at Williamsburg, he made a stand for his personal fashion sense on the eve of graduation at West Point. It seems that he was not satisfied with the design for his class' post-graduation uniforms. Furthermore he did not approve of alleged nepotism involving the Academy's superintendent and its clothier. Regardless he, as usual, acted positively on his beliefs. First, he lobbied for the superintendent himself to give permission for Hancock to call in the clothier of his choosing. Having failed at that endeavor, the typically determined cadet took it upon himself to solicit the services from a Boston clothier of his liking anyway:

> I have spoken to nearly all of the first class on the subject- and they are anxious that you should make us a visit. I am confident that all of them will patronize you, and I hope you will not disappoint us.[51]

It is not clear if he was ultimately successful in his bid to assert what he felt was his right. Yet he clearly demonstrated the steadfast belief in his own judgment that would ultimately shape historic moments like the battle of Gettysburg. When he made his stand, contrary to orders, at Williamsburg, and when he hurried the First Minnesota to its pyrrhic charge at Gettysburg, he exercised not only his quick eye, but his resolute self assurance as well. As one witness recalled:

> There was a dash to him. What he did he did in a hurry, with his eyes wide open; he didn't wait to consider, he moved right in and won.[52]

His conviction to fairness and reason helped make him the ever-attractive and compelling leader that persuaded powerful, egotistical men and vast throngs of soldiers to act on his every word. But it was more than those things that gave him such authority.

The Charismatic

The most common assertions about Hancock by his contemporaries, next to accounts of his battlefield actions, are those praising his charisma. General W. F. "Baldy" Smith recalled:

> Of his peculiar qualities on the field of battle, I can say that his personal bearing and appearance gave confidence and enthusiasm to his men, and perhaps no soldier during the war contributed so much of personal effect in action as did General Hancock. In the friendly circle his eyes were warm and genial, but in the hour of battle became intensely cold and had immense power on those around him.[53]

Smith's statement cites two distinct spheres of Hancock's magnetism: first, the "personal bearing and appearance" on the battlefield, and second, the "warm and genial" quality Hancock had "in the friendly circle." Nelson Miles, a subordinate of Hancock who eventually rose to command of the United States Army, also recognized the two areas of Hancock's appeal:

> His presence was always dignified and commanding, and though he possessed the indomitable and inflexible spirit of a great commander, yet there throbbed within his manly breast a heart as tender as that of a woman.[54]

General Franklin recognized these separate realms of Hancock's appeal when he noted "His very appearance was inspiring- in action he was Mars himself- and his behavior forced all who saw him to be as one with him" and also that Hancock was "as a man, a loyal and constant and generous friend."[55] Even General Howard, when describing Hancock in the context of a personal disagreement, noted both Hancock's "peculiar, gallant style" as well as his "usual frank and cordial manner."[56]

Most of the tens of thousands he led would not personally meet him, but know him largely as a figure on horseback. Yet, what they did see of him was striking and magnetic. Regarding this, McClellan recalled Hancock's "superb presence."[57] Hancock staffer Henry Bingham wrote:

> Major General Hancock stands six (6) feet one (1) inch in height, had broad square shoulders, with erect and commanding carriage and presence. His splendid personal appearance attracts attention wherever he is seen and doubtless this is one of the adjuncts which gives him such thorough command over troops....
>
> It was his habit to remain mounted at all times on the battle field, and no one who ever saw him on such occasions will forget his chivalrous bearing & knightly appearance, as he rode along his lines encouraging all to stand fast & give no ground.[58]

General Meade's son, George, noted that "His bearing was so striking that it would have prompted anyone, ignorant of who he was, to inquire [as to whom he was]."[59] One observer stated simply that Hancock was "the most superb looking man I ever set eyes upon."[60] Private Ralph Orson Sturtevant of the Thirteenth Vermont, who wrote his regiment's history, raved:

> One of the inspiring and encouraging sights on that field [Gettysburg] was the dash of General Hancock coming down the line near us followed by a single aide or orderly.... No braver man or better fighter or more perfect speciman [sic] of manly beauty and soldierly appearance took part on that field than General Winfield S. Hancock.[61]

Hancock's appearance struck another Vermonter, George Grenville Benedict, in a similar way.

> But my eyes were upon Hancock's striking figure—I thought him the most splendid looking man I ever saw on horseback, and magnificent in the flush and excitement of battle...."[62]

Corporal John Day Smith believed Hancock's presence was so commanding that he need not have had an emblem of rank to get his way:

> General Hancock, the gallant commander of the Second Corps, was the best looking officer in the army. He was tall and well proportioned, had a ruddy complexion, brown hair, and he wore a moustache and tuft of hair upon his chin.... Had General Hancock worn citizen's clothes, his order would have been obeyed anywhere, for he had the appearance of a man born to command.[63]

Although Corporal Smith felt Hancock's regal bearing spoke for itself, the general added to the effect by always dressing the part. First Lieutenant Haskell made the connection between Hancock's manner of dress and his commanding presence:

> Upon horseback, I think he was the most magnificent looking general in the whole Army of the Potomac, at that time. With a large, well shaped person, always dressed with elegance, even upon that field of confusion, he would look as if he was "monarch of all he surveyed," and few subjects would dare to question his right to command, or do aught else but obey.[64]

As if that was not convincing enough, Haskell also observed:

> Hancock is the tallest and most shapely, and in many respects is the best looking officer of them all. His hair is very light brown, straight and moist, and always looks well; his beard is of the same color, of which he wears the moustache and a tuft upon his chin; complexion ruddy, features neither large nor small, but well cut, with full jaw and chin, compressed mouth, straight nose, full, deep blue eyes, and a very mobile, emotional countenance. He always dresses remarkably well, and his manner is dignified, gentlemanly, and commanding.[65]

At Gettysburg, Hancock wore a black felt slouch hat that held its shape and an officer's undress uniform coat buttoned at the top and open at the waist.[66] This unusual manner of buttoning a coat displayed his most remarkable aspect of dress: an always immaculate white shirt. That his shirt seemed perpetually bright white is especially remarkable given the rigors of army life at the time: largely outdoors and on the move in an unpaved world. Credit for the seeming imperviousness to mud and dust goes to Hancock's English valet, "Mr. Shaw."[67] While historian Tucker notes the servant "spent much of his time over the scrubbing board," Jordan notes that Mr. Shaw's intimacy with Hancock's personal effects led him to partake of the general's cigars, drink, and personal papers.[68] Mr. Shaw's licentiousness chagrined Hancock, but the general apparently permitted his behavior.[69] The "monarch of all he surveyed" perhaps reasoned it a fair price for the steady supply of fresh white shirts.

Mr. Shaw was not the only one of the general's acquaintances who benefited from his generosity. Besides the overall geniality noted earlier, Hancock had the rare ability to relate to, on a personal level, even the lowest ranking and most common people who made his acquaintance. John W. Barlow noted:

> No one was so low in his life as to be passed by without a genial, kind remembrance. In enjoying the acquaintance of Gen. Hancock, in meeting him personally, you could not fail to feel that he was personally interested in you[70];

Staff member William P. Wilson agreed that Hancock had a knack for loosening people up in intimate settings, despite his intimidating rank and reputation:

> I can distinctly recall my trepidation on entering his office, and how quickly it was dispelled by his cordial greeting. His kindness at once won my confidence....[71]

Even more important than the warmth he radiated on a personal level was the respect he extended to the new volunteer element of the army at the beginning of the Civil War. Walker recalled that "although a 'regular' in every fiber of his being, Hancock was altogether destitute of that snobbishness regarding volunteers which was exhibited by so many small minds."[72] It seems ludicrous that in an army, which would grow from less than 17,000 to over a million men, anyone would scoff at those who answered the call for volunteers. However, Walker notes that such practice was common and that Hancock would have none of it:

> He recognized the fact that the war was to be waged by volunteers; and that, however much the regular army had to give to the vast masses of earnest soldiers swarming in from East and from West to the defense of the Union, it was, after all, these men who were to bear the heat and burden of the great conflict. He saw that it was of supreme importance to promote the self-respect and self-confidence of volunteer regiments; to lead them to think that they could do anything, and were the equals of anybody; and that to be everlastingly talking about the regular army, bewailing the lack of its methods and forms, instituting odious comparisons, and sneering at the deficiencies of the new troops, was a very poor way of accomplishing that object.
>
> Hancock not only never sneered at volunteers- he did not, incredible as it may seem, even patronize them. He made them feel- by his evident respect, his hearty greeting, his warm approval of everything they did well- that he regarded them as just as fully, just as truly, just as honorably, soldiers of the United States Army as if they had belonged to the old Sixth Infantry.[73]

He also went to great lengths to give credit where it was due. This was especially effective as a managerial tool in the Victorian era, where society placed honor and reputation among its highest values. And army tradition, especially in the intense period of Civil War, elevated this culture of honor to an obsessive level. Whether he did it out of kindness or as a deliberate effort to evoke loyalty and obedience, Hancock's men knew he would recognize their good work. Aide-de-camp Miller wrote:

No commander more fully appreciated the services of his subordinates than Gen. Hancock, none more generous in awarding praise when it was deserved, yet too honest to bestow it when it could not truthfully be given. In his official report he never forgot the good conduct of the orderlies attached to the staff, none were overlooked or forgotten.[74]

He did not limit the accolades in his reports to the headquarters staff. Just a glimpse at any of his reports show that he went to great lengths to acknowledge the work of regiments and their commanders, whose names and titles he always mentioned. After the action that earned him "The Superb" moniker at Williamsburg, he wrote a letter to his wife that included glowing tributes to his men. "On this occasion my men behaved beautifully," he raved, "and captured the first color yet taken. My loss was 126 in killed and wounded, a great number showing hard and determined fighting."[75] Even while incapacitated by the Gettysburg wound that would almost kill him and keep him out of command until winter, Hancock inquired from his bed in Philadelphia as to the identity of a unit which he wanted to credit for gallant service:

> Circular]   Philadelphia, Pa.,
>   July 7, 1863
>
> Major-General Hancock desires to know the designation of a certain regiment, and the name of its commander, belonging to the First, Second, or Twelfth Corps which, at the instance of General Hancock, charged a rebel regiment which had passed through our lines on Thursday evening, 2d instant. The conduct of this regiment and its commander were so marked … that General Hancock desires properly to notice the subject.
>
> By order of Major-General Hancock[76]:

The commander's encouragement came not just in after-action reports, but in the heat of battle as well. During the rear-guard action at Chancellorsville, Hancock was so pleased with the performance of then-Colonel Nelson Miles, that he ordered "Captain Parker, ride down and tell Colonel Miles that he is worth his weight in gold."[77]

Performance Under Pressure

Finally, Hancock had more than the series of disparate qualities detailed above. He had the rare quality we attribute to our greatest champions. He was a clutch performer. That is, he had the uncanny tendency to raise his abilities to their highest level when he needed them most. In an assessment echoing the opening passage of this chapter, a contemporary of his asserted "…he possessed like Marshal Massena the rare faculty of growing more clear-sighted the hotter the battle raged."[78]

When the Gettysburg campaign came around, as the two great armies maneuvered toward their greatest battle, Hancock was ready. His talent, upbringing, training, and experience had prepared him to put his stamp on history. He had an extraordinary combination of *tactical* skill, *discipline, decisiveness,* and *charisma,* as well as a gift for *excelling under pressure.* It is within this context that one will best understand the story of Hancock at Gettysburg.

3

Arrival

*His arrival upon the field of battle was most opportune.
Wreck, disaster, disorder, almost the panic that precedes disorganization, defeat and retreat, were everywhere. He
assumed command; soldiers retreating stopped, skulkers
appeared from under their cover, lines were reformed; in the
language of the writer: "And as the sun showing through a rift
in the clouds may change a scene of gloom to one of beauty,
so this prince of soldiers brings life and courage to all."*[1]

—Henry H. Bingham

Hancock's Second Corps reached Taneytown, Maryland, some thirteen miles south of Gettysburg, and bivouacked at 11:00 a.m. on 1 July 1863. There Hancock visited his new commander and old friend, General Meade.[2]

They discussed what became known as the Pipe Creek line, Meade's plan to arrange the Army of the Potomac in a defensive position roughly along Pipe Creek in Maryland. Meade's belief was that the Pipe Creek line would serve well both strategically and tactically, in that it protected the area of Baltimore and Washington, D.C., and that it would be a very difficult position for Lee to attack. Meade knew that Lee's Army of Northern Virginia sprawled largely north and west of Gettysburg, Pennsylvania, but that the vicinity of his own army had relieved any threat to Philadelphia and the Pennsylvania state capital of Harrisburg.[3]

Upon Hancock's departure from Meade's headquarters, the two men were likely still pondering an upcoming battle of Pipe Creek, not Gettysburg, which would be fought in the vicinity of where he and his corps now stood. However, Meade shortly thereafter got news of an engagement just west of Gettysburg involving Major General John Reynolds' First Corps. He became concerned that Reynolds would fail to cover the road between Gettysburg and Taneytown, an action that would be critical to the development of a line along Pipe Creek.[4]

To relieve this concern Meade issued Hancock a written order to move

Major General George Gordon Meade's equestrian statue stands on Cemetery Ridge. It was owing to his high opinion of Hancock that he sent his fellow Pennsylvanian ahead to take command of the field on 1 July and report back (photograph by William Bretzger).

the Second Corps toward Gettysburg, ensure that the road there is covered, and then retire back to Frizellburg, Maryland, a point roughly along the planned Pipe Creek line.[5] The date of the order was 12:30 p.m.[6]

However, Meade again received word of further developments from Gettysburg. This time he went to Hancock's headquarters himself to issue new orders.[7] The news was jolting. General Reynolds had been either killed or badly wounded.[8] Meade's wishes now were for Hancock to proceed immediately to Gettysburg, without his corps, to take command of the field should the report of Reynolds' disability be true.[9] There were several irregularities in Meade's orders to Hancock. First, Meade knew that General Oliver Otis Howard was at Gettysburg commanding the Eleventh Corps, and that Howard was senior to Hancock. Also, Meade specifically ordered Hancock to place his Second Division leader General John Gibbon in command of the Second Corps while Hancock went to Gettysburg. This put Gibbon above First Division commander John C. Caldwell, who was senior to Gibbon. Hancock pointed out these irregularities but Meade responded that Secretary of War Edwin Stanton had authorized him to make such appointments to command as he saw fit.[10] So Meade stood by the orders. They seemed clear and rational to Hancock but would soon be a source of one of the many controversies of Gettysburg that persist to this day.

Hancock received written orders echoing their verbal discussion dated 1:10 p.m. and a follow up instructing him to hold the Second Corps "ready to move" dated 1:15 p.m.[11] His official report states "at 1:10 o'clock I was on the road to Gettysburg."[12] An eyewitness to Hancock's mission was his inspector general and chief of staff Lieutenant Colonel Charles H. Morgan. Morgan rode with the general to Gettysburg and provides some of the best information about the trip. Morgan wrote that Hancock was "accompanied by his personal staff, and two or three other officers on duty at his headquarters."[13]

Morgan left at least two written observations of Hancock on this initial trip to Gettysburg. The first of Morgan's accounts is a report for historian John B. Bachelder, probably written in 1886, on his experiences at Gettysburg:

> General Hancock left Taneytown within ten minutes of one o'clock. I rode with him the first three or four miles in the ambulance examining the maps and his orders, but the ambulance though driven very rapidly could not keep pace with the General's anxiety, so we took our horses and made as rapid progress as the intense heat of the day would permit. The nature of the ground on either side of the road was continually scanned by the General with a view to the retreat on Pipe Creek, should he deem it advisable.[14]

A second account by Morgan appears as an appendix to *Reminiscences of Winfield Scott Hancock*, the memoir by Winfield's widow published in 1887:

He rode in an ambulance for the first two or three miles, for the purpose of examining the maps and the instructions concerning the proposed formation on Pipe Creek. The rest of the journey was performed at a rapid gait on horseback. The ground was closely scanned by General Hancock as he rode along, with a view of noting the defensive positions which would be available should a retreat be made along the road.[15]

As Hancock and his entourage made their way toward Gettysburg, the situation was thus: Union defenders had been executing a defensive action west of Gettysburg since mid-morning. As the day wore on, the fight grew larger. What started as a chance engagement between two divisions eventually became a conflagration involving about 49,000 men at arms.[16] The action stretched in an arc, clockwise, from Gettysburg's western approaches to the fields north of town.

The Union contingent consisted of the First Division of the Cavalry Corps and the First and Eleventh Corps of infantry. Brigadier General John Buford led the cavalry. Reynolds commanded the First Corps and, by virtue of being commander of the "left wing" of the army, commanded all troops present. Howard commanded the Eleventh Corps until the passing of Reynolds put Howard in command of the entire field. At that point, Major General Carl Schurz ascended to command of the Eleventh Corps. Major General Abner Doubleday took over the First Corps upon Reynolds' death.

Their opposition grew to include various divisions from the Confederate Second and Third Corps. It was Hancock's old friend, Henry Heth, now a Confederate major general commanding a division, who had begun the engagement with an advance on Buford's dismounted cavalry. The grim reality of the battle reached Hancock well before he got to Gettysburg. Morgan describes:

> Four or five miles from Gettysburg we met an ambulance containing a dead body wrapped in a blanket and escorted by a single staff officer. The General asked whose body it was and was answered "General Reynold's, sir." We rode in silence.[17]

Hancock found little other evidence of a raging battle until he got quite close to it. As he described it, the odd silence seems to have been due to what we now refer to as an "acoustic shadow":

> Owing to the peculiar formation of the country, or the direction of the wind at the time, it was not until we had come within a few miles of the field that we heard the roar of the conflict then going on.[18]

It would not be long, however, before the first living refugees from the battle of Gettysburg prompted Hancock into action. Said Morgan:

> Near Gettysburg the road began to be blocked up with trains, which on inquiry proved to belong to the Eleventh Corps.... They were ordered peremptorily to the rear by General Hancock.[19]

The new corps commander had made his first major order at the battle of Gettysburg:

That order, though seemingly routine and not directly affecting action on the battlefield, is of some significance. First, it illustrates Hancock's vigilance and attention to logistics and detail. Morgan derisively noted that the Eleventh Corps' "trains and pack animals had contributed no little to the stampede at Chancellorsville."[20] In other words, Hancock was clearing the escape route from Gettysburg in a positive effort to avoid disorder, should the two corps need to retreat. Second, the order to move those support wagons to the rear indicates that Hancock was still operating under the guide of the Pipe Creek plan. Any decision to stay at Gettysburg still would have required a bold conclusion that the unplanned conditions there were more advantageous than the safety of the comparatively well-planned Pipe Creek line. Third, Hancock's direct instructions to Eleventh Corps elements demonstrate that he was superseding General Howard who was, by ordinary procedure, senior to Hancock. This is pertinent because a controversy would quickly develop over who had command on that first day of battle and, therefore, who would get credit for the eventual victory at Gettysburg.

The removal of wagons and pack animals from the vicinity of Gettysburg was a footnote compared to the work that lay ahead. Hancock soon ascended Cemetery Hill. There he began forty-eight hours of combat leadership that would define his career and alter the battle to an extent that was arguably more substantial than any figure on the Union side.

When Hancock reached the top of Cemetery Hill, he could see the town in the shallow valley below and the first day's battlefield on the gentle ridges beyond. His arrival there precipitated his controversial meeting with General Howard. In short, the controversy over what transpired between Hancock and Howard when they met is overrated and moot. While many attribute great import to the question of who officially held command of the field, the overwhelming evidence is that Hancock is the one who the *soldiers recognized* as being in command.

Hancock met Howard shortly after he crested the hill. Descriptions of their conversation vary enormously. But there is no question regarding what happened when Hancock went into action. Large bodies of the Union troops, previously engaged on the other side of town, were streaming away from the battle. They passed through the town and up the north slope of Cemetery Hill, where they met Hancock, who had ascended the south face. Morgan is one of many who described how the general stemmed the rush of fleeing men and turned them to face the enemy.

> … riding up on Cemetery Hill the whole field was before us.
> The remnants of the 1st Corps was forming near the Taneytown road. To what extent the 11th Corps had formed on the right and left of the Baltimore Turnpike,

On 1 July, Major General Oliver Otis Howard (top left) ascended to command of all troops on the field upon the death of Major General John Reynolds. Major General Carl Schurz (top right) took Howard's place in command of the Eleventh Corps. Major General Abner Doubleday (bottom right) took over command of the First Corps. Hancock sent the Twelfth Corps division under Brigadier General John Geary to the northern base of Little Round Top when it arrived on the field (Library of Congress reproduction numbers LC-USZ62–52494, LC-DIG-pga–04183, LC-DIG-cwpb–04466, LC-DIG-cwpb–06117).

I do not know, but I do know that the road was literally full of men many appearing to be organized regiments going to the rear, and that General Hancock and his staff rode in among them and by hard work succeeded in turning them into the field behind the stone wall.[21]

Elsewhere, Morgan concludes "By threats and persuasion the tide flowing along the Baltimore Turnpike was diverted, and lines of battle formed behind the stone walls on either side of the road."[22]

Second Lieutenant Sidney Cooke of the First Corps' 147th New York wrote:

> But if organization was lost, it needed but an organizer to restore it among these veterans. Hancock was there to meet the crisis. I happened to come near enough to note his bearing in that trying moment, and to hear some of his remarks and orders. The enemy was emerging from the streets of the town below, and forming line as if to drive us from our coveted position. Every man knew how hopeless resistance would be, but Hancock sat his horse, superb and calm as on review; imperturbable, self-reliant, as if the fate of the battle and of the nation were not his to decide. It almost led us to doubt whether there had been cause for retreat at all. His dispositions were prompt. A skirmish line was at once organized and advanced down the hill in the face of the enemy. Others were quickly deployed to extend its line to the left and right. To General Doubleday, who sat

The equestrian statue of Hancock on East Cemetery Hill depicts his arrival there on 1 July. Unveiled on 5 June 1896, it shows him, firmly but calmly, extending his hand to halt the retreat of Union forces (photograph by William Bretzger).

on his horse by his side, he said "General, move a brigade to the hill across the road on the right." "But general," he replied "I have no brigade." "Then take the first thousand men here. Never mind where they belong." No excitement in voice or manner, only cool, concise, and positive directions, given in a steady voice and a conversational tone.

The tired and discouraged men responded to the will of their master. The semblance of an organization was produced at once, and a show of strength made which might well impress the enemy, as it did, with the idea that we had at last received reinforcements. No charge was made. The position was saved.[23]

Brigadier General Gouverneur K. Warren was Chief of Engineers of the Army of the Potomac and would soon earn the moniker "Savior of Little Round Top." He later explained to congress' Joint Committee on the Conduct of the War "General Hancock made a great deal of personal effort to get our troops into position; and I think his personal appearance there did a great deal toward restoring order."[24]

Even General Schurz, who was Howard's second in command and maintained that Hancock never superseded Howard as commander of the field, explained:

> … under these circumstances the appearance of General Hancock was a most fortunate event. It gave the troops a new inspiration. They all knew him by fame, and his stalwart figure, his proud mien, and his superb soldierly bearing seemed to verify all the things that fame had told about him. His mere presence was a reinforcement, and everyone on the field felt stronger for his being there. This new inspiration of self-reliance might have become of immediate importance, had the enemy made another attack—an eventuality for which we had to prepare.[25]

Lieutenant Francis Wiggin of the Sixteenth Maine gushed:

> When the shattered forces of the First Corps reached the Ridge, one of the first things we saw, was the magnificent form of General Hancock, who was mounted on a noble charger. He was surrounded by his staff, and he was busy issuing orders and directing the location of troops as they arrived…. He had quickly grasped the situation and had gotten matters so well in hand that the Confederates would certainly have met with a very warm reception had they tried that night to take Cemetery Ridge.[26]

Lieutenant Edward Whittier of the Fifth Maine Battery of the First Corps observed the effect of Hancock's presence:

> … on horseback, unmoved by all the confusion among retreating soldiers, sat a man, born to command, competent to evolve order out of chaos, the master of the first position that day found for successful resistance. I shall never forget (for I reported to him for orders) the inspiration of his commanding, controlling presence, and the fresh courage he imparted. I recall even his linen, clean and white, his collar open at the neck, and his broad wristbands rolled back from his firm, finely moulded hand. This was General Hancock.[27]

It is this recognition by the troops of Hancock as their commander that renders moot the question of who officially held command. Still, it is a controversy that lives to this day, and therefore earns discussion herein.

The Hancock–Howard Controversy

The accounts of the meeting between Hancock and Howard not only vary, many starkly contradict one another. On one end of the spectrum is the contention that Hancock proclaimed Meade had placed him in command of the field and that Howard acquiesced. The other extreme is the assertion that Howard stubbornly rejected any of Hancock's claims to command and that it was actually Hancock who acquiesced. However, there is agreement that they met immediately, if not shortly after, Hancock's arrival on Cemetery Hill. There is also little contention that any alleged disagreement between them caused confusion or delay in the field operations.

The debate began that evening, after cessation of the day's major combat, when Howard wrote to Meade that the order for Hancock to supersede him in command "has mortified and will disgrace me."[28] The issue simmered for years. Hancock, who received wide recognition as a Gettysburg hero immediately after the battle, had little motivation to involve himself in a public spat with Howard. Even when Congress, in January 1864, passed a resolution thanking Hooker, Meade, Howard, and no other individual for the victory at Gettysburg, Hancock did not take his views public.[29] The resolution, in its odd singling out of the three men to the exclusion of others, provoked a public debate among partisans of those involved. In April 1866, Congress passed a resolution to include Hancock as well.[30]

It was not until Howard published his version of the events at Gettysburg in the July 1876 issue of the *Atlantic Monthly* that Hancock felt chagrined enough to pen his own public response. He did so with a characteristically clear, detailed, and well-sourced response in *The Galaxy* magazine of December that year. Other participants in the public debate over the years included Abner Doubleday, General Howard's brother and staff member Charles Howard, and members of Hancock's staff such as Morgan and Walker. Historians picked up the issue and have kept it alive until the present.

It was the public exchange between the two men in 1876, however, that was the controversy's hottest moment. Howard stated, in his *Atlantic Monthly* article, that:

> General Hancock greeted me in his usual frank and cordial manner, and used these words: "General Meade has sent me to represent him on the field." I replied,

"All right, Hancock. This is no time for talking. You take the left of the [Baltimore] pike and I will arrange these troops on the right." He said no more, and moved off in his peculiar, gallant style to gather scattered brigades and put them into position…. It did not strike me then that Hancock, without troops, was doing more than directing matters as a temporary chief of staff for Meade.[31]

So he asserts that Hancock made no claim to command of the field. Howard would echo this account in his 1904 autobiography.[32] Later in his article, Howard states that it was not until "just before night, when the order from General Meade came to me, superseding me in command of the field by a junior in rank…."[33]

Hancock, however, responded in *The Galaxy* that:

As soon as I arrived on the field, at about 3:30 p.m. I rode directly to the crest of the hill where General Howard stood, and said to him that I had been sent by General Meade to take command of all forces present; that I had written orders to that effect with me, and asked him if he wished to read them. He replied that he did not, but acquiesced in my assumption of command.[34]

Hancock then implies that Howard was insincere in stating that Hancock made no claim to command when they originally talked. Howard's letter complaining to Meade that Meade's order replacing him as commander of the field "has mortified and will disgrace me" also noted "General Hancock's order to assume command reached here in writing at seven (P. M.)." About that, Hancock wrote:

The apparent intention of that sentence is to convey the impression that he had no knowledge of the existence of that order at that time. But while it may be that 7 P. M. of that day was the time he received from the Adjutant General of the army his copy of the written order, it was not the first time that day he had the opportunity to see that order, because, as I have stated, I offered to show him the original in writing when I first met him on the field and assumed command at about 3:30 P. M. He then said he did not desire to see it, and immediately yielded command to me.[35]

Hancock continued that if Howard "pretended to transfer the command to General Slocum at 7 P. M." that:

He knew that he was not vested with the command at that time; he knew that he had yielded it to me, without protest, when I arrived on the field and informed him that I had an order from General Meade to assume command of our forces; he knew that, by virtue of that order and his own relinquishment, I was formally vested with the command, and had actively exercised it from the moment of my arrival until the close of the day…."[36]

The many other statements by Hancock, Howard, and other writers, some claiming to be eyewitnesses, do little to clear up the matter. Howard's brother,

Charles, held the rank of major and was the general's senior aide-de-camp. He later supported the contention that Hancock and Howard had amicably decided to split command, but differed from his brother's contention that Hancock had only claimed to "represent" Meade or act "as a temporary chief of staff for Meade."

> Meeting General Howard near the [Baltimore] pike he [Hancock] said that General Meade had sent him to take command of the left wing and added, apologetically, something to the effect that he wished General Howard to understand it was by no means seeking of his, but wholly an act of General Meade who had explained to him fully his plans.* Howard replied that it was now no time for talking, that he would be glad of Hancock's co-operation and suggested that he locate the troops south of the pike and he (Howard) would attend to the north side.
> *Hancock had reference to the fact that Howard out-ranked him.[37]

Major Eminel Halstead was on the staff of the First Corps and was seeking reinforcements from Howard when he claims to have witnessed the meeting at issue. He writes "There was no person present besides myself when the conversation took place between Howard and Hancock."[38] His account also supports the notion that Hancock made Howard aware of Meade's orders; but it also contends that the two came to an agreement that did not conform to those orders:

> I returned to where General Howard sat, just as General Hancock approached at a swinging gallop. When near General Howard, who was then alone, and with great animation, as if there was no time for ceremony, said General Meade had sent him forward to take command of the three Corps [the First, Eleventh, and his own, the Second]. General Howard replied that he was the senior. General Hancock said: 'I am aware of that, General, but I have written orders in my pocket from General Meade, which I will show you if you wish to see them.' General Howard said: 'No; I do not doubt your word, General Hancock, but you can give no orders here while I am here.' Hancock replied: 'Very well, General Howard, I will second any order that you have to give....'[39]

General Doubleday, who had taken over the First Corps upon the death of Reynolds, wrote several pieces which contained observations on the matter of what transpired between Hancock and Howard. While he appears to have been nearby when they met, he does not seem to have been close enough to have overheard anything. However, Hancock made direct responses to some of Doubleday's contentions which are worth discussing.

For instance, there is a copy of one of Doubleday's published writings in which Hancock scribbled several disagreements in the margins. On one page, where Doubleday asserts "Howard refused to submit to Hancock's assumption of authority, and quite a scene occurred," Hancock scribbled "Gen. Howard made no objection whatever. No scene occurred."[40] Furthermore, Doubleday continues "Hancock then said he would go back to headquarters and report, but Howard asked him to remain and help him organize the troops." Hancock drew a line on the page to indicate the general section of text that contains both of the above passages and labeled it with the words "This is all wrong."[41]

It is especially unlikely, given what we know about Hancock's character, that he would, after clear orders from Meade and a two-hour ride, meekly suggest returning to headquarters. It is equally unlikely that he would sheepishly shrink from rallying a fleeing army until invited by another general.

In fairness to Doubleday, he also highly praised Hancock:

> Hancock then rode over to me…. As he ranked me, and I had the greatest confidence in his ability, I was happy to serve under him. He said, "General Doubleday, I command this field…."[42]

The above passage is also significant, regarding the controversy, in that it has Hancock claiming command of the field. This is another blow to the credibility of Doubleday's other statements.

Historians can endlessly debate the credibility of differing versions of the discussion between Hancock and Howard. But there are more important, more consistent, and more credible statements that indicate who was really in command. These are the several recollections indicating that, when the Federals were either disorganized or in flight and the Confederates threatened to extend their advance even further, Hancock was simply a more *engaged* and *active* leader. First, Hancock himself made this case in *The Galaxy*, indicating that he was, far and away, the more active commander even immediately after his meeting with Howard:

> As it was necessary at once to establish order in the confused mass of his troops on Cemetery hill and the Baltimore pike, I lost no time in conversation, but at once rode away and bent myself to the pressing task of making such dispositions as would prevent the enemy from seizing that vital point…. I exercised positive and vigorous command over all the troops present, and General Howard, so far as my knowledge goes, gave no orders save to the troops of his own corps, the Eleventh.[43]

Even General Howard reinforced the idea that Hancock, not Howard, was being more "positive and vigorous":

> I noticed that he sent Wadsworth's division, without consulting me, to the right of the eleventh corps, to Culp's Hill; but as it was just the thing to do, I made no objection,—probably would not have made any in any event….[44]

He does recall that he "worked away, assisted by my officers, organizing batteries and infantry along the stone wall and fences toward Gettysburg, and along the northern crest of the ridge."[45] But Howard does not explain why it was Hancock, who had just gotten there, and not himself, having been there all day, who placed Wadworth's division in an effective position. One should also note that Howard speaks of working on a localized front: "along the stone wall and fences toward Gettysburg, and along the northern crest of the ridge" while it was Hancock who thought of the neighboring Culp's Hill, and eventually the distant Little Round Top.

Comparisons between their vigor and effectiveness at that critical hour do not end there. William Swinton traveled with the army as a reporter for the New York Times and wrote, in a book published in 1866, that:

> In such an emergency it is the personal qualities of the commander alone that tell. If, happily, there is in him that mysterious but potent magnetism that calms, subdues, and inspires, there results one of those sudden moral transformations that are among the phenomena of battle. This quality Hancock possesses in a high degree, and his appearance soon restored order out of seemingly hopeless confusion—a confusion which Howard, an efficient officer, but of a rather negative nature, had not been able to quell.[46]

Elsewhere, Swinton commented again on the rallying of the army on Cemetery Hill, "In this duty General Howard's success had not been eminent; but Hancock soon made the magnetism of his personal presence felt."[47]

J. W. Hoffman was in the First Corps and observed the effect that Hancock's presence had on Brigadier General Lysander Cutler, commanding a brigade in Wadsworth's division of that corps. According to Hoffman, it was Hancock's character and reputation that made him commander, regardless of the official chain of command. When Hoffman approached Cutler on Cemetery Hill for directions on which way to go, Cutler responded, "Wait a moment, there's Hancock, I'll go see."[48] Hoffman observed: "General Cutler could not possibly have known that Hancock was in command, for he had evidently just arrived, and Cutler doubtless knew that he was not the ranking officer on the field, his own manner and action was simply the result of the confidence inspired by Hancock's presence. Nor was he the only one so impressed—for a short time Hancock had wrought order from chaos."[49]

Eminel Halstead who, as noted above, claims to have been the only eyewitness to the controversial meeting between Hancock and Howard, also attests to the sharp contrast in demeanor between Hancock and Howard. "General Doubleday sent me to General Howard for reinforcements and orders. I found him in the Cemetery, near the gate. He looked the picture of despair."[50]

After a few more lines which imply that Howard had a sulking, defeatist attitude (and also that he mistook a line of advancing Confederates for rail fences) Halstead's account bounces with excitement when describing the arrival of Hancock: "I returned to where General Howard sat, just as that brilliant, dashing soldier, General Hancock, the hero of Gettysburg, approached at a swinging gallop."[51] Even in accounts that interpret Howard's static presence as admirably resolute, not despairing, Hancock's dynamic aura outshines Howard. For instance, J. A. Watrous of the Sixth Wisconsin later reported:

> As we reached the cemetery hill, about the first general officer we saw was Howard, sitting upon his horse with about as much coolness as though he was watching a Fourth of July parade, and just beyond him, all excitement—not nervous—looking in a thousand ways every minute and giving directions as carefully and precisely as though he was preparing for a great parade, was Gen. Hancock … he was young and fresh and bright and constantly active, who meant what he said, and said what he wanted to say so that everybody who heard it would understand. He was saying to this man and that: "Take your guns in that direction"; "Collect your men"; "Prepare for immediate action."[52]

What the army needed at that moment was not a stoic totem like Howard, but a proactive and engaged leader like Hancock.

There is also evidence that Howard had failed to establish positive leadership all day, despite having known since 11:30 a.m. or earlier, that he had official command of the field.[53] For instance, he was observing the action from atop the Fahnestock building in the middle of town when he heard that command fell upon him. Instead of riding to the front to establish himself, reconnoiter, and meet with his men in the field, he retreated to Cemetery Hill to establish his headquarters.[54]

Cemetery Hill offered a fine (though distant) view of the battle and a safe, stable base from which to direct the action, but removing to it was not the kind of morale-building hands-on leadership that someone like Hancock would likely have performed. In fact, General Buford reported to Meade, in a note dated 3:20 p.m. that "General Reynolds was killed early this morning. In my opinion there seems to be no directing person."[55] A member of Buford's staff also contended that Buford wrote a dispatch saying, "For God's sake send up Hancock, everything is going at odds and we need a controlling spirit."[56]

The point here is not necessarily that Howard was incompetent or performed poorly, but that Hancock's dynamism was much more effective and appropriate for the situation. Howard's "efficient" nature, as Swinton put it, was sufficient under ordinary conditions. But at that extraordinary moment it took Hancock's presence to establish control and instill the troops with a sense that their sacrifice was coordinated toward a worthy and attainable objective.

Their respective equestrian statues on East Cemetery Hill today reflect the difference in the nature of the two generals. Howard's likeness sits his horse firmly facing the enemy. He appears courageous, but motionless. Only feet away, however, the bronze Hancock is in motion, riding toward the Baltimore Pike with his hand extended to stop and calm the retreating army.

Regarding their recollections of their initial conversation: Howard's contentions are inconsistent and, given Hancock's personality, unlikely. Meanwhile, Hancock's statements on the matter are both consistent and plausible. Therefore the thrust of Hancock's argument is of much greater credibility. One important conflict in Howard's statements is between his official report, dated 31 August 1863, and the narratives of his later years, when he appears to have settled on a story. His official report states that Meade had superseded him with Hancock while mistakenly believing that Hancock was his senior: "General Hancock came to me about this time, and said that General Meade had sent him on hearing the state of affairs; that he [Meade] had given him [Hancock] his instructions while under the impression that he was my senior."[57]

But in his 1876 *Atlantic Monthly* article, however, and in his autobiography of 1904, Howard claims that Hancock had arrived with orders from Meade only to "represent him on the field."[58] To this, Hancock responded in *The Galaxy*: "This proves that General Howard contradicts himself. In this report he admits that when I arrived upon the field he knew General Meade had sent me to supersede him…. If he stands by his report, he falls by his article; if he stands by his article, he falls by his report."[59]

In *Atlantic Monthly*, Howard also wrote: "as I understood the matter at the time, General Meade really intended, and Hancock so implied in his conversation with me, that he (Hancock) was to represent Meade, as Butterfield, the chief of staff, would have done, on the field of battle."[60]

Hancock quoted that passage and responded:

> In the first place General Meade could not have so intended, for, in his conversation with me at Taneytown, and in his written order directing me to assume command of the forces on the field, it is clear as sunlight that he "really intended" and so directed, that General Howard should be superseded; and in the second place, knowing that General Meade had assigned me to that duty, having his written order in my pocket, it is impossible that I could have conveyed to General Howard the implication above quoted.[61]

He continues: "My action and orders on the field show that I had no such idea of my duties as now occurs to General Howard. When I moved off, as he says, 'to gather scattered brigades and put them into position' … he knew I was exercising authority which no staff officer would have dared to personally exercise under any circumstances."[62]

And in case one speculates that in all the excitement and noise on Cemetery Hill that Hancock might not have been so clear as to his intentions, he wrote: "I assert positively that I never implied in any conversation with General Howard that when I arrived at Gettysburg on that occasion I 'was to represent Meade as Butterfield, the chief of staff, would have done, on the field of battle.'"[63]

Doubleday's account of Hancock asserting, "General Doubleday, I command this field" is further testimony to the lack of ambiguity in Hancock's actions or statements that afternoon on Cemetery Hill.[64] Relative to this, Hancock wrote: "General Doubleday, commanding the First corps, after the fall of Reynolds, can give positive evidence that I assumed immediate command and directed the disposition of his troops, as soon as he fell back to Cemetery Hill."[65]

In his article, Hancock also addresses Howard's assertion that they agreed to split command, with Hancock taking "the left" of the Baltimore Pike and Howard "the right": "The only pretext for his statement of such an understanding is, that as I was about riding away to the left I understood him to indicate to me that he would prefer the right, where his troops were then posted, for his own position, and he said that he would be found there personally; but there was no division of command between Howard and myself."[66]

Hancock then recalls that he issued commands to Howard's units, further indicating that he commanded the field with Howard's acquiescence: "Indeed, one of the first orders I gave on assuming command was for the troops of the Eleventh corps (Howard's) to be pushed forward to the stone walls in the next field to give room for development, and to deter the enemy's advance."[67]

In conclusion, Hancock's actions not only show that he was in command regardless of his rank and what transpired between him and Howard, but that Howard must have been aware of the arrangement, despite what Howard would soon be saying. But perhaps most importantly, it was Hancock's vigorous and positive comportment that drew the forces present to his leadership.

4

Hancock Sets the Table

Hancock at once appreciated the value of this curved ridge as a defensive position for our army, and resolved to hold it, if possible. By posting troops far on the right and left he gave the enemy the impression that we had a long line and had been heavily reinforced. They accordingly delayed their attack until the next day, and the ridge remained in our possession.

This was the first great service on that field rendered by Hancock.[1]

—Abner Doubleday

Regardless of whether or not Howard was conscious of it, Hancock assumed command of the field. Before he turned command over to General Slocum, upon Slocum's arrival some three hours later, Hancock performed three major tasks. One task was the transformation of the First and Eleventh Corps from a defeated and fleeing crowd into an army reorganized to deter a possible attack. Several others participated in this endeavor, including Howard, but Hancock was its spiritual and tactical leader. Another task was the widening of the army's front to protect its flanks. To accomplish this Hancock ordered units to the formidable heights that flanked Cemetery Hill: Culp's Hill to the east and Little Round Top to the south. Some maintain that this also helped present, to the enemy, the appearance of a larger force.[2] This task not only helped deter any further enemy advance, but presciently determined the major points of the Union line for the next two days. Finally, Hancock made at least two dispatches to General Meade, informing him of the situation and the quality of the ground. This helped Meade decide to continue a general movement of the army to Gettysburg and offer a general engagement there.

To understand the task that Hancock and the other officers faced in rallying the troops, one should know the condition of those troops. The First Corps had been engaged west of town since as early as 10:30 a.m. Theirs was a group of much greater repute and *élan* than the Eleventh, but their beloved commander had been killed almost as soon as the fight began and their casualties grew to staggering figures as the bitter day wore on. The Eleventh had marched hard to join the fight and was not fully engaged until well into the afternoon. But they had barely attained a coherent formation north of town before the enemy flanked their right and drove them back into Gettysburg.

Since its inception, the Eleventh Corps contended not only with Confederates but with ethnic prejudice by other Federals. With about half of its regiments being German, and its officer corps filled with names like von Gilsa, von Steinwehr, and Schimmelfennig, the corps faced disproportionate derision and scapegoating. Having suffered a decisive rout at Chancellorsville had pulled the corps' reputation and morale to a new low in the weeks preceding Gettysburg.

Morgan made several derisive statements about the Eleventh Corps on its retreat to Cemetery Hill that are consistent with that corps' reputation: "The Eleventh Corps, whatever may have been said of it, was entirely unreliable and quite unmanageable.... General Howard himself was apparently despondent and his brother, Major Howard could not restrain his mortification at the behavior of the corps."[3]

Elsewhere he states: "To show the disorder into which General Howard's troops had been thrown by the unequal conflict they had waged during the day, it is only necessary to mention that 1,500 fugitives were collected by the provost guard of the Twelfth Corps, some miles in rear of the field."[4]

General Schurz, himself a German native and acting commander of the Eleventh Corps at that moment, remembered it differently:

It has been represented by some writers, Southerners, that the Union forces on the first day of the battle of Gettysburg were utterly routed and fled pell-mell into the town. This is far from the truth. That there were a good many stragglers hurrying to the rear in a disorderly fashion, as is always the case during and after a hot fight, will not be denied. Neither will it be denied that it was a retreat after a lost battle with the enemy in hot pursuit. But there was no element of dissolution in it. The retreat through the town was more or less disorderly, the streets being crowded with vehicles of every description, which offered to the passing troops exceedingly troublesome obstructions. It is also true that the Eleventh Corps men complained that when they entered the town, it was already full of First Corps men, and vice versa, which really meant that the two corps became more or less mixed in passing through. It is likewise true that many officers and men ... became entangled in the cross streets, and alleys without thoroughfare, and were captured by the enemy pressing after them. But, after all, the fact remains that in whatever shape the troops issued from the town, they were promptly reorganized, each was under the colors of his regiment, and in as good a fighting trim as before, save that their ranks were fearfully thinned by the enormous losses suffered during the day.[5]

General Doubleday wrote from the perspective of his own Corps:

> The First Corps was broken and defeated, but not dismayed. There were but a few left, but they showed the true spirit of soldiers. They walked leisurely from the Seminary to the town, and did not run. I remember seeing Hall's battery and the Sixth Wisconsin regiment halt from time to time to face the enemy, and fire down the streets.... Many of the Eleventh Corps, and part of Robinson's division, which had been far out, were captured in the attempt to reach.... Cemetery Hill, which was the rallying point.[6]

Doubleday, like Morgan, had unflattering things to say about the Eleventh Corps. Soon after the troops reached Cemetery Hill, he says Howard "rode over to ask me, in case his men (Steinwehr's division) deserted their guns, to be in readiness to defend them."[7] While that was only an implied indictment, he continued with a direct criticism: "General Schurz about this time was busily engaged in rallying his men, and did all that was possible to encourage them to form line again.... It seemed to me that the discredit that attached to them after Chancellorsville had in a measure injured their morale and *esprit-de-corps*, for they were rallied with great difficulty."[8]

Regardless of partisan claims as to which corps was more resilient, it is clear that it would be a daunting task to rally all of them and discourage or repel further pursuit by the Confederates. In retreat, the two corps converged and crammed, with supply trains, artillery, pack animals, and other encumbrances, into the narrow streets of a town whose population was a small fraction of their own.

Hence, there should be no doubt that the rallying of the army was a remarkable, if not heroic, achievement. But that is not the only feat that Hancock performed in the waning daylight of 1 July. Stopping the retreat and attaining some semblance of order would not alone be enough to repel or discourage a further Confederate advance. The troops needed to be arranged in a tactically sound and expedient manner. Furthermore, Hancock had to assess the situation and make Meade aware of it as soon as possible. Essentially, the selection of a battlefield was still not done. Communication with Meade would have to wait, however, as Hancock decided the need for tactical arrangements to be more immediate.

He combined the two tasks of restoring order and setting up a defense into one. That is, by dispersing units to different areas of the field, Hancock not only relieved crowding and confusion on Cemetery Hill, he simultaneously formed a workable defensive position. Organizing Cemetery Hill was the most immediate matter. Hancock wrote in *The Galaxy*: "Indeed, one of the first orders I gave on assuming command was for the troops of the Eleventh Corps (Howard's) to be pushed forward to the stone walls in the next field to give room for development, and to deter the enemy's advance. And about the same time I addressed a few words to his own troops on the left of the pike with a view to encourage them to hold the position while our lines were forming."[9]

His official report states: "I arrived at Gettysburg and assumed the command. At this time the First and Eleventh Corps were retiring through the town, closely pursued by the enemy.... Orders were at once given to establish a line of battle on Cemetery Hill, with skirmishers occupying that part of the town immediately in our front."[10]

After he addressed the most immediate threats, Hancock began to expand his influence and establish order on a larger scale. In *The Galaxy* he continues: "I then rode on to place the First corps further to the left, in order that we should cover the whole of Cemetery Hill, only a small portion of which was occupied when I arrived upon the field.[11]

He credits others, as well, for the stabilizing of Cemetery Hill: "In forming the lines, I received material assistance from Major-General Howard, Brigadier-Generals Warren and Buford, and officers of General Howard's command."[12]

He then looked east toward Culp's Hill. Accounts vary as to whether his actions were preemptive or in response to an observed Confederate movement, but it is clear that Hancock was the one who had ordered the hill covered. Morgan reports:

> A line of battle with skirmishers out was plainly seen east of the town, making its way toward Culp's Hill, and so far as I could see we had not even a skirmisher to meet it.
> Pointing out the line to General Hancock, he directed me to get a brigade from the 1st Corps to occupy the western slope of the Hill.[13]

Major Henry Edwin Tremain was the senior aide to General Dan Sickles of the Third Corps. He had ridden ahead of his corps to inform Howard of its imminent arrival and to reconnoiter the situation for Sickles. In the process he had witnessed much of the activity on Cemetery Hill and also noticed the emerging Confederate line: "From a fine vantage point east of the highway an extensive view could be had; and while I was studying its features; a column of men in the distance could be discerned moving apparently around our extreme right flank.... So I ventured to go to General Hancock and report what I had seen. He rode towards the spot and saw the same thing; but apparently without surprise. Hancock was one of the most alert of our generals."[14]

By one of General Doubleday's accounts, the movement of troops to Culp's Hill was one of the first things Hancock did after assuming command: "He says he assumed absolute command at 3:30 p.m. I know he rode over to me and told me he was in command of the field, and directed me to send a regiment to the right, and I sent Wadsworth's division there, as my regiments were reduced to the size of companies."[15]

Morgan claims that Doubleday showed more reluctance and defeatism than Doubleday admits:

> The enemy's line of battle was seen advancing up the ravine between the town and Culp's Hill, and General Hancock sent one of his staff to General Doubleday for troops with which to meet the threatened advance. The staff-officer was met with a series of excuses: that the men were out of ammunition, that they were disorganized by their losses, that they had no officers, etc. General Hancock rode up behind General Doubleday, and overheard these remarks, and rising in his stirrups, with his hand raised, said; "Sir, I am in command on this field; send every man you have got."[16]

In a personal report to historian John Bachelder, Morgan reveals himself to be the above-mentioned "staff-officer" but remains critical of Doubleday's reaction:

> I delivered my message to the corps commander, informing him of the emergency, who with the beaten demeanor that characterized some persons on that field protested that his men were worn out, cut up, had no ammunition &c., &c. How long he would have hesitated, I do not know, but it seems General Hancock, who had followed behind me overheard the conversation, for I heard him suddenly roar out, "General.... I want you to understand that I am in command here, send every man you have." Wadsworth's division was sent and occupied the ground assigned to it during the remainder of the battle. The 5th Maine battery accompanied it and opened on the enemy as did one of General Howard's batteries to which I carried the order.[17]

The need to occupy Culp's Hill was obvious, whether Confederates were already advancing toward it or not. Nevertheless, no one did it until Hancock ordered it. This does not mean that, without Hancock, no one else would have gotten around to it. Nevertheless it was Hancock who initiated the defense of Culp's Hill, earning for himself the credit for it.

A less obvious, yet astute, tactical move was the placement of artillery on what became known as Stevens' Knoll. The part of Cemetery Hill east of the Baltimore Pike is commonly known as East Cemetery Hill. Unlike the north face of the hill, which has a gentle slope, the east face of East Cemetery Hill is quite steep. Therefore, artillery on the hill cannot cover the approach from that side for inability to fire steeply downward. Realizing this, Hancock saw that flanking fire from the area between Culp's and East Cemetery Hills would protect the otherwise uncovered valley. Captain Greenleaf T. Stevens commanded the Fifth Maine Battery of the First Corps. His battery came up East Cemetery Hill with the throng that had retired through town. He co-authored an article on his battery, which refers to himself in the third person. It contains this description of how Hancock placed the battery:

> He [Hancock] arrived on Cemetery Hill about four o'clock, and was by the gate of the Cemetery as the Fifth Maine battery came up. He called for the captain of "that brass battery." Captain Stevens heard what he said and put himself in Hancock's presence, he ordered Stevens to take (his) battery to that hill," pointing to Culp's Hill, and "stop the enemy from coming up that ravine." "By whose order?" was the inquiry. "General Hancock's," was the reply…. This position commanded completely the easterly slope of Cemetery Hill and the ravine at the north.[18]

First Lieutenant Edward Whittier was in the Fifth Maine Battery of the First Corps and wrote: "The 'dead angle' made by the abrupt slopes of Cemetery Hill had been changed, by the act of General Hancock, who placed the 5th Maine light twelves on the side of the salient created by the north face of Culp's Hill, into a most deadly angle.[19]

The battery, in its key position, helped repel the Confederate assault on East Cemetery Hill on the night of 2 July by raking its eastern slope. By that time, Lieutenant Whittier had replaced Captain Stevens, who took a bullet through both legs, as commander of the battery. But it was Stevens' name that stuck to the knoll on which Hancock had placed the battery.

One should note that Hancock is not the only one who has a claim to establishing Stevens' Knoll as a key artillery position. Colonel Charles S. Wainwright commanded First Corps' Artillery Brigade. He, like the rest of the First Corps and most of the Eleventh, was involved in the day's earlier fight and the ensuing retreat through town. He claims that when he arrived on Cemetery Hill that General Howard "expressed pleasure at seeing me, and desired me to take charge of all artillery, and make the best disposition I could of it."[20] Wainwright describes placing almost all the guns which ended up in the Cemetery Hill area including those of Stevens' Fifth Maine: "On the neck of Culp's Hill I posted Stevens, who thus had a fire along my north front."[21]

Wainwright's claims may be sincere, but they are suspect. Hancock had much more opportunity to assess the terrain and situation, as Wainwright had been busy getting his brigade through the crowded town and only took "charge of all artillery" upon arriving on the hill. Hancock would also have received greater recognition as the overall commander, he being a top corps commander while Wainwright had led but a single artillery brigade.

Hancock's official report recognizes the particular advantage of the position: "As soon as the line of battle mentioned above was shown by the enemy, Wadsworth's division, First Corps, and a battery (thought to be the Fifth Maine) were placed on the eminence just across the turnpike, and commanding completely this approach."[22]

Hancock's use of the passive voice ("a battery ... were placed" versus "I placed a battery") is consistent with the style of his official report and therefore does not suggest that someone else placed the battery.

General Hancock and the others present had now checked the most immediate threats. Eleventh Corps elements guarded the Baltimore Pike where it rose from town up Cemetery Hill. Most of the First Corps covered the Taney-town Road, which ascended from town on the left of the Baltimore Pike. Cemetery Hill bristled with artillery. On Culp's Hill, to the right, stood Wadsworth's division of the First Corps which also supported Stevens' battery on the knoll between the two hills. General John Buford's cavalry division had been occupying the plain southeast of town since before Hancock's arrival. At about this time elements of the Twelfth Corps began arriving via the Baltimore Pike. Hancock's official report noted: "A division of the Twelfth Corps, under Brigadier-General Williams, arrived as these arrangements were being completed, and was established, by order of Major-General Slocum, some distance to the right and rear of Wadsworth's division."[23]

Hancock himself, however, located another Twelfth Corps division in such a way that further demonstrated his tactical skill, if not foresight. His report continues: "Brigadier-General Geary's division of the Twelfth Corps, arriving on the ground subsequently, and not being able to communicate with Major-General Slocum, I ordered the division to the high ground to the right of and near Round Top Mountain, commanding the Gettysburg and Emmitsburg road, as well as the Gettysburg and Taneytown road to our rear."[24]

Geary's official report roughly corroborates that of Hancock: "Not finding General Howard, I reported to Major-General Hancock, commanding Second Corps, who informed me that the right could maintain itself, and the immediate need of a division on the left was imperative. By his direction, upon this threatening emergency, I took up a position on the extreme left of the line of battle."[25]

Hancock also elaborates in his *Galaxy* article:

> I sent Geary's division of the Twelfth corps, which had just arrived, to occupy the ground to the left, near Round Top, commanding the Gettysburg and Emmettsburg road, as well as the Gettysburg and Taneytown road to our rear. This was part of General Slocum's corps; and although I had not been directed by General Meade to assume command of other than the First, Third, and Eleventh corps, I felt that the urgency of the case (not having heard of General Slocum's arrival in person), and seeing that division approaching the field, my duty as commander required me to place it at that point where it would best protect our left and rear.[26]

Hence, Hancock had placed a division at the northern base of Little Round Top. The position became controversial the following morning when

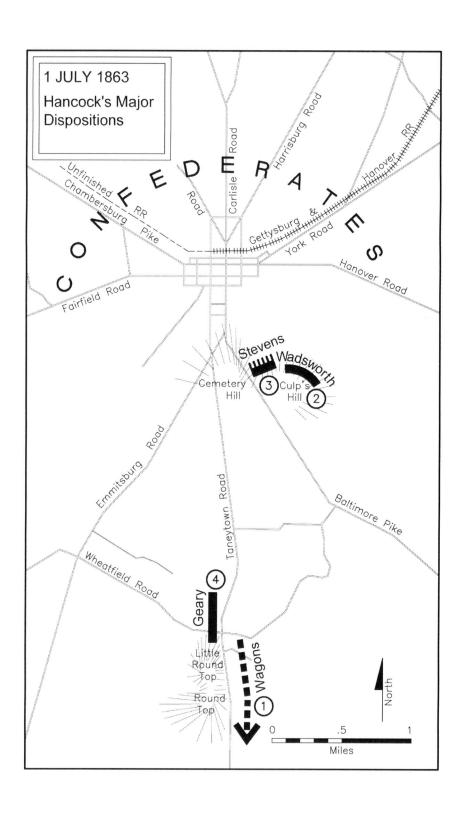

1 JULY 1863

Hancock's Major Dispositions

CONFEDERATES

Unfinished RR

Chambersburg Pike

Carlisle Road

Harrisburg Road

Hanover RR

Road

Gettysburg & York Road

Hanover Road

Fairfield Road

Stevens

Wadsworth

Cemetery Hill

③ Culp's Hill ②

Emmitsburg Road

Taneytown Road

Baltimore Pike

Wheatfield Road

Geary ④

Little Round Top

Wagons

①

Round Top

North

0   .5   1

Miles

Meade ordered Sickles' Third Corps to replace Geary their. Sickles' decision to abandon it in favor of the "Peach Orchard Salient" became one of the battle's greatest and most enduring controversies. When commentators criticize Sickles' 2 July action, they are not just endorsing Meade's line of that day, but the one that Hancock established on 1 July.

It is also notable that Hancock recognized the importance of Little Round Top when only three of the army's seven corps were present and the fighting was limited to Gettysburg's immediate environs some two or three miles north of it. The anxious studies and observations he made en route to Gettysburg, in which he surely noticed Little Round Top, shaped the entire three-day battle, not just the first day. The sending of Geary to the base of Little Round Top was the last major tactical disposition of Hancock on 1 July; and *it outlined the famed fish hook line that the Union army held for the rest of the battle*. The shaft of the hook ran from Geary's division near Little Round Top to Cemetery Hill, and became filled with troops from the Second, Third, Fifth and Sixth Corps the next day. The hook curved around Cemetery Hill with the First and Eleventh Corps and terminated at the Twelfth Corps' right on Culp's Hill.

Upon reaching this moment of relative stability, Morgan writes: "The lines having been so established as to deter the enemy from further advance, General Hancock dispatched his senior aide, Major Mitchell, with a verbal message to General Meade that General Hancock could hold Cemetery Hill until night-fall, and that he considered Gettysburg the place to fight. Major Mitchell left Gettysburg about 4 o'clock, and arrived at Taneytown before 6 o'clock. Having delivered his message to General Meade, the latter replied, 'I will send up the troops.'"[27]

Morgan's statement strongly implies that Hancock's take on the situation at Gettysburg prompted Meade to determine to fight there. It may or may not be valid. He was not an eyewitness to the exchange and his contention seems more like Second Corps partisanship than historical reporting. The question of when Meade decided to abandon the Pipe Creek plan in favor of Gettysburg and what prompted him to do so is yet another controversy.

This controversy became very public in January 1864, when Congress passed the resolution thanking three Union generals for the victory at Gettys-

Opposite: 1. Hancock sends wagon trains to the rear; **2.** Hancock orders General Wadsworth's First Corps division to Culp's Hill; **3.** Hancock orders the Fifth Maine Light, Battery E, commonly called "Steven's Battery," to the low rise between Culp's Hill and East Cemetery Hill. The place eventually takes on the name "Stevens' Knoll"; **4.** Hancock orders General Geary's Twelfth Corps division "to the high ground to the right of and near" Little Round Top. Note: other Union units present are not shown; maps drawn by the author.

burg.[28] It recognized Hooker for his management of the campaign until shortly before the battle, Meade for conducting the battle, and Howard for selecting the battlefield. It was Senator James W. Grimes of Iowa who had moved to include Howard in the document.[29] Said Grimes: "As I have read the history of that campaign, the man who selected the position of where the battle of Gettysburg was fought, and who, indeed, fought it the first day, was General Howard, and to him the country is indebted as much for the victory as to any other person."[30]

Several took exception to the selection of Howard for congressional recognition as well as the contention that he chose the battlefield. According to Abner Doubleday, "It was Hancock's recommendation that caused Meade to concentrate his army on the ridge, but Howard received the thanks of Congress for selecting the position. He, doubtless, did see its advantages, and recommended it to Hancock. The latter immediately took measures to hold it as a battle-ground for the army, while Howard merely used it as a rallying point for his defeated troops."[31]

Who Selected the Battlefield?

One may dismiss this as another unanswerable or even trivial question akin to "who fired the first shot?" or "who got the farthest in Pickett's Charge?" Some attribute the origin of the battle of Gettysburg to Winfield's old friend, Confederate General Henry Heth and an alleged quest for shoes. Some credit Buford for his decision to have it out with Heth west of town. Others say it was Reynolds, who commanded the left wing of the Union army and elected to support Buford, thus escalating the engagement to a true battle. Still others credit Howard. After all, he placed a division on Cemetery Hill while sending the rest of his corps to the aid of Reynolds and Buford. Those who hold that all responsibility lies at the top would state that Meade and Lee made the ultimate determination. After all, either one could have, at any time before or during the fight, withdrawn his army.

For this discussion, that is, the matter of Hancock and his effect on the events of Gettysburg, there are more finite ways to frame the issue. There is no dispute that Meade sent Hancock to Gettysburg on 1 July because he trusted Hancock's judgment and he knew Hancock was aware of his intentions. As Hancock put it: "I was sent to Gettysburg to relieve General Howard of the command of all our forces there, and to determine and inform General Meade whether or not, in my opinion, Gettysburg was the place to fight the battle."[32]

Knowing this and knowing that Meade's army did, shortly thereafter, concentrate at Gettysburg, it is reasonable to ask the following:

Did the Army of the Potomac concentrate at Gettysburg by

a) its own momentum set by events beyond any one person's control,
b) Meade's order, independent of Hancock's input, or
c) Meade's order, as a result of Hancock's input?

The answer to this question is more determinable than "who got the farthest in Pickett's Charge?" but is still not absolute. Like other questions, the uncertainty lies not in a lack of eyewitnesses, but in an abundance of alleged eyewitnesses who contradict one another.

For instance, Major Halstead claims to have witnessed Hancock's initial meeting with Howard on Cemetery Hill (see Chapter 3). He directly answered the question of who chose Gettsyburg, but his account seems woefully idealized:

> Hancock replied: "…General Meade has also directed me to select a field on which to fight this battle in rear of Pipe Creek." Then, casting one glance from Culp's Hill to Round Top, he continued: "But I think this is the strongest position by nature upon which to fight a battle that I ever saw, and if it meets your approbation I will select this as the battle-field." General Howard responded: "I think it a very strong position, General Hancock; a very strong position!" "Very well sir, I select this as the battle-field."[33]

This romantic account seems like an attempt to make an unmistakable and decisive historical moment out of something that had more complexity. Similarly, Morgan's claim that Meade, upon hearing Major Mitchell's report promptly replied, "I will send up the troops" is also suspiciously simple. General Howard lived long after the battle and left several accounts of it. The details of each vary. But if one is to accept his autobiography, published in 1908, then it was he who chose to fight on Cemetery Hill even before he knew of Reynolds' death. As he tells it, he was perusing the hills south of town on the morning of 1 July, understanding that he was only to "keep within supporting distance" of Reynolds.[34] Upon reaching Cemetery Ridge, he writes: "Colonel Meysenberg was my adjutant general. We sat on our horses, side by side, looking northward, when I said: 'This seems to be a good position, colonel,' and his own prompt and characteristic reply was: 'It is the only position, general.' We both meant **position for Meade's army**."[35] (The emphasis is in Howard's text.)

Unfortunately for Howard, even if one could verify this account, it would not prove that he selected the battlefield. Since he had no authority over the army, and almost no discussion with or influence on Meade, his exchange with Colonel Meysenberg would constitute only an accurate prediction, not a *selection of the battlefield*.

He goes on to emphasize, correctly, that he alone established Cemetery Hill as a military position. However, before the day was over, most of his corps was on the other side of town and all but one brigade and one battery remained on Cemetery Hill.[36] Howard should receive credit for noticing the value of Cemetery Hill. But there is no evidence that he did, or even had the authority to, order a general concentration there and therefore select the battlefield.

In fairness to General Howard, he was not alone in making shaky claims to that distinction. Even the words of Meade himself, whose testimony one should suspect would clarify the matter, are self-contradictory and ambiguous. While his original contentions were clear, his accounts became muddy and contradictory as the months went by.

For instance, his official report dated 1 October 1863 includes the following: "Major General Hancock arrived [at Gettysburg], whom I had dispatched to represent me on the field, on hearing of the death of Reynolds."[37] His report then goes on to clearly state that he relied on reports from the front and waited until quite late before committing to Gettysburg.

> About 7 p.m., Major-Generals Slocum and Sickles, with the Twelfth Corps and part of the Third, reached the ground, and took post on the right and left of the troops previously posted. Being satisfied with the reports received from the field that it was the intention of the enemy to support with his whole army the attack already made, and the reports from Major-Generals Hancock and Howard on the character of the position being favorable, I determined to give battle at this point; and, early in the evening of the 1st, issued orders to all the corps to concentrate at Gettysburg....
>
> At 10 p.m. of the 1st, I broke up my headquarters, which until then had been at Taneytown and proceeded to the field, arriving there at 1 a.m. of the 2d.[38]

Meade's statement before the joint congressional Committee on the Conduct of War on 5 March 1864 is fairly consistent with his official report: "Early in the evening of July 1, I should suppose about 6 or 7 o'clock, I received a report from General Hancock, I think in person, giving me such an account of a position in the neighborhood of Gettysburg, which could be occupied by my army, as caused me at once to determine to fight a battle at that point."[39]

However, when he testified to the committee less than a week later he gave a substantially different account. On 11 March Meade specified that even though he had sent Hancock largely to evaluate the Gettysburg area as a battlefield, he decided to move the army there before he got word from Hancock.

> I directed General Hancock to proceed to Gettsyburg and take command of the troops there, and particularly to advise me of the condition of affairs there, and the practicability of fighting a battle there.... But from information received from the field, from officers returning, I became satisfied that the enemy were in such force there that it was evident that General Lee was about to concentrate his army there. I therefore did not wait for the report from General Hancock, as I can

prove from my staff officers who took my orders, but immediately commenced to move my troops to the front, being determined to fight a battle there.[40]

One might attribute the change in Meade's testimony to political pressure. He had come under a publicity attack by Generals Hooker and Sickles, who sought to discredit Meade in an effort to bolster their own reputations. Hooker was suffering the disgrace of presiding over the humiliating defeat at Chancellorsville. Sickles was fending off implications that his actions on the second day at Gettysburg were insubordinate and blunderous. Regardless, their camp was pushing a rumor that Meade had never wanted to fight at Gettysburg, and that even once the army was there he had attempted to order a retreat. It is possible that Meade had grown more wary of this between the two testimonies above. Therefore it is possible that he sought to make the record show him as more decisive and aggressive.

The actual written communications by Meade, not his accounts made after the fact, are the most reliable clues to how the battle came to be fought at Gettysburg. The most specific of these is the orders he addressed to both Hancock and Doubleday, dated 1 July, 6 p.m. A passage from which reads, "It seems to me we have so concentrated that a battle at Gettysburg is now forced on us."[41]

More evidence that Meade himself decided relatively early to fight at Gettysburg comes from a message he sent to General-in-Chief Halleck, also dated 6 p.m. on 1 July: "The First and Eleventh Corps have been engaged all day in front of Gettysburg. The Twelfth, Third, and Fifth have been moving up, and all, I hope, by this time on the field.... At any rate, I see no other course than to hazard a general battle."[42]

Those messages seem to indicate that Meade made a clear decision, early on, to fight at Gettysburg. Furthermore, they seem to indicate that he did so based on the occurrence of several corps already concentrating there. However, Meade's message to Halleck also left open the possibility for a withdrawal or other change of plans as it continued: "Circumstances during the night may alter this decision."[43] Also, despite the fact that Meade alerted Halleck of the likelihood of a general engagement being at Gettysburg, he does not appear to have committed the Fifth and Sixth Corps there until later. His written order for the Fifth Corps to march there is dated 7 p.m., and a similar order for the Sixth Corps is dated 7:30.[44]

Then the question remains: How critical was Hancock's assessment of the situation at Gettysburg to the decision to fight there? Since the question of what *did* happen yields so many varying answers, perhaps what *did not* happen is more telling. For instance, when he arrived atop Cemetery Hill, Hancock *did not* decide the situation there was untenable. Despite the defeated and disorganized condition of the First and Eleventh Corps, and the fact that they were still fleeing from an enemy in close pursuit, Hancock did not advise Meade that the Gettysburg area had been lost; and he did not order the troops to continue their flight. Hancock was in a position to order a retreat and cause a reversal of any general concentration at Gettysburg. Even if Meade had ordered such a concentration before he received word from Hancock, the reversing of those orders and a counter-march would have been entirely possible. Hence, Hancock helped select the battlefield through what he did *not* do.

Such a decision may have been quite logical under the circumstances that Hancock found when he first crested Cemetery Hill. Several facts indicate that a Union concentration at Gettysburg was far from inevitable, and may have even been unwise. Many Confederates later contended that their General Richard Ewell could have occupied Culp's Hill with no resistance and Cemetery Hill almost as easily. Hancock himself had ordered the Taneytown Road cleared of trains so as not to complicate a retreat.

General Slocum's tentativeness is another illustration of the situation's uncertainty. Howard had repeatedly, throughout 1 July, sent word to him asking for his help. Had he moved his Twelfth Corps to Gettysburg with any kind of zeal or urgency, Slocum should have arrived north of town in plenty of time to aid in the fight there. However, he was curiously slow in getting there.

Both explanations for Slocum's tardiness demonstrate the uncertainty of the day. Slocum points to Meade's so-called "Pipe Creek Circular" as the reason for his hesitance to move any closer to Gettysburg than Two Taverns, some five miles away. "Pipe Creek Circular" is the name historians have given Meade's orders to all corps commanders early on 1 July. It designates positions for each corps along the Pipe Creek line should that plan go into effect. But the orders are tentative and perhaps even self-contradictory.

General Reynolds had made an aggressive response to his situation, moving forward to reinforce Buford outside of Gettysburg. Had he lived, Reynolds could have easily explained his actions as consistent with the orders in the circular, perhaps citing the line "Developments may cause the commanding general to assume the offensive from his present positions."[45] General Slocum, on the other hand, could cite "General Slocum will assume command of the two corps at Hanover and Two Taverns, and withdraw them."[46] Charles Howard, however, who desperately wanted relief in the Eleventh Corps' tangle with increasingly overwhelming odds all day, attributed Slocum's absence to a dishonorable lack of fortitude. According to him, Slocum did not like what he understood about the situation at Gettysburg and lacked the courage to join what Slocum perceived was a messy, unwinnable contest. The brother of the Eleventh Corps' commander later wrote that when he finally found him personally, Slocum responded, "I'll be damned if I will take the responsibility of this fight."[47] Charles Howard also wrote of Slocum, "he was about 2 miles away but he was too willing to demonstrate the fitness of his name *Slow come*."[48]

Again, Slocum's hesitance is demonstrative of the variability of the moment, whether it was proper or not. If Charles Howard was right, and the situation was too unmanageable for Slocum to stomach, then a general concentration of the army at Gettysburg would have been foolish. On the other hand, Slocum may have simply been obeying the circular, which directed him to "withdraw." Either case reinforces the contention herein that it was plausible for Hancock to call for either a full withdrawal or a forward concentration. What Hancock opted for was the following: He committed a great deal of effort to organizing the troops and assessed the situation. He then sent Meade the aforementioned verbal message. Finally, he found time to dictate a written message to Meade, dated 5:25 p.m.:

> GENERAL: When I arrived here an hour since, I found that our troops had given up the front of Gettysburg and the town. We have now taken up a position in the cemetery, and cannot well be taken. It is a position, however, easily turned. Slocum is now coming on the ground, and is taking position on the right, which will protect the right. But we have, as yet, no troops on the left, the Third Corps not having yet reported; but I suppose that it is marching up. If so, its flank march will in a degree protect our left flank. In the meantime Gibbon had better march on so as to take position on our right or left, to our rear, as may be necessary, in some commanding position. General G. will see this dispatch. The battle is quiet now. I think we will be all right until night. I have sent all the trains back. When night comes, it can be told better what had best be done. I think we can retire; if not, we can fight here, as the ground appears not unfavorable with good troops. I will communicate in a few moments with General Slocum, and transfer the command to him.
>
> Howard says that Doubleday's command gave way.
>
> General Warren is here.
>
> > Your obedient servant,
> > WINF'D S. HANCOCK
> > Major-General, Commanding Corps.[49]

So Hancock communicated to Meade the facts as he saw them and did not directly recommend a course of action for the army. He reported that a withdrawal or a stand were both possible. But it may be the one recommendation he did make that helped sway General Meade. That recommendation is the suggestion to move his own Second Corps toward Gettysburg ("In the meantime Gibbon had better march on so as to take position on our right or left.... General G. will see this dispatch").

To conclude, it was up to Meade to make the final decision. However, Hancock was acting as Meade's eyes and ears. Also, the situation that Hancock witnessed, then helped stabilize, was far from secure upon his arrival on Cemetery Hill. Had he deemed it proper, Hancock could have helped continue the withdrawal that was already occurring and sent word to Meade that Gettysburg was lost. Even if Meade did decide that "we have so concentrated that a battle at Gettysburg is now forced on us" without Hancock's consultation, Meade had the ability to call the army back toward Pipe Creek if Hancock had so recommended. This is evident in Meade's words to Halleck: "Circumstances during the night may alter this decision." In view of all this, it is logical to conclude that Meade made the final decision to fight at Gettysburg, but only after he had positive word from Hancock that such a move made sense.

Anecdotes and Activities

Hancock stayed at Gettysburg for two to three hours, depending on what assumptions one makes and who one believes. He made a lot of strong impressions during his first brief visit. Colonel Orland Smith commanded the only infantry brigade that Howard had left to hold Cemetery Hill as fighting raged on the other side of town. He noted:

> After taking my position, and when everything looked like disaster, General Hancock arrived. He immediately rode along my lines and complimented the men and the dispositions. He saw Captain Madeira and inquired who commanded that brigade. On being told, he desired to see me. I was called and introduced. Said he: "My corps is on the way, but will not be here in time. This position should be held at all hazards. Now, Colonel, can you hold it?" Said I "I think I can." "Will you hold it?" "I will." And we did.[50]

One who, many years later, warmly recalled Hancock on that day was J. A. Watrous:

> As we reached cemetery hill … I had a squad of army wagons and thought it was no more than right to report to Hancock for orders. I saluted. Said he: "Great God, what have you got here? What have you got a wagon here for? You haven't been out into action?" Said I: "Yes sir, just came back with the rear guard." "Well," he said, "did you lose all your ammunition?" "No, sir; distributed nearly all of it." "Lose any of your wagons?" "Well, I got back with some of them." "You did well Sergeant," said he; "just move your wagons down there and report to me in half an hour." All who served there will agree with me in this, that we felt a great deal safer when Hancock and his corps were around.[51]

Another person who spoke of him in detail was General Carl Schurz. He recalls some quiet moments with Hancock after Hancock had made his major dispositions:

This done, General Hancock sat down on a stone fence on the brow of the hill from which he could overlook the field, on the north and west of Gettysburg, occupied by the Confederates. I joined him there, and through our fieldglasses we eagerly watched the movements of the enemy. We saw their batteries and a large portion of their infantry columns distinctly. Some of those columns moved to and fro in a way the purpose of which we could not clearly understand. I was not ashamed to own that I felt nervous, for while our position was a strong one, the infantry line in it appeared, after the losses of the day, woefully thin. It was soothing to my pride, but by no means reassuring as to our situation, when General Hancock admitted that he felt nervous, too. Still he thought that with our artillery so advantageously posted, we might well hold out until the arrival of the Twelfth Corps, which was only a short distance behind us. So we sat watching the enemy and presently observed to our great relief that the movements of the rebel troops looked less and less like a formation for an immediate attack. Our nerves grew more and more tranquil as minute after minute lapsed, for each brought night and reinforcements nearer.[52]

Did Ewell Squander a Confederate Opportunity?

The failure of the Confederates to fully exploit their victory and allow the Federals to regroup on Cemetery and Culp's Hills became yet another source of controversy. As months and years went by, a chorus of criticism developed against Lieutenant General Richard S. Ewell, commanding the Confederate Second Army Corps.

Why did Ewell, out of all the Confederate officers who arguably failed to press the advantage their army gained that afternoon, become such a central target of criticism? Beside some eccentricities that made him an easy target, he was one of the few, if not only commander, who received direct, albeit conditional and discretionary orders from Robert E. Lee to take Cemetery Hill. Lee likely sent these orders while at the distant eminence of Seminary Ridge. They were verbal, so there is no direct copy of them. By the Commander-in-Chief's own account however, he sent instructions for Ewell: "to carry the hill occupied by the enemy, if he found it practicable, but to avoid a general engagement until the arrival of other divisions of the army, which were ordered to hasten forward."[53]

Most debates about Confederate leaders are beyond the scope of this discussion, but the Ewell matter relates substantially enough to Hancock to merit discussion here. The controversy is relevant to Hancock in at least two ways. First, the failure of the Confederates to further exploit their victory that day is a substantial reflection on Hancock's labors. Second, critics of Ewell famously used some words from Hancock himself as a major component of their argument. Hancock penned those words in a letter to former Confederate general Fitzhugh Lee dated 17 January 1878: "in my opinion, if the Confederates had continued the pursuit of General Howard on the afternoon of the 1st July at Gettsyburg, they would have driven him over and beyond Cemetery Hill."[54]

Fitzhugh Lee included that passage in his article in the *Southern Historical Society Papers* "Reply to General Longstreet" in 1878. Hancock enjoyed enormous respect from both sides of the Mason-Dixon line. Therefore, observers took his words as solid support to the popular contention that General Ewell had blundered by failing to pursue the fleeing Federals through Gettysburg and drive them off the coveted heights south of town. The entirety of Hancock's letter to Fitzhugh Lee, however, specifies that any Confederate opportunity was fleeting. The letter continues: "After I had arrived on the field, assumed the command, and made my dispositions for defending that point (say 4 P. M.), I do not think the Confederate force then present could have carried it. I felt certain at least of my ability to hold it until night, and sent word to that effect back to General Meade, who was then at Taneytown."[55]

His words may be self-serving, but his contention that Cemetery and Culp's Hills were vulnerable for only a very brief time is credible. There may never be a consensus about Hancock's time of arrival on the hill relative to that of the retreating men of the First and Eleventh Corps. But there is no known contention that any disorder there lasted more than a few minutes. One also has to consider that disorder typically does not just occur among the retreating troops, but on their pursuers as well. This would be especially so in this case where narrow unknown streets came into play.

Since the town lay between the advancing Confederates and the heights to the south, and since the disorder on those heights lasted only a few minutes, the Confederate pursuit would have to have been as fast as the Federals' flight. This precludes the option for Confederates to stop and reform. Not only would they have had to form into column to get through the town, they would have had to reform into battle line as they emerged from town directly under the guns on Cemetery Hill.

Hence, the hypothetical "continued pursuit" of which Hancock speaks needed to have been essentially that of one mob chasing another. The benefits of such an undertaking are highly debatable. One also has to consider that the two Federal corps might simply have retired to the Pipe Creek line in good order, depriving the Confederates of a fully convincing victory over the Army of the Potomac.

Schurz summarized all this well:

> There has been much speculation as to whether the Confederates would not have won the battle of Gettysburg had they pressed the attack on the first day

after the substantial overthrow of the First and Eleventh Corps. Southern writers are almost unanimous in the opinion that Lee would then without serious trouble have achieved a great victory. It is indeed possible that had they vigorously pushed their attack with their whole available force at the moment when the First and Eleventh Corps were entangled in the streets of the town, they might have completely annihilated those corps, possessed themselves of Cemetery Hill, and taken the heads of the Federal columns advancing toward Gettysburg at a disadvantage. But night would soon have put an end to that part of the action; that night would have given General Meade time to change his dispositions, and the main battle would in all likelihood have been fought on Pipe Creek instead of Gettysburg, in the position which General Meade had originally selected.

Nor is it quite so certain, as Southern writers seem to think, that the Confederates would have had easy work in carrying Cemetery Hill after the First and Eleventh Corps had passed through the town and occupied that position. When they speak of the two corps as having fled from the field in a state of utter demoralization, they grossly exaggerate. Those troops were indeed beaten back, but not demoralized or dispirited. Had they been in a state of rout such as Southern writers describe, they would certainly have left many of their cannon behind them. But they brought off their whole artillery save one single dismounted piece, and that artillery, as now posted, was capable of formidable work. The infantry was indeed reduced by well-nigh one half its effective force, but all that was left, was good. Besides, the Confederates, too, had suffered severely. Their loss in killed and wounded and prisoners was very serious. Several of their brigades had become so disordered during the action that it required some time to re-form them.[56]

Return Trip

Hancock felt satisfied that the position at Gettysburg was stable and that his work there was done. His official report explains:

> Between 5 and 6 o'clock, my dispositions having been completed, Major-General Slocum arrived on the field, and, considering that my functions had ceased, I transferred the command to him. The head of the Third Corps appeared in sight shortly afterward, on the Emmitsburg road.
> About dark I started for the headquarters of the army, still at Taneytown, 13 miles distant, and reported in person to General Meade.[57]

Before he reached Meade, he encountered his own Second Corps, still under the temporary command of General Gibbon. It had marched from Taneytown to about three miles south of Gettysburg in Hancock's absence. According to Morgan, it was "in a position to secure the left flank against any turning movement around Round Top."[58] Many officers were anxious to learn what the general had seen on his trip to the front, and even though he must have been anxious to see General Meade, he obliged them. Lieutenant Haskell of Gibbon's staff reported:

While I was engaged in showing the troops their positions, I met General Hancock, then on his way from the front to General Meade, who was back towards Taneytown; and he, for the purpose of having me advise General Gibbon, for his information, gave me a quite detailed account of the situation of matters at Gettysburg, and of what transpired subsequently to his arrival there.

He had arrived and assumed command there, just when the troops of the First and Eleventh Corps, after their repulse, were coming in confusion through the town. Hancock is just the man for such an emergency as this.[59]

Lieutenant Colonel Franklin Sawyer of the Eighth Ohio wrote: "We met Gen. Hancock, who was returning to Gen. Meade's headquarters. In a conversation with Col. Carroll [commanding First Brigade, Third Division, Second Corps], he gave the outline of the battle up to the time he had left the field; the driving back by the rebels of the First and Eleventh Corps through Gettysburg, and the probability of a great battle the next day. 'But,' said Gen. Hancock, 'I have selected a position from which LEE cannot drive us, and there the battle will be fought.'"[60]

Private William Kepler of the Fourth Ohio remembered the specifics differently, but agreed with Sawyer on the overall sense of the conversation: "just at dark we met our Corps Commander, General Hancock, in whose generalship and judgment all had unbounded confidence.... Just as the General was riding away Carroll asked: 'General, have we a good position?' and received the instant reply, in a firm tone, 'If Lee does not attack before all our forces are up, we can hold the position I have selected against the whole Confederacy.'"[61]

Hancock later said he had wanted "to report to General Meade in detail what I had done, in order to express my views clearly to him, and to see what he was disposed to do."[62] Certainly Meade was interested in hearing from Hancock. However, it seems the eventuality of their meeting was anti-climactic. As Hancock put it: "I rode back and found General Meade about 9 o'clock. He told me he had received my messages and note, and had decided, upon the representations I had made, and the existence of known facts of the case, to fight at Gettysburg, and had ordered all the corps to the front. That was the end of operations for that day."[63]

But for Meade, another day was just beginning: "At 10 p.m. of the 1st, I broke up my headquarters, which until then had been at Taneytown, and proceeded to the field, arriving there at 1 a.m. of the 2d."[64]

Hancock took the moment as an opportunity to get some sleep. According to Morgan, the general's rest was well deserved but would be brief.

Being somewhat exhausted by the labors of the day—for it is to be remembered that he had ridden from Unionville to Gettysburg, and after riding many miles to and fro from the field, back to Taneytown again—he laid down for a couple hours to rest, General Meade himself starting for Gettysburg.[65]

Morgan also noted that the labors of the day took their toll not just on the general, but his entire staff as well. And perhaps it was their horses who made the greatest sacrifice. "I made my way back [to Taneytown] as best I could on an exhausted horse, who had lost two of his shoes on the way. I passed one of the Generals aides lying by the side of the road, his horse having given out. I reached Army Headquarters about midnight and an hour or two afterwards the General started back to the field getting there at an early hour in the morning. Nearly every horse belonging to the General or his staff on this day died from hard riding."[66]

So ended the first day of the battle of Gettysburg and so began one of the most tumultuous days in American history.

5

The Battle of Bliss Farm

One of the bravest spirits in our Armies during the war was General Alexander Hays, of Pittsburg, Penna. He joined the 2nd Army Corps with his division near Centreville, Virginia, on the march to Gettsyburg and during that battle his troops held the ground immediately on the left of the Taneytown road on our front line of battle. His skirmishers were deployed in the valley before him. A large barn stood on this plain just beyond his skirmish line which was held by the "Reb" skirmishers in considerable force & from which they maintained a galling fire.[1]

—Henry Bingham

The hours before daybreak on 2 July must have been relatively uneventful for Hancock, since there is virtually no historical record of them. Even Morgan's writings, through which one can almost locate Hancock at any minute on 1 July, do not adequately account for the first six hours or so of 2 July: "Soon after midnight General Hancock returned to Gettysburg, rejoining the Second Corps before its arrival on the field at 7 a.m."[2] Given that two hours is a conservative estimate for getting from Taneytown to Gettysburg, there is a gap in the historical record.

The general may have tended to matters typical of his particular character, like clerical chores or aspects of personal appearance. Perhaps he just got more sleep. Maybe he did all these things. Military history tends to overlook matters of human necessity and comfort. Nevertheless, it is apparent that he did not involve himself in any matters of tactical importance during this time, except for the fact that some relief and a good meal would have contributed greatly to his performance in the coming critical hours. Hancock's brief disappearance from historical accounts indicates that he had substantial confidence in both the position of the army and the man he left in charge of the Second Corps, General Gibbon. Schurz confirmed that it was a relatively quiet night on Ceme-

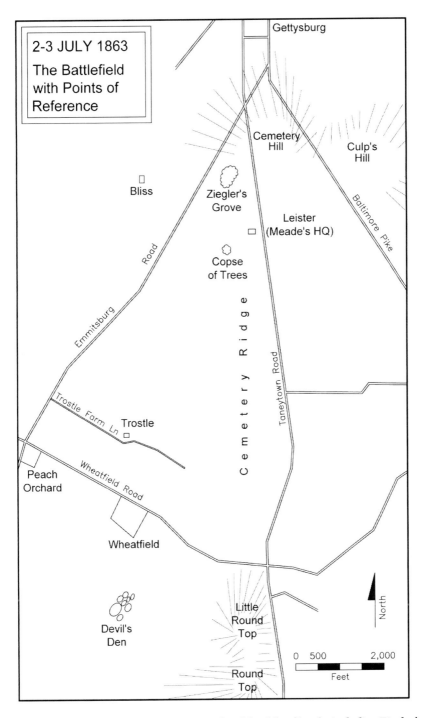

2-3 JULY 1863

The Battlefield with Points of Reference

Gettysburg

Cemetery Hill

Culp's Hill

Bliss

Ziegler's Grove

Leister (Meade's HQ)

Baltimore Pike

Copse of Trees

Emmitsburg Road

Cemetery Ridge

Taneytown Road

Trostle Farm Ln

Trostle

Peach Orchard

Wheatfield Road

Wheatfield

Devil's Den

Little Round Top

North

0 500   2,000

Feet

Round Top

This map shows features critical to the second and third days' battle, including Ziegler's Grove and the Bliss farm. Map by the author.

tery Hill, especially considering the promise of such great and terrible events to follow: "It was rather a commonplace, business-like 'good-night,' as that of an ordinary occasion. We of the Eleventh Corps, occupying the cemetery, lay down, wrapt in our cloaks, with the troops among the grave-stones. There was profound stillness in the graveyard, broken by no sound but the breathing of men and here and there the tramp of a horse's foot; and sullen rumblings mysteriously floating on the air from a distance all around."[3]

Gibbon, leading the Second Corps from its bivouac south of the Round Tops, agreed that things were well under control even after operations of the second day began:

> We were all astir early in the morning and would have been on the road by daylight but for some detention caused by the leading division. We got off, however, soon after, and to facilitate the march and shorten the column, the road was left, as before, to the artillery and ambulances, the infantry marching through the grain and grass fields on each side. In this way the corps reached the field about 6 o'clock. I reported to Gen. Meade near by the house where his Headquarters were afterwards established. Reports were then constantly reaching him and everything betokened preparations for a coming battle. I heard Meade say that Ewell was reported to be concentrating a force on our right. Soon after our arrival, the corps was directed to go into position…. About the time the 2nd Corps took up its position, Hancock resumed command of it and I reverted to my division.[4]

Hancock later recalled, before the Joint Committee on the Conduct of the War, that the reported concentration by Ewell precipitated a short-lived placement of the Second Corps in a position largely forgotten by history: "In fact, when I arrived on the ground in the morning, General Meade thought there would be a formidable attack by the enemy on the right of our line, and when my corps arrived on the ground it was formed facing in that direction, but shortly afterwards was marched over to the position which we held during the subsequent battle."[5]

After going into its place in the line of battle, the Second Corps, like the rest of the army, found the Confederates had failed to organize for a significant early attack. Hancock stated, "Some time after daylight, I again reported to General Meade, at Gettysburg, and assumed command of my own corps after it arrived."[6] He does not recount surveying the field with Meade, but it seems likely that he would have.

An account by a soldier in Robinson's (Second) Division of the First Corps' notes a visit from Hancock:

> Upon waking in the morning, we found everything astir with excitement and preparation. Thousands of troops had gathered in the night, presenting a formidable appearance in the gray morning light. As we were gazing about, a party of officers were seen approaching, among whom was General Hancock. Some of

the boys, regardless of danger, were exposing themselves on top and at the sides of the earthworks that we built last night, when, in a mild, pleasant voice, General Hancock said, "Keep down, boys; that is the way with you Massachusetts boys—too much d——d curiosity; keep down![7]

As for Meade, one of his staff recorded he "was occupied during the night in directing the troops, and as soon as it was daylight, he proceeded to inspect the position occupied, and for making arrangements for posting the several corps as they should arrive."[8]

Once he got over his concern for the right flank, Meade posted the Second Corps in the center of the battle line. Its right lay in Ziegler's Grove, on the western edge of Cemetery Hill. From there the corps extended south, in an essentially straight line, along Cemetery Ridge to the vicinity of the Weikert farm house. There the left of the Second Corps met the right of the Third Corps, at least for the moment. The Third Corps' left was to rest at the base of Little Round Top, where Hancock had put Geary's division the previous evening. Geary's division had, in the interim, rejoined the Twelfth Corps on Culp's Hill.

The Second Corps formed its three divisions as follows. The Third Division, under Brigadier General Alexander Hays, was on the right. A substantial portion of which was in Ziegler's Grove. Gibbon's Second Division fell in line as the corps' center. On the left, remaining in column because there was no immediate threat, was the First Division under Brigadier General John C. Caldwell. Including artillerists, the Second Corps had something over eleven thousand men for the impending fight.[9]

The widely accepted view of Gettysburg's second day holds that there was no substantial fighting until Confederate General Longstreet attacked the Union left in the late afternoon. That contention is true, as long as one accepts that skirmishing is not "substantial fighting."

For those on the Second Corps skirmish line, however, killing and dying began quite early in the morning.[10] There was particularly sharp skirmishing, made so largely by the struggle for possession of the Bliss farm buildings. These buildings lay midway between the Union and Confederate lines, which were slightly less than a mile apart. The position and the especially large size of the Bliss barn gave it special tactical importance. A Connecticut soldier remarked that the barn was "almost a citadel in itself. It was an expensively and elaborately built structure ... seventy five feet long and thirty-three feet wide."[11] Historian Elwood Christ later wrote,

> Due to the structural strength of the barn and the house, these buildings along with the orchard, all situated on a slight hillock, provided the only significant cover for troops operating over 1,200 yards of relatively flat, open farm lands between the battle lines. The soldiers who could hold the house, barn, and

orchard had an excellent view of the opponent's main position and fortifications, could monitor their activities more accurately, and any sharpshooters stationed there could rain havoc on the enemy's troops all in relative safety.[12]

It is not clear which side first occupied the Bliss farm in force. But as Lieutenant John L. Brady of the First Delaware notes, daylight had hardly broken before his regiment became engaged in a struggle for the complex:

> Shortly after daylight on the morning of July 2d, 1863, the regiment was sent forward, and at once deployed as skirmishers, with Lt. Col. E. P. Harris, of the 1st Delaware in command of the line. For sake of convenience, I shall divide the regiment into "wings" i.e., the "right" and "left" respectively, and say: that the left wing, of which my company "E" (being the one to which I was attached) formed a part moved forward, under a brisk fire from the enemy, in front, and occupied a position in a large field of wheat, on the left of or south end of the barn, while the right wing extended north of that building into a peach orchard.
> Here we (of the left wing) remained under a rattling fire from the enemy, which was repaid with interest, until about 8 o'clock a.m.[13]

Thus began an intense and deadly back-and-forth struggle for the yard and buildings of the Bliss farm. Overseeing this contest under Hancock was General Hays, since it was his division's front on which the Bliss farm stood. Hancock and Hays had known each other since West Point, where they were quite close. Hays was already a graduate of Allegheny College when he became a cadet.[14] According to twentieth century historian Glenn Tucker: "Probably Hays was Hancock's closest friend at the Academy, though the relationship was a bit paternal, for Hays was a few days short of twenty-one when he entered, Hancock's senior by nearly five years."[15]

Physical size also helped shape the nature of their friendship. Hancock, as William Franklin recalled "was then a small boy scarcely of the regulation height" and Hays was a large man.[16] No story better illustrates the closeness and "paternal" nature of their relationship than that of Hays' fist fight with a schoolmate who bullied Hancock. Although Winfield demonstrated his will to defend himself, Alex Hays saw fit to intervene on Hancock's behalf against William Logan Crittenden (this was not one of the Crittendens famous in antebellum politics or the Civil War itself).

Crittenden and Hays first sparred verbally over the former's mistreatment of Hancock, who was still a diminutive plebe. Crittenden did not yield, and agreed to settle the matter with Hays via a contest of bare fists. The two brawny

Opposite: **A bronze statue in Ziegler's Grove depicts the indomitable Brigadier General Alexander Hays gazing out at the field in front of Cemetery Ridge. Commanding the Third Division of the Second Corps, he directed much of the fighting at the Bliss farm, which he considered his "Reb trap" (photograph by William Bretzger).**

young men met behind the Kosciuzko Monument to settle their differences.[17] Their battle is said to have been brutally long and ferocious, leaving both cadets on the ground.[18] However, Hays eventually walked away while Crittenden needed several days of bed rest.[19]

After graduation, the careers of Winfield and Alex took parallel but separate paths. Both men distinguished themselves in the Mexican War, between wars, and in the Civil War itself. The morning of 2 July 1863 was a reunion of sorts, as Hays and several of his units were new to the Second Corps. Hancock, although new to its command, had been with the corps through most of its hard-won glory.[20] The battle of Bliss farm would be their first major collaboration since their days as cadets.

Unfortunately, the fortitude which came so naturally to Hays and Hancock escaped Colonel Harris on the skirmish line. Lieutenant Brady's account continues:

> I at once proceeded along the line, in quest of Lt. Col. Harris, whom, in the meantime, we of the left had lost sight of. Upon finding that officer in the basement of the barn, where he had established his headquarters, I at once explained to him the state of affairs, as existing on the right.
>
> Whereupon he, after carefully venturing from this, his safe retreat, and taking a very hasty glance over the situation, turned and fled precipitately, towards our main lines, leaving that portion of the field, in the immediate charge of 1st Lieutenant Charles B. Tanner, and myself.[21]

For those Harris left behind, the situation was indeed hazardous, as Brady laments: "Here it was that Capt. Martin W. B. Ellegood ... yielded up his young life.... And here to, 'pari passer' it was that my old friend, Captain Ezechial C. Alexander, together with several of the 'boys' received tickets for gratuitous admission to partake in the hospitalities of Libby Prison at Richmond Va."[22]

Hence, the "skirmishing" that history so frequently forgets was not so forgettable to its participants. Hancock did not overlook these actions either, as Harris soon discovered. Harris' exhibition of self preservation was natural but not acceptable in the context of war, especially in Hancock's corps, as Brady recalled: "Upon returning to the main line, after the enemy had succeeded in taking the barn, and cutting off our left wing, I found Lieutenant Col. Harris, in the apple orchard, confronted by General Hancock, who, standing erect in his stirrups, was interviewing him in the most choice and forcible language deemed suitable for the occasion, which resulted in Harris, being then and there 'ordered under arrest for cowardice in the face of the enemy.'"[23]

Hancock's old West Point pal shared his hands-on approach. Colonel Clinton MacDougall of the 111th New York recalled the rare sight of a division commander on the skirmish line: "I can never forget the first act of superb gallantry I noticed in General Hays. The line of skirmishers on our right was hard pressed and gave way. In an instant the general rode down at a gallop mounted on his fine bay 'Dan,' with an orderly carrying his division flag, followed by his other orderlies. The line was at once re-established.... It was the first and last time I ever saw a division commander with his flag and staff on the skirmish line—they were targets for hundreds of sharpshooters."[24]

Opposing skirmishers repeatedly exchanged possession of the Bliss farm throughout the day. By Brady's account,

> Time about 10 o'clock a.m. July 2d, 1863. The "barn" that endless "bone of contention" was now in possession of the 12th N. Jersey, who at sometime succeeded in capturing somewhere between ninety and one hundred prisoners, among whom were several commissioned officers.
>
> Shortly after this the enemy in force, made a charge upon and re-captured the barn, whereupon detachments from the 1st Delaware, and the 12th New Jersey, were ordered to "Move in." This movement was accomplished with little, if any loss, and being subsequently reinforced, by a small detachment from the "Berdan Sharpshooters" we retained possession until about 6 o'clock p.m. July 2d; at which time a largely increased force of the enemy, was seen approaching, under the cover of Steven's Run, (being a small canyon or gulch lying contiguous to the barn) when we, then under command of Capt. T. J. Thompson 12th New Jersey "moved out," and falling back on our main line rested during the night.[25]

The New Jerseyans may have been done for the day, but several other regiments and companies maintained heavy pressure on their Confederate enemies in and around the Bliss farm. These Union units included the 106th Pennsylvania and First Delaware as well as part of Berdan's Sharpshooters. Most notably, however, were the Eighth Ohio and parts of the 4th. The Eighth Ohio, in particular, began an audaciously forward stand that lasted some twenty-four hours, arguably becoming a fly in the ointment of top Confederate aspirations.[26] But mysterious actions by the Union Third Corps, on the other end of Hancock's line, were shaping the battle to a much greater degree. The trouble brewing there would put the Union army in the worst position it would find itself throughout the entire battle.

6

Sickles Advances

*The object of General Sickles moving to the front I could not
conceive.*[1]

—Winfield Scott Hancock

On the evening of 1 July 1863, General Winfield Scott Hancock had collected the Union troops present near Gettysburg, and laid them out on roughly
the line they would hold until the end of the battle two days later. The strength
of the position Hancock laid out for the army late 1 July is irrefutable. Curling
counter-clockwise from Culp's Hill to Cemetery Hill, then stretching down
Cemetery Ridge to Little Round Top, the army anchored itself on commanding
heights and connected those heights with relatively short straight lines. It
required only the Second and Third Corps to fill the space between Cemetery
Hill and Little Round Top. The arrival of the Fifth Corps provided ample
strength to fully cover the Round Tops and still hold the hard marching Sixth
in reserve. The failure of General Lee's all-out assault of 3 July against this line
proved it unbreakable.

On 2 July however, the well-meaning but ill-conceived actions of Third
Corps commander General Sickles thwarted the design of his own army's command. When Sickles arrived at Gettysburg, his biography already had enough
color and controversy to stake a notable place in American history, for better
or worse. Born in New York City in 1825, Daniel Edgar Sickles became a lawyer
and politician in New York's Tammany Hall political machine.[2] According to
modern historian William Glenn Robertson: "Sickles soon gained a reputation
as a rake, a spendthrift and a partisan politician of high visibility. Election to
the New York state assembly in 1847 offered a new arena to Sickles, who scan-
dalized polite society by escorting a known prostitute into the legislative cham-
bers. Sickles ignored censure by his peers, and both his political and legal careers
prospered."[3]

He won election to the New York state senate in 1855 and the United

States Congress in 1856.[4] By Robertson's account, "He lived far beyond his means, continued his rakish indiscretions, and generally made himself notorious in Washington society."[5] In 1859, he really made things interesting. When he found Phillip Barton Key, son of Francis Scott Key, was having an affair with his wife, he shot and killed him.[6] The ensuing trial resulted in the first ever successful use of the plea of innocent by reason of temporary insanity.[7] His exoneration kept him out of jail but he did not run for re-election in 1860.[8]

Sickles turned the outbreak of war in 1861 into an opportunity to resurrect his public career. Former politician became patriotic soldier upon helping raise first a New York regiment, then the "Excelsior Brigade."[9] Though he was inexperienced, his impetuous nature served him well as a soldier. His political connections and friendship with the similarly fast living General Hooker helped him rise to the rank of major general and command of the Third Corps by February 1863.[10]

His experience at the battle of Chancellorsville, merely two months before Gettysburg, probably had great influence on his ill-advised actions at the latter engagement. On 2 May 1863, he observed a Confederate column marching across his front. When he aggressively moved his corps forward to engage it, Hooker called him back.[11] The Confederate column later proved to be that of Stonewall Jackson on its legendary flank march, which resulted in the rout of the Union right flank under General Howard. The next day, Sickles' frustration increased when Hooker ordered Sickles to retire from the heights of Hazel Grove. The enemy quickly occupied the abandoned position and used it to launch a deadly artillery barrage against its former occupants.[12] It is therefore entirely possible that when he led his corps to Gettysburg, the headstrong Sickles was highly doubtful about the judgments higher command made from its relatively isolated headquarters. It is similarly possible that he felt more convinced than ever that aggressiveness was the way to deal with mysterious enemy activity. Finally, it is almost certain that he became acutely aware of what the enemy's guns could inflict on him from a seemingly dominant position.

When he received orders early 2 July to replace Geary's division of the Twelfth Corps and extend the battle line from Hancock's left to Little Round Top, he did not like the position. Had he taken the position as ordered, there is some truth to his contention that he would have faced higher ground in his front. His center would have been looking up a gentle rise to the Peach Orchard along the Emmitsburg Road, just less than a mile west. Furthermore, he believed the enemy was moving around his left flank and intended to attack there. By 4:00 p.m. the obstinate political general had advanced his corps to a long and winding position which included the aforementioned Peach Orchard.

Francis Amasa Walker served on Hancock's staff, though he was not at

Gettysburg; and later chronicled his commander and the Second Corps. He described Hancock observing the Third Corps advance: "Hancock had, with great anxiety, seen the throwing forward of Sickles' corps to the Emmitsburg road. As he watched the movement of Humphreys' division he turned to his staff and said: 'Gentlemen, that is a splendid advance. But' he added after a moments pause, 'those troops will be coming back again very soon.'"[13]

Amasa included a critique in his writings that well exemplify the criticism of Sickles' actions by both his contemporaries and modern observers:

> This was done without notification to General Hancock, so that a gap of some hundreds of yards appeared between the right of the Third Corps and the left of the Second. Moreover, the advance of General Sickles to the Emmettsburg road … not only brought the Third Corps into a very advanced position, but left its flank "in air," offered to the enemy's blows. To remedy this defect General Sickles resorted to the next most dangerous device in warfare, namely, the formation of an angle, both lines of which were subject to an enfilading fire.… As this movement of General Sickles led to momentous consequences, it has become the subject of much controversy.[14]

Walker does not stop there:

> General Sickles alleges that he had not as many troops to hold the left as should had been given him. But the smaller General Sickles' force, the stronger would seem to be the reasons against doubling, as he did, the length of the line he was to hold. General Sickles further says that the Round Tops formed the key of the position at Gettysburg; that General Meade had neglected to occupy them, and that his movement was to cover and protect that position. But General Sickles did not, in his movement, cover either of the Round Tops, his line ceasing at the Devil's Den; so that when the enemy … began to swarm up the slopes of Little Round Top, it was not the troops of the Third Corps, but troops of the Fifth … which they encountered.[15]

Finally, says Walker:

> Again, the commander of the Third Corps alleges that the ground he was asked to occupy, on the extension of Cemetery Ridge toward Little Round Top, was low and untenable, and that the position to which he advanced was strong and commanding. It is true that for half or three-quarters of a mile the line assigned to General Sickles was not a good one. It will happen , in battle, that, in order to hold the best line for the whole army, some one body of troops may be required to take a position not in itself desirable. The forces which disposed the surface of the earth have generally so acted as to produce few lines which have not a weak point. In occupying a position, the army must take the bad with the good, the weak with the strong. The general line from Culp's Hill, across Cemetery Hill down Cemetery Ridge to Little Round Top, was, on the whole, a very strong one.… General Sickles' attempt to piece out one line with the other, and to combine the strong points of both, proved futile and disastrous.[16]

Commentators have debated the prudence of Sickles' move since the day he made it. Experts typically conclude that Sickles made a grave mistake and that the Federals escaped defeat that day despite his actions, not because of them. However, historians have not fully examined how Sickles was able to make the ill-advised advance in the first place. How did the Army of the Potomac manage to misplace 10,000 men? How did an entire corps become so badly located while posted next door to the ever alert General Hancock?

The timing of the advance is critical to this issue. If the Third Corps had advanced early and conspicuously, there would have been plenty of time to correct the error before the enemy attacked and therefore no explanation for Hancock's apparent inaction. If they did not advance until just before they came under attack around 4:00 p.m. it would have been impossible for anyone, including Hancock, to rectify the situation on time.

The character of the advance is also important. Was it gradual or abrupt? If it was gradual, one understands how it might go unnoticed. Most descriptions paint a picture of a grand military spectacle, with endless lines of soldiers, bands playing and flags flying. According to Colonel St. Clair Mulholland of the 116th Pennsylvania in Caldwell's division, the advance was a giant parade-like spectacle which interrupted a quiet afternoon:

> The boys had partly recovered from their fatigue, and were actually beginning to enjoy life; some of them indulged in a quiet game of euchre, while others toasted their hard-tack or fried a little bacon at the small fires at the rear of the lines. Shortly after 3 o'clock a movement was apparent on our left ... and when it became evident that something was going to take place, the boys dropped their cards regardless of what was the trump, even the men who held the bowers and the ace- and all gathered on the most favorable positions to witness the opening of the ball. Soon the long lines of the Third Corps are seen advancing, and how splendidly they march. It looks like a dress parade, a review. On, on they go.[17]

Mulholland's words were always colorful, and therefore subject to suspicion of embellishment. Perhaps an observation by Hancock himself is a more reliable testimony to the abruptness and spectacle of the movement: "Everything remained quiet, except with artillery and engagements with pickets in our front, until about 4 o'clock in the afternoon, when General Sickles moved out to the front. I happen to be present with my corps at the time.... I recollect looking on and admiring the spectacle."[18]

Major Tremain disagreed with the common sentiment regarding the advance: "The 'spectacle' that has been described by participants and others—often in exaggerated language—as attendant upon this 'grand advance' of the 'Third Corps going into battle' was in reality no 'advance' at all. It was simply the movement forward of the infantry battalions to the locations essential to be held for the support of the skirmishers at their front, and for the defense of the night's camping ground."[19]

Was it, as Tremain asserted, "in reality no 'advance' at all"?[20] Or was it a "spectacle," as Hancock put it and a "ball" as Mulholland described?[21] To answer this, an examination of the Third Corps' actions and aspirations from very early in the day is in order. The Third Corps consisted of two divisions. Major General David Bell Birney commanded the First Division and Brigadier-General Andrew Atkinson Humphreys led the Second Division. General Birney's official report describes his original position as follows: "At 7 a. m., under orders from Major-General Sickles, I relieved Geary's division [the Twelfth Corps unit Hancock had positioned the previous evening], and formed a line, resting its left on Sugar Loaf Mountain [Little Round Top] and the right thrown in a direct line toward the cemetery, connecting on the right with the Second Division of this corps. My picket line was in the Emmitsburg road, with sharpshooters some 300 yards in advance."[22]

Meanwhile, Humphreys' report describes his first position as such: "At an early hour of the morning, my division was massed in the vicinity of its bivouac, facing the Emmitsburg road, near the crest of the ridge running from the cemetery of Gettysburg, in a southerly direction, to a rugged, conical-shaped hill, which I find goes by the name of [Little] Round Top, about 2 miles from Gettysburg."[23]

Thus the corps began the day as Meade wanted, completing the army's line from Hancock's left to Little Round Top. Birney was the far left, with his left flank at the base of Little Round Top. Humphreys was on Birney's right, connecting the corps to Caldwell's division of the Second Corps. The massing Humphreys described, as opposed to a battle line, was similar to Caldwell's division. In the absence of an immediate threat or plan to attack, it left the troops able to move quickly in response to any unforeseen development.

But the Third Corps never had a stable formation of any type. While the rest of the army seems to have settled into defensive placements almost immediately, the Third Corps was unsettled, fluid, and active all day. This unsettled posture dated back to the previous evening, as Tremain recalls: "The Third Corps had simply gone into bivouac, pretty much of it in the gloom of the evening 'on the left of the Second Corps.' Neither the batteries nor the infantry were occupying special posts selected for defence or offence."[24]

Part of the cause for tentativeness at dawn was the fact that the whole corps had not yet arrived on the field. Also, the latecomers were arriving via the Emmitsburg Road, a route they perceived to be under Confederate threat.[25] However, the Third Corps' desire to hold the Emmitsburg Road persisted well after the entire corps had arrived safely. Years later, Tremain revealed this command decision in a speech to surviving veterans of the Third Corps: "Lest surprise and destruction should reach you it became essential to decide if the Emmitsburg road, by which we had marched, was to be held or abandoned. I was sent to General Meade to ask that question, and I asked it. In the absence of explicit orders to abandon it, military necessity and good discipline required it should be held. The picket and skirmish line, therefore, of your division held it."[26]

But holding the road was a tall order for such a small corps, especially if it was to form where Meade wanted it, almost a mile east of the road on the Cemetery Ridge line.

Either because of Sickles' incompetence, or the impossibility of achieving all the objectives his corps was aspiring to, his corps behaved in a confused and indecisive manner. A colonel of the Eleventh New Jersey reported, "*July 2.—Morning dawned....* Troops moving in different directions, apparently taking up several positions."[27] A major of the Twenty-sixth Pennsylvania reported: "On the morning of July 2, my regiment was detailed to clear away the fences in front of the division, to facilitate the movement of our troops."[28]

Tremain held the backwards notion that the main body was to support the skirmishers, instead of vice-versa. He explained that the Third Corps advance "was simply the movement forward of the infantry battalions to the location essential to be held for support of the skirmishers at their front."[29] And of his thinking during the moment in question, he recalled: "But first of all, the pickets! Where should they be posted? ... What lines should be covered? My first duty concerned this feature."[30]

An illustration of how disorganized the corps was is the plight of the Third Brigade of Sickles' Second Division, with Colonel George C. Burling commanding. His report is a tale of turmoil:

> We joined the corps and division at 9 a.m., July 2nd. The brigade was massed in columns of regiments, and remained in that position until nearly 12 m., when General Humphreys ordered us to our position as a reserve to the First and Second brigades of our division. Shortly after, I received orders from General Humphreys to march to the left, and report to General Birney, commanding First Division, Third Corps. I did so, and was ordered by him to mass the brigade in a piece of woods in the rear of the division.[31]

This was tolerable, but was just the beginning: "In a short time skirmishing commenced very heavily along his front. I was then ordered by General Birney out of the woods on an open field. Immediately on our unmasking, the enemy opened with a terrific artillery fire on our left flank, at a distance of not more than 1,000 yards."[32]

This led to another relocation: "After remaining in this position for half an hour, upon the solicitation of several regimental commanders…. I ordered the brigade to fall back about 100 yards, where they would have the protection of a small rise of ground, which was done in perfect order."[33]

More disarrangement followed: "At this moment Captain Poland, of General Sickles' staff, rode up to me, and, in an excited manner, inquired by whose authority I moved the brigade. I answered 'By my own.' He ordered me to take the brigade back again. I started with it, when an aide from General Birney ordered me to change direction to the left, and take a position behind a piece of woods, my front now being at right angles with my former front."[34]

Then, the fragmentation of Burling's brigade began: "I now received orders from General Birney to detail two of my largest regiments to report to General Graham, in compliance with which I detailed the Second New Hampshire and Seventh New Jersey Volunteers."[35]

The dismembering continued: "Shortly after this, I received orders from General Birney to detail the strongest regiment to report to General Humphreys for picket, in compliance with which I sent the Fifth New Jersey volunteers, leaving me three small regiments."[36]

They were struggling just to find some semblance of a continuous battle line. "I was now ordered by General Birney to form a line across a small wheatfield on my left," wrote Burling, "to connect two brigades of the First Division."[37]

But the fragmentation continued: "Before I had executed this order, I received an order from General Birney to send the largest regiment to General Ward's support, on my left, and while I was attending to that, the Eighth New Jersey Volunteers was taken from me without my knowledge, leaving me with the One hundred and fifteenth Pennsylvania Volunteers, numbering 140 muskets."[38]

Burling's brigade had become so divided that he finally availed himself for other services: "My command being now all taken from me and separated, no two regiments being together, and being under the command of the different brigade commanders to whom they had reported, I, with my staff, reported to General Humphreys for instructions, remaining with him for some time."[39]

The constant relocation and complete redistribution of Burling's men indicates an apprehensive and uncertain corps command. But Sickles did seem certain about one thing: he wanted to advance his corps to the Peach Orchard. In hindsight, Sickles seems to have tipped his hand around noon when he moved his own headquarters forward to the Trostle farm yard, well in advance of the main battle line. According to modern historian Kathleen G. Harrison: "As a result of his own deliberations, Sickles no longer waited for a decision from General Meade. He made preparations for a general movement forward to occupy higher ground. He moved his headquarters from Cemetery Ridge to a spot near the Trostle barn along the farm lane, from which he and his staff would personally oversee the movement of his brigades and batteries to battle positions."[40]

As for the question concerning the nature of his corps' advance—whether it was abrupt or gradual—it was gradual and piecemeal throughout most of the day but culminated in a spectacular forward movement. By Birney's account, it appears his division began the Third Corps advance after some of his advanced skirmishers found some enemy apparently sidling around his left flank:

> At 12 m., believing from the constant fire of the enemy that a movement was being made toward the left, I received permission [to advance skirmishers] and feel the enemy's right.... The skirmishers of the enemy were driven in, but three columns of their forces were found marching to our left....
> Communicating this important information to Major-General Sickles, I was ordered by that officer to change my front and meet the attack. I did this by advancing my left 500 yards, and swinging around the right so as to rest on the Emmitsburg road at the peach orchard.[41]

Hence, Birney had moved forward five hundred yards and wheeled his right flank to the Emmitsburg Road, an enormous relocation. The far right of the position was close to a mile in front of where Hancock had placed Geary's division the night before. So why did Hancock not sound an alarm? He probably could not see most of the movement because of intervening woods and a drop in elevation. Morgan, writing about Sickles, remembered, "From our line we could see little beyond the left of his right division (Humphreys)."[42] Humphreys himself said that even he could not see in that direction: "I ... had no knowledge of the general position of the other troops except what I could see on my right; the ground on my left was hidden by trees."[43] Hancock should have been able to, however, see the force of Birney's which was at the Emmitsburg Road. There is no clear explanation as to why he did not respond with some apprehension to the advance. Perhaps he reasoned that the advanced contingent was small, being that he could not see the rest of Birney's men.

Humphreys then began to assemble a more battle-ready formation, according to his report: "Shortly after midday, I was ordered to form my division in line of battle, my left joining the right of the First Division of the Third Corps, Major-General Birney commanding, and my right resting opposite the left of General Caldwell's division, of the Second Corps, which was massed on the crest near my place of bivouac. The line I was directed to occupy was near the foot of the westerly slope of the ridge [Cemetery Ridge] I have already mentioned."[44]

Being "near the foot of the westerly slope of the ridge," Humphreys was neither on Cemetery Ridge nor that ridge on which the Emmitsburg Road ran.

Rather, he was in the shallow valley between them. In 1864, when the Congressional Committee on the conduct of the War questioned him, it was probably this position under discussion in the following excerpt from the committee's transcript:

> Question. Your position was in advance of the general line somewhat?
> Answer. Yes; my division was.
> Question. So as to expose its flanks?
> Answer. Not at that time. My orders first were to form with my right resting on the left of the 2d corps, and my left touching general Birney's right and in line with him; but I could not do both; and when I learned from General Caldwell that he had no orders to move forward, I reported it to General Sickles, and was ordered to form as I did. It was at that time, I think, that I was authorized to call on General Caldwell for support. We were both of opinion that the distance I was then in front of him would make no very great difference. We were in a hollow, and this was simply a preliminary position of the troops.[45]

In an attempt to improvise a connection between Birney's extremely forward right and Caldwell's left, Humphreys took to stacking his units, one in front of the other: "The front allotted to me admitted of my forming the First Brigade ... in line of battle.... The Second Brigade ... was formed in line of battalions in mass 200 yards in rear of the first line, and the Third Brigade ... was massed 200 yards in rear of the second line, opposite its center."[46]

This arrangement proved brief when, as Humphreys told, he sent the hapless Burling to Birney's sector: "Shortly after these dispositions were made, I was directed to move my Third Brigade to the rear and right of General Birney's division, and make it subject to his order for support, which was accordingly done. I was at the same time authorized to draw support, should I need it, from General Caldwell's division, Second Corps, and by General Hunt, chief of artillery, was authorized to draw from the Artillery Reserve should I require more."[47]

Another factor that may have contributed to a lack of alarm from Hancock and other observers is the heavy skirmishing that had been going on near the Emmitsburg Road all day. "On the east side of the Emmitsburg road, opposite the middle of my line, was a log house surrounded by an orchard" reported Humphreys, "This I occupied with the Seventy-third New York (Fourth Excelsior)."[48] Witnesses may have mistaken the advance of troops as simply contributors to the heavy skirmishing.

It is probably the "advance" Humphreys describes below which severed any semblance of connection to the Second Corps, and got the attention of all who could see it: "About 4 p.m., in compliance with General Sickles' orders, I moved my division forward, so that the first line ran along the Emmitsburg road a short distance behind the crest upon which that road lies. At the same

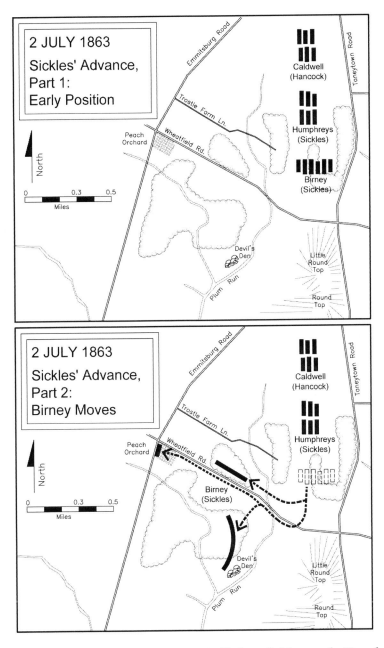

Sickles' Advance, Part 1: Early in the morning Sickles' two divisions, under Humphreys and Birney, respectively, massed to the left of Caldwell's division of Hancock's corps. Although they did not cover the Round Tops, they were roughly in the location Meade had wanted them. Sickles' Advance, Part 2: Fearing a Confederate flanking maneuver, Birney and Sickles agree to develop a defensive posture forward of Birney's former location. Woodlots and a falloff in elevation concealed most of the movements from view of most of the rest of the army. Maps by the author.

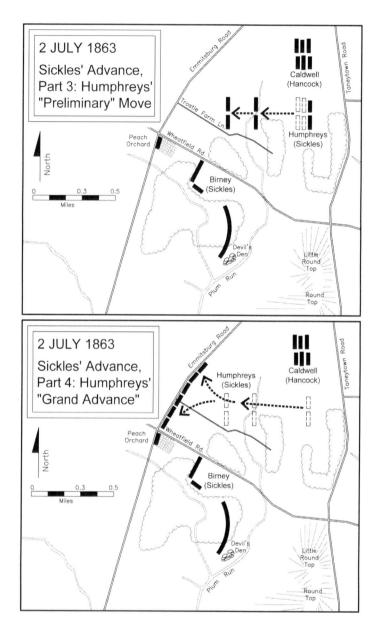

Sickles' Advance, Part 3: Sickles orders Humphreys to form in line of battle, connecting the flank of Birney's division with that of Caldwell. Humphreys responds by stacking his three brigades, one in front of the other. Humphreys later testified that the position was "preliminary" and that he and Caldwell agreed "that the distance I was then in front of him would make no very great difference." Note: this movement may have been simultaneous to those of Birney. Sickles' Advance, Part 4: At about 4:00 p.m. Sickles orders Humphreys to advance to the Emmitsburg Road. It is probably this audacious movement, abandoning any pretense of connection to the rest of the army and in plain view of thousands, which elicits marvel and concern. Maps by the author.

On 2 July, Major General Dan Sickles (top left) led his Third Corps on a controversial advance forward of the line Meade intended for him. Major Henry Edwin Tremain (top right) was Sickles' senior aide, and he defended the advance as a "military necessity." The two Third Corps division commanders were Major General David Bell Birney (bottom left) and Brigadier General Andrew Atkinson Humphreys (bottom right) (Library of Congress reproduction numbers LC-DIG-cwpb–05563, LC-USZ61–2143, LC-USZ62–104947, LC-DIG-cwpb–04932).

time I ordered Lieutenant Seeley to place his battery in position on the right of the log house."[49]

It was such an impressive sight that Gibbon's aide Haskell thought it to be the entire Third Corps: "It was magnificent to see these ten or twelve thousand men—they were good men—with their batteries, and some squadrons of cavalry upon the left flank, all in battle order, in several lines, with flags streaming, sweep steadily down the slope, across the valley, and up the next ascent, towards their destined position! From our position we could see it all…. The Third Corps now became the absorbing interest of all eyes."[50]

"No one supposed at first that he was taking a new line," wrote Morgan.[51] They simply found it hard to fathom that even Sickles would be so audacious as to separate his corps so severely from the rest of the army. And when they realized that he was, it was too late. "As the division moved forward in two lines, as heretofore described," remembered Humphreys "the enemy opened with artillery."[52] Thus there is a credible explanation for Hancock and others to not have noticed Sickles' ill-advised advance: Birney's half occurred behind the cover of trees, while Humphreys' movement was piecemeal and gradual until the last act, when it was too late to rectify. Also, the heavy skirmishing near the Peach Orchard provided the appearance that Sickles was just feeding troops into that engagement. The first unmistakable act occurred as Humphreys remembered, "About 4 p.m., in compliance with General Sickles' orders, I moved my division forward."[53]

One may even suppose that Sickles *intentionally* made the advance inconspicuously, so no one would stop him. Regardless, the rest of the army, particularly the Fifth Corps and Hancock's Second, would have to deal with the reality of it, like it or not. It was to cause the greatest crisis of the battle.

7

The Third Corps Collapses

General Sickles, I am afraid you are too far out.[1]
—George Gordon Meade

It was not until Sickles' advance was all but complete that Meade summoned his corps commanders to his headquarters. Sickles was immersed in the details of his own corps' dispositions and tried to be excused from the proceedings. However, Tremain explains, "the troops of the corps had practically assumed their assigned positions. Except for an occasional shot there was in the air the silence of expectancy. An aide of General Meade rode up and told General Sickles—and this was the second message of the same purport—that General Meade wished to see him at his headquarters. The corps commanders had been summoned there. Nothing was to be done but comply at once."[2]

By the time Sickles arrived at Meade's headquarters (the "Leister House," a small home on the Taneytown Road at the bottom of Cemetery Hill), Tremain recalls,

> the sound of musketry from Birney's front was quite marked, although it had not yet attained the volume signifying battalion collisions. It was, however, to the experienced ear sufficiently significant of their approach. The interview, therefore, between Generals Sickles and Meade was very brief. The artillery also had announced the commencement of the action. The Council of War had dispersed. General Meade met General Sickles in front of his quarters, and informed him he need not dismount; and that it was too late; that his presence was needed at his own front. General Meade said he would meet him there in a few minutes. We were off again in short order, because of the significance of the firing; and by the time we reached our starting point it was clear that the battle was thoroughly opened.[3]

Indications from both Meade's and Sickles' staff are that the advanced location of the Third Corps was an unpleasant surprise to Meade when he saw it. Said James Biddle, a member of Meade's staff:

When he arrived on the ground, at about four P.M., he found that General Sickles, instead of connecting his right with the left of General Hancock, as he had been ordered to do, had thrown forward his line three quarters of a mile in front of the Second Corps, leaving Little Round Top unprotected, and was, technically speaking, "in air"—without support on either flank. General Meade at once saw this mistake, and General Sickles promptly offered to withdraw to the line he had been intended to occupy, but General Meade replied: "You cannot do it. The enemy will not let you get away without a fight."[4]

Tremain, of Sickles' staff, concurs with Biddle's account of the conversation, but without alleging a mistake on Sickles' part. "General Meade said: 'General Sickles, I am afraid you are too far out.' General Sickles responded: 'I will withdraw if you wish, sir.' General Meade replied: 'I think it is too late. The enemy will not allow you. If you need more artillery call on the reserve artillery. (Bang! a single gun sounded.) The Fifth Corps—and a division of Hancock's—will support you.'"[5]

He goes on to explain that the behavior of Meade's horse abruptly ended the conversation:

> The conversation could not be continued. Neither noise nor any destruction had arrested it. Attracted by the group, it was a shot at them [by Confederate artillery].... The great ball went high and harmlessly struck the ground beyond. But the whizzing missile had frightened the charger of General Meade into an uncontrollable frenzy. He reared, he plunged. He could not be quieted. Nothing was possible to be done with such a beast except to let him run; and run he would, and run he did. The staff straggled after him; and so General Meade, against his own will, as I then believed and afterwards ascertained to be fact, was apparently ingloriously and involuntarily carried temporarily from the front at the formal opening of the furious engagement of July 2, 1863.[6]

It was as if Meade's horse had sensed impending catastrophe, as some believe beasts are apt to do, and sought flight to safety.

Sickles had done what he thought was best for his corps, but his dispositions were highly flawed, at best. In summary, his advance had

a) separated his right flank from the support of Caldwell's division of Hancock's Second Corps,

b) created a salient, that is an angled line which allows an attacker the ability to both enfilade the line and focus a frontal attack on the same point from two different directions,

c) greatly expanded the area his force needed to cover, stretching his line so thin that it left gaps at some points, and

d) abandoned Little Round Top. In doing so, he ignored the most naturally strong and commanding position on the entire field while leaving his left flank exposed.

It may be, for reasons the previous chapter explains, that neither Hancock nor his subordinates sounded any advance alarms about the folly of Sickles' advance.

However, it is also clear that Hancock and his officers were not in passive admiration of the spectacle as it unfolded, especially after firing became substantial. Having failed to prevent Sickles' blunder, the army could only try to alleviate its consequences. Other than the Fifth Corps' crucial defense of Little Round Top, no one's effort in covering for Sickles' gaff was as profound as that of Hancock and his corps.

The Confederate assault on Sickles' vulnerable position sent Hancock into a furious whirl of activity that lasted into the night and saved the Army of the Potomac from possible defeat. His actions at this time may have been the most important service Hancock rendered at Gettysburg. Years later, however, an appreciative nation placed Hancock's equestrian statue on East Cemetery Hill to commemorate his service on 1 July. And shortly after the war, historian John Bachelder helped popularize the Confederate assault on 3 July as "the high water mark" of the Confederacy itself. These interpretations of history, though not necessarily inaccurate, overlook the tenacious and brilliant service Hancock rendered in the twilight of the 2 July, when the Union cause was arguably in its greatest jeopardy of the battle.

Perhaps Hancock told Meade about the Third Corps advance at the corps commander meeting, and it was his report that prompted Meade to adjourn the meeting and ride to the site himself. Regardless, once Sickles' advance developed, and the Confederates began swarming over his exposed position, the Second Corps alertly made a series of emergency dispositions. But they were between two very unsatisfactory options. One was to try to save the Third Corps, which was arguably impossible, considering the place it had put itself. The other was to wait and prepare for the Confederate tsunami to reach their line. But that left the enormous gap between the Second Corps and Little Round Top completely vulnerable to Confederate occupation, and the splitting of the Union army.

Haskell explained: "These ten or twelve thousand men of the Third Corps fight well, but it soon becomes apparent that they must be swept from the field, or perish there where they are doing so well, so thick and overwhelming a storm of rebel fire involves them.... To move down and support there with other troops is out of the question, for this would be to do as Sickles did, to relinquish a good position and advance to a bad one."[7]

Nevertheless, something of a worst case scenario would later develop and force the Second Corps into a series of desperate measures, anyway. Besides, the security of the army as a whole now depended on the Third Corps holding on as well as possible, regardless of how uncomfortable it would have made the Second Corps to venture from its secure perch atop Cemetery Ridge. Hence, Meade quickly ordered Hancock to send an entire division from the safety of Cemetery Ridge to the aid of Sickles' men. Hancock reported: "Having been directed by General Meade to send a division to the assistance of the Third Corps, with orders to report to General Sykes, commanding the Fifth Corps, the First Division, under the command of Brigadier-General Caldwell, was dispatched to the scene of the conflict. The division was assigned to its position by one of Major-General Sykes' staff officers."[8]

The Gettysburg Campaign had reached a dramatic moment for the men in Caldwell's division. After weeks of marching, and days knowing that a battle was imminent, they had watched their Third Corps neighbors march splendidly into a head-on collision with the Confederates. Now they received the command to jump headlong into the cauldron of combat themselves. The recollections of Colonel St. Clair Mulholland, commanding the 116th Pennsylvania of Caldwell's Second or Irish Brigade, were never short of dramatic flair:

> Now help is called for, and Hancock tells Caldwell to have his division ready. "Fall in!" and the men run to their places. "Take arms!" and the four brigades of Zook, Cross, Brook and Kelly are ready for the fray. There is yet a few minutes to spare before starting, and the time is occupied in one of the most impressive religious ceremonies I have ever witnessed. The Irish brigade, which had been commanded formerly by General Thomas Meagher, and whose green flag had been unfurled in every battle in which the Army of the Potomac had been engaged, from the first Bull Run to Appomattox, and was now commanded by Colonel Patrick Kelly, of the Eighty-eighth New York, formed a part of this division. The brigade stood in regiments, closed in mass. As a large majority of its members were Catholics, the chaplain of the brigade, Rev. William Corby, proposed to give a general absolution to all the men before going into the fight. While this is customary in the armies of Catholic countries in Europe, it was, perhaps, the first time it was ever witnessed on this continent, unless, indeed, the grim old warrior, Ponce de Leon, as he tramped through the everglades of Florida in search of the Fountain of Youth, or De Soto, on his march to the Mississippi, indulged in this act of devotion. Father Corby stood upon a large rock in front of the brigade. Addressing the men, he explained what he was about to do, saying that each one could receive the benefit of absolution by making a sincere act of contrition and firmly resolving to embrace the first opportunity of confessing their sins.[9]

But Mulholland, as he continued, indicated that Father Corby's mission was not just to save souls, but implore the men to fight,

> urging them to do their duty well, and reminding them of the high and sacred nature of their trust as soldiers and the noble object for which they fought, ending by saying that the Catholic Church refuses Christian burial to the soldier who

A bronze statue captures the moment Father William Corby gave general absolution to the Irish Brigade, purportedly on the very rock he stood on 2 July. A copy of the same likeness appears at Notre Dame University, where he served twice as president after the war (photograph by William Bretzger).

turns his back upon the foe or deserts his flag. The brigade was standing at "Order arms." As he closed his address every man fell on his knees, with head bowed down. Then, stretching his right hand toward the brigade, Father Corby pronounced the words of absolution: "Dominus noster Jesus Christus vos absolvat, et epo, auctoritate ipsius, vos absolvo ab omni vinculo excommunicationis et interdicti in quantum possum et vos indigetis, deinde ego absolvo vos a peccatis vestris in nomine Patris, et Filio, et Spiritus Sancto. Amen."[10]

To Mulholland, as well as many non-Catholics, the ideals of Christianity were in perfect congruity with those of war:

> The scene was more than impressive, it was awe-inspiring. Near by stood Hancock, surrounded by a brilliant throng of officers, who had gathered to witness this very unusual occurrence, and while there was profound silence in the ranks of the Second corps, yet over to the left, out by the Peach Orchard and Little Round Top, where Weed and Vincent and Hazlitt [sic] were dying, the roar of battle rose and swelled and re-echoed through the woods, making music more sublime than ever sounded through the cathedral aisle. The act seemed to be in harmony with all the surroundings. I do not think there was a man in the brigade who did not offer up a heartfelt prayer. For some it was their last; they knelt there in their grave clothes—in less than half an hour many of them were numbered with the dead of July 2.[11]

Corby himself agreed with Mulholland about the magnificence of the event: "A more impressive scene—perhaps never took place on any battlefield. It was indeed so earnest and truly sublime that non-Catholics—prostrated themselves in humble adoration of the true God while they felt that perhaps in less than half an hour their eyes would open to see into the ocean of eternity."[12]

Hancock had commanded this division until just three weeks previous. Bingham described Hancock's relationship with Colonel Edward Cross, then commanding the division's First Brigade: "General Hancock had made many efforts to obtain Col. Cross' promotion to the rank of Brigadier General of Volunteers for his conspicuous bravery and services, but was not successful. The Colonel was not right with his own state authorities politically (whose preferences were regarded by the appointing powers), and ... was not slow to give vent to his likes and dislikes, talked too plainly perhaps."[13]

Bingham continued:

> Just before the action began at Gettysburg General Hancock said to him that he regretted that thus far he had not been able to procure his promotion but that he felt quite confident that battle would make him a Brigadier. "No General" said Cross "this is my last fight, I shall be killed here," and sure enough, the brave old colonel was shot through the body in that day's battle and died within a few hours thereafter. He had been severely wounded in different battles, at least six or eight times previously.[14]

Caldwell reported that the appearance of the other troops, also coming to Sickles' aid, cancelled his initial movement to the left: "Early in the afternoon ... I was ordered to [the Third Corps'] support. I had moved but part of the distance required, when a column of the Fifth Corps appeared ... and by order I resumed my former position."[15]

But the Fifth Corps alone proved insufficient in its attempt to pull the Third Corps out of the mess it was in: "The battle was raging with considerable fury at the left, where, between 4 and 5 o'clock, I received orders to report with my command to General Sykes [commanding Fifth Corps]. I moved off immediately by the left flank, and sent forward my aide ... to find General Sykes, but he did not succeed in finding him. Before reaching the position designated for me, I met a staff officer (I think the adjutant-general of General Sykes), who told me he had orders to place me."[16]

As Caldwell's report continued, it detailed how the effort of his First Division, Second Corps was desperate and, initially, successful:

> I moved forward rapidly, a portion of the time at double-quick, as the Third Corps was said to be hard pressed. The position assigned me was on the right of the Fifth and the left of the Third Corps, and I was ordered to check and drive back the enemy who were advancing at that point. I ordered Colonel Cross, commanding the First Brigade, to advance in line of battle through a wheat-field, his left resting on the woods which skirted the field. He advanced but a short distance when he encountered the enemy, and opened upon him a terrific fire, driving him steadily to the farther end of the wheat-field.
>
> In the meantime I had put the Second Brigade in on the right of the First, and they advanced in like manner, driving the enemy before them. The Third Brigade I ordered still farther to the right, to connect with the Third Corps, while I held the Fourth Brigade in reserve. The First, Second, and Third Brigades advanced with the utmost gallantry, driving the enemy before them over difficult and rocky ground, which was desperately contested by the slowly retreating foe.[17]

So far so good. And Caldwell's report continued:

> The First Brigade, which had been longest engaged, had expended all its ammunition, when I ordered Colonel Brooke to relieve it. He advanced with his usual gallantry, and drove the enemy until he gained the crest of the hill, which was afterward gained by the whole of my line. In this advantageous position I halted, and called upon General Barnes [commanding First Division, Fifth Corps], who was some distance in the rear, to send a brigade to the support of my line. He readily complied, and ordered the brigade of Colonel [Sweitzer] forward into the wheat-field. I then galloped to the left to make a connection with General Ayres [commanding Second Division, Fifth Corps], and found that I had advanced some distance beyond him. He, however, gave the order to his line to move forward and connect with my left. Thus far everything had progressed favorably. I had gained a position which, if properly supported on the flanks, I thought impregnable on the front.[18]

Satisfied that his left was secure, Caldwell soon realized the situation dire on his other flank: "But I found on going to the right that all the troops on my right had broken and were fleeing to the rear in great confusion. As soon as they broke, and before I could change front, the enemy in great numbers came in upon my right flank and even in my rear, compelling me to fall back or have my command taken prisoners. My men fell back under a very heavy cross-fire, generally in good order, but necessarily with some confusion. I reformed them behind a stone wall until relieved by the Twelfth Corps."[19]

Thus, Hancock's First Division had suffered the same kind of defeat that the entirety of Sickles' Corps would soon face under Longstreet's inexorable charge. This led to what Morgan believed was unjust criticism:

> Shortly after the division retired from Sykes's front, General Sykes informed General Hancock that it had not behaved well. He doubtless spoke in ignorance of the fact that its flank was turned, as afterwards happened to Ayres, but he did great injustice to Caldwell and to the troops. This was the division which, organized under Sumner, had attested its valor under Richardson at Antietam, and which, under Hancock, had made, as we have seen, the most determined and desperate assault of the war at Fredericksburg. When, therefore, General Hancock heard this charge, he replied, with great indignation, that if the division had not done well it was not the fault of the troops. Subsequent investigation showed that General Caldwell had not only conducted himself with great coolness and bravery, but that he had handled his troops with great skill, and that the reverse reflected no dishonor upon either the troops or their commander.[20]

Continuing his written defense of the division, Morgan testified to the signature emblem of honor in Victorian Era warfare: casualties.

> Its losses were great, over 1,200 out of a little more than 3,000 engaged. Two of the brigade commanders, General Zook and Colonel Cross, were mortally wounded, and a third brigade commander, Brooke, wounded, but kept on the field. General Zook was an able and valuable officer, Colonel Cross was a very eccentric character, but an invaluable officer. He was a rigid disciplinarian, and used to say his regiment, the Fifth New Hampshire, **dared not** fall back without orders. It would seem as if someone had neglected to give them these orders at Gettysburg, for that heroic regiment, numbering about 150 muskets, had over one hundred casualties, and the killed out-numbered the wounded. If Colonel Cross ever knew fear, no one ever discovered it. He had been several times wounded, and was prominent on every field for his defiant bearing....
>
> Besides these officers, Colonel Roberts, One hundred and Fortieth Pennsylvania, and Lieutenant-Colonel Meriam, Twenty-seventh Connecticut Volunteers, were instantly killed, and Colonel Morris, Sixty-sixth New York, wounded.[21]

"By direction of Major-General Hancock," reported Caldwell, "I marched my command back to the ground it had occupied in the earlier part of the day."[22] But that was not until later, after fighting on that part of the field had ended. The First Division, or as Caldwell put it, "what was left of the division" was essentially done fighting at Gettysburg.[23] According to Morgan:

> On returning to his Corps, Caldwell was obliged to take up a position somewhat to the left, to cover the ground abandoned by Sickles, and the interval between his right and Gibbon's division was filled by other troops (First Corps) sent up to reinforce the line. It thus happened that Caldwell's division was separated, and took no active part in the attack of the 3d. Had the division resumed its proper place, the attack of the 3d would have been met entirely by the Second Corps, and its measure of glory would have been still greater, if possible.[24]

But on 2 July, the division's departure from Cemetery Ridge had expanded the yawning gap between the Second and Third Corps. Behind the disintegrating Third Corps, the gap between the Second Corps on Cemetery Ridge and the Fifth Corps on Little Round Top was, ridiculously, about a mile.

8

Hancock Prepares

*Dispositions must be made to meet the enemy in the event
that Sickles is overpowered.*[1]

—Frank Aretas Haskell

The collapse of the Third Corps started at Birney's line, which ran in a
tattered arrangement from Devil's Den to the Peach Orchard, and angled northward along the Emmitsburg Road. The Confederate surge then spread to
Humphreys' Division, which extended Birney's line still farther north up the
road. As the retreating troops and their triumphant pursuers made their way
east and north toward Cemetery Ridge, the adjustments that Gibbon initially
resisted became necessary. Before reinforcements from the Union right arrived,
the Second Corps needed to deploy units forward and to the left to, at least,
delay what seemed like an unstoppable tide.

These deployments were of two general types at two different periods.
The first series of measures were *preparatory* attempts to protect Sickles'
exposed right flank and stitch together a connection between the Second and
Third Corps. Gibbon and Meade, as well as Hancock, contributed to this phase.
Shortly thereafter, when threats became actual Confederate breakthroughs,
Hancock was on the scene to make a series of maneuvers in reaction to them.
Chapter 9 discusses these *reactive* deployments.

Preparatory Deployments

Hancock and Gibbon collaborated to improvise at least four distinct
deployments to slow the imminent rout of Humphreys' division:

1. Teaming up with Meade, the group elects to send forward the Nineteenth
Massachusetts and Forty-second New York.[2]
2. Gibbon advanced the Fifteenth Massachusetts, Eighty-second New York,
and Battery B, First Rhode Island Light.[3]

3. Gibbon (probably) ordered the First Minnesota left and forward to support Lieutenant Evan Thomas' Battery C, Fourth United States.[4]

4. Hancock advanced Lieutenant Gulian Weir's Battery C, Fifth United States and the Nineteenth Maine Volunteer Infantry.[5]

Haskell explained the thinking behind these defensive preparations: "Dispositions must be made to meet the enemy in the event that Sickles is overpowered. With this corps out of the way, the enemy would be in a position to advance upon the line of the Second Corps, not in a line parallel with its front, but they would come obliquely from the left."[6]

The Nineteenth Massachusetts and Forty-Second New York

A Massachusetts History Committee reports:

> Gen. Meade comes up just at this time, with Hancock and Gibbon, and stands near the Nineteenth Massachusetts, which is occupying a position in the front of the Second Division, Second Corps, just to the left of the now justly celebrated Copse of trees. It is soon apparent that something must be done to assist Humphrey [*sic*].
>
> Turning to Hancock, Gen. Meade says: "Something must be done. Send a couple of regiments out in support of Humphrey." Hancock turned to Gibbon, and, without a word between them, the latter says to Col. Devereux, "Take the Forty-Second New York with you."[7]

The Fifteenth Massachusetts, Eighty-Second New York and Battery B, First Rhode Island Light

According to Haskell, "the left of the Second Division of the Second Corps is thrown back slightly, and two regiments, the Fifteenth Massachusetts—Colonel Ward—and the Eighty-second New York–Lieutenant-Colonel Horton— are advanced down to the Emmettsburg road, to a favorable position nearer us than the fight has yet come, and some new batteries from the artillery reserve are posted upon the crest near the left of the Second Corps. This was all General Gibbon could do."[8]

Charles Morgan described this deployment as a means "to protect General Sickles' right flank and partially fill the gap between it and the Second Corps."[9] As an aide to Hancock, not Gibbon, Morgan was critical of the move: "This well meant movement cannot be regarded otherwise than as an error, particularly the placing of the battery in front of the main line. The chief of artillery [commander of the Second Corps Artillery Brigade], Capt. Hazard was justly apprehensive concerning this battery, and General Hancock himself disapproved of its being sent out, but said nothing to General Gibbon concerning it."[10]

Haskell explains that the departure of Caldwell's division prompted Gibbon to insert his reserve brigade: "The division moved as ordered, and disappeared from view in the woods ... and the reserve brigade—the First, Colonel Heath temporarily commanding—of the Second Division was thereupon moved up, and occupied the position vacated by the division."[11]

The First Minnesota regiment, part of the First Brigade of the Second Division, took part in the latter movement. Its relocation from a remote point near Meade's headquarters to a spot in the main line moved it closer to where it would soon make its terrible sacrifice.

As for the battery, its Sergeant John H, Rhodes described its movement to a forward position: "the guns of Battery B, at four o'clock, were advanced to the right and front, a few hundred rods, to a ridge in front of the main battle line at General Gibbon's (Second Division of Second Corps) left front, known as the 'Godori's [sic] field' ... by orders from General Gibbon."[12]

"The Fifteenth Massachusetts and the Eighty-second New York regiments lay along the road beside the fences," added Rhodes.[13]

The First Minnesota and Battery C, Fourth United States

It is ironic that the First Minnesota, which was to attain legendary status within hours, had a bitter run-in with Charles Morgan himself just days before Gettysburg. The report by the "Minnesota Board of Commissioners" contains the following account:

> Early on June 29th we crossed the Monocacy, our division taking the advance of the corps. About three hours on the road, we came to a considerable creek, crossed by fording something more than knee-deep, and having a timber, hewn on top, crossing it, on rough stone supports on each side of the road, for pedestrians. To allow the men to cross on these timbers would impede the march, and Col. Charles H. Morgan, the efficient inspector general of the corps, remained here, directing each regimental commander to march his command right through the water. The direction was given to Colvill as we approached, and followed by his command, "Close order. March!" But a few of the men and line officers scurried across on the timbers, losing no time, and saving themselves from scalded feet in the long day's march before them. Morgan became angry, and having some further trouble with the Fifteenth Massachusetts Regiment which followed next behind, and being groaned by that regiment when he passed our brigade at a halt shortly after, and believing that an act of insubordination, he caused Col. Colvill

to be placed in arrest. This act produced a strong feeling of resentment in the men, who felt their colonel was most unjustly dealt with.[14]

The report also notes that on 2 July, "Early in the morning, just after we reached the battlefield, Col. Colvill was relieved from arrest, and assumed command of the regiment."[15]

After the brigade moved to occupy the former location of Caldwell's division, Company F moved ahead as skirmishers and, according to the Board, "the remaining eight companies of the regiment, numbering two hundred and sixty-two men (Company C was also absent, being the provost guard of the division), were sent ... to support Battery C of the Fourth United States Artillery. No other troops were then near us, and we stood by this battery, in full view of Sickles' battle in the peach orchard half a mile to the front, and witnessed with eager anxiety the varying fortunes of that sanguinary conflict."[16]

"Orders directed the First Minnesota to support Lieutenant Evan Thomas' Battery C Fourth U.S. Artillery," wrote historian John Quinn Imholte, "located a half-mile to the south along the ridge and a half-mile east of the Peach Orchard."[17] Hancock does not mention this deployment. General Gibbon probably ordered it. Neither took direct credit for it. Regardless, it led to the legendary charge of utmost importance and sacrifice.

The Nineteenth Maine and Battery C, Fifth United States

Then there was the advance of Weir's Battery (Fifth United States Battery C) and the Nineteenth Maine infantry. Weir's battery was part of the Artillery Reserve, and in the afternoon it, according to his report, "moved to the front, by order of General Tyler [commanding the Artillery Reserve]."[18] Weir reports how Hancock then took over: "About 4 o'clock was ordered by Major-General Hancock to take up a position about 500 yards to the right and front, with orders to watch my front, as our troops were falling back on the left at the time."[19]

According to John Day Smith of the Nineteenth Maine, these preparatory measures had stranded his regiment, at least for the moment: "The First Minnesota was taken from the brigade.... The Fifteenth Massachusetts and Eighty-second New York were then taken.... In the meantime the Nineteenth Massachusetts and Forty-second New York had been taken out of the Third Brigade line.... The First Division, under General Caldwell had also been withdrawn.... That left the Nineteenth Maine practically alone on the particular part of the field it then occupied."[20]

Weir's Battery C was also alone, but Hancock was not one to leave a battery without infantry support. The Nineteenth's Captain Silas Adams wrote:

"About five P. M., our regiment was detached by General Hancock and conducted to a position forming a continuation of the line from Cemetery Ridge to Little Round Top, and ordered to hold it. The order was given to Colonel Heath, after the regiment was located, with a directness that implied that we might expect some serious work before the fight was over, and, 'I expect you to hold it at all hazards.'"[21]

It is not completely certain that the Nineteenth Maine's placement was in support of Weir's battery, but it appears quite likely. Adams recalled that "our right extended well up toward the ridge with Weir's United States Battery."[22] Also, Hancock coupled the two units in a post-war letter, writing, "I have always been of the impression that the battery was Weir's … and that the regiment was the Nineteenth Maine."[23]

According to Heath, a mishap occurred while maneuvering that drew Hancock's ire:

> While this movement was going on Genl. Hancock gave way to a curious outbreak of temper. He had ordered a battery to change position about this time and the regiment & battery came into contact. Wishing to hasten the movement I had files broken to the rear to let the guns & horses pass. Genl. Hancock spoke in a good deal of passion to the officers in command of the battery saying "if I commanded this regt. I'd be God Damned if I would not charge bayonets on you"— After taking the position assigned by Genl. H. the regt. was ordered to lie down as shots from the vicinity of the fight near the "peach orchard" were reaching us.[24]

It appears that the genial general had switched to combat mode. After the Nineteenth Maine "advanced rapidly to the front," John Day Smith provides another anecdote:

> There were no troops then between its left company and the First Minnesota, about sixty rods [990 feet] General Hancock rode along and jumped from his horse and took the first man on the left (who was George Durgin of Company F) and conducted him forward about a couple of rods and a little to the left. He said to Durgin, "Will you stay here?" Durgin who was a short heavy man, looked up into the General's face and replied, "I'll stay here, General, until h—l freezes over." The general smiled and ordered the Colonel to dress his regiment on that man, jumped upon his horse and galloped away.[25]

Meanwhile, the Third Corps was heavily engaged. Lieutenant Haskell recalled: "We have more apparent reason to fear for ourselves. The Third Corps is being overpowered; here and there its lines begin to break; the men begin to pour back to the rear in confusion; the enemy are close upon them and among them; organization is lost to a great degree; guns and caissons are abandoned and in the hands of the enemy; the Third Corps, after a heroic, but unfortunate fight, is being literally swept from the field."[26]

The preparatory actions that Meade, Hancock, and Gibbon had thus far taken were desperate and forlorn. They must have occupied Hancock for a substantial period as he galloped here and there in the gap between the two corps, trying, with limited resources, to fashion both material support for the Third Corps and a connection between it and his Second Corps. However, he did, according to Haskell, find time to bolster the morale of his forces: "Generals Hancock and Gibbon rode along the lines of their troops; and at once cheer after cheer, not rebel mongrel cries, but genuine cheers, rang out along the line, above the roar of battle, for 'Hancock' and 'Gibbon' and 'our Generals.' These were good. Had you heard their voices, you would have known these men would fight."[27]

Sickles Falls

Hancock was likely to get involved in the fight well before it reached the main line of his corps, especially since an entire division and several of his regiments were in the thick of it. However, fate hastened Hancock's participation when the Third Corps' wayward commander fell terribly wounded. As he sat mounted near his headquarters, observing the fight and issuing orders, a cannon shot all but severed General Sickles' right leg. Though he coolly transferred command of his corps to Birney, word of his incapacitation must have quickly reached General Meade. It does not appear to have been long before Hancock learned of his new responsibilities: "after General Meade received notice that General Sickles was wounded so as to be unable to continue in command, he sent word to me to go and take command of the 3d corps. I then turned command of the 2d corps over to General Gibbon."[28]

Gibbon observed: "In the midst of the confusion and turmoil of the fight, Gen. Hancock received an order from Gen. Meade to take command of the 3rd Corps, it being understood that Sickles had been wounded. Hastily turning over the 2nd Corps to me, he started off toward the 3rd and I was not surprised that he should utter some expressions of discontent at being compelled at such time to give up command of one corps in a sound condition to take command of another which, it was understood, had gone to pieces."[29]

Hancock reports two more preparatory dispositions occurring just before taking the helm of the Third Corps: "I had just before received an order from General Meade to send a brigade to the assistance of General Birney (whose division had occupied the extreme left of Sickles' corps), and to send two regiments to general Humphreys, who commanded the right of that corps. I immediately led the brigade (Third Brigade, Third Division, under Colonel Willard)

At Gettysburg, Hancock's staff included Major William G. Mitchell (top left, post-war image), who carried one of Hancock's messages from the front to General Meade on July 1; Captain W. D. W. Miller (top right), who was shot twice on 2 July by Wilcox's Brigade; Chief of Staff Lieutenant Colonel Charles H. Morgan (bottom left), who wrote an important narrative of the Gettysburg campaign; and Captain Henry H. Bingham (bottom right, post-war image), who tended to Confederate Brigadier General Lewis Armistead upon the general's mortal wounding on 3 July (*Reminiscences of Winfield Scott Hancock*, 1887, courtesy Digital Scanning).

intended for General Birney toward the left of the original line of battle of the Third Corps."[30]

Hancock sent a staffer to his Third Division leader General Hays for a brigade as Meade had requested. The messenger found Hays with his Third Brigade commander Colonel George Willard and announced, "General Hancock sends you his compliments and wishes you to send one of your best brigades over there [pointing to the Third Corps' left]." Hays then faced Willard, and with characteristic bombast, implored, "Take your brigade over there and knock the H— out of the rebs."[31]

As Hancock set off to the left with new responsibilities and Willard's brigade in tow, it fell on General Gibbon to find two regiments apt for dispatching to Humphreys. The Nineteenth Massachusetts and Forty-second New York were the two regiments Gibbon selected.

As General Humphreys realized his Emmitsburg Road line was about to face overwhelming odds, he reports that he had "dispatched one of my aides, Lieutenant Christiancy, to General Hancock ... with the request that he would send a brigade, if possible, to my support."[32] According to his official report, Gibbon, "on the application of General Humphreys, sent two of my regiments to his assistance."[33]

In summary: the deployment of Caldwell's entire First Division to the vicinity of Birney's line had increased the size of the gap between the Second and Third Corps. As the Confederate onslaught spread from Birney's division to Humphreys,' the Second Corps completed a series of preparatory deployments. These deployments were each part of an attempt to support Sickles' exposed right flank and re-establish a connection between it and the Second Corps. But the Third Corps was disintegrating. Its fleeing troops

Undated image of Hancock (from the collection of the Historical Society of Montgomery County).

streamed into the gap behind it, along with rows of Confederate pursuers. The deadly weight of Longstreet's colossal assault was about to fall on the Second Corps' flank and shortened front. Hancock rode ahead of Willard's brigade toward the corps newly under his command. It was a place where chaos reigned and Confederates were victorious.

9

Hancock Reacts

The Third corps had been driven back, broken and shat-tered, its commander wounded and carried from the field, the troops that had gone to its support fared no better, and every man felt the situation was grave.

HANCOCK TO THE RESCUE.

However, all was not yet lost. Meade had again thought of Hancock, and as yesterday he sent him to stop the rout of the First and Eleventh corps, so to-day he orders him to assume command on the left. Once more he is in the fight.[1]

—St. Clair A Mulholland.

The left of the Third Corps, under Birney, was collapsing. Hancock's First Division, under General Caldwell, was suffering the same fate, though it had first swept Confederate attackers from what became known as "The" wheatfield, in Birney's line. Caldwell had become the victim of his own success. His triumphant charge through The Wheatfield had out-gained his flank support. At that time the Confederates managed to get around Caldwell's right, almost behind him, and force him back to the base of Little Round Top in relative disarray.

The inadequacy of attempts to shore up Humphreys' line with assorted Second Corps units was becoming apparent. Having broken Birney, Confederates were beginning to roll back the left flank of Humphreys. Adams recalled how the Nineteenth Maine struggled to avoid the influence of the disintegrating Third Corps: "As soon as we formed we were ordered to lie down.... Fearing the Nineteenth Maine might catch the spirit of the defeated troops in our front, and be swept away in the current, Colonel Heath walked rapidly along in front of the regiment, cautioning the men to lie still and keep their places and allow the broken and disorganized troops to pass over us to the rear."[2]

Behind this action, back on Cemetery Ridge, Willard's brigade was southbound. It was a new brigade, though its regiments were experienced. Its four regiments were all from New York state: the Thirty-ninth (the "Garibaldi Guards"), 111th, 125th and 126th. Most importantly, however, some referred to them as the "Harpers Ferry Cowards." All four regiments had been among the Union garrison at Harpers Ferry which surrendered to Stonewall Jackson during the Antietam Campaign. The decision was not theirs, but they sat out the fighting until their exchange late in 1862, when they remained inactive as part of the defenses of Washington, D.C. As they headed toward the fight they were eager for redemption.[3]

Reactive Deployments

It would be Birney himself who advised Hancock that his division was beyond rescue, and convince Hancock to abort his leftward mission. Hancock reported:

> I immediately led the brigade (Third Brigade, Third Division, under Colonel Willard) intended for General Birney toward the left of the original line of battle of the Third Corps, and was about proceeding with it to the front, when I encountered General Birney, who informed me that his troops had all been driven to the rear, and had left the position to which I was moving. General Birney proceeded to the rear to collect his command. General Humphreys' small command yet remained in position. The force which had turned General Caldwell's right and driven the left of the Third Corps now approached the line of battle as originally established.[4]

The storm had arrived. This was the transition between *preparatory* and *reactive* deployments. The enemy Hancock referred to was General William Barksdale's Brigade, McLaw's Division, First (Confederate) Army Corps. It was not, as Hancock believed, the same group that turned Caldwell's right. But Barksdale had made a splendid charge, smashing through the Sickles' line on the Emmitsburg Road. Now it was surging toward the seemingly unoccupied spot on Cemetery Ridge itself. Hancock continued: "I established Colonel Willard's brigade at the point through which General Birney's division had retired, and fronting the approaching enemy, who were pressing vigorously on. There were no other troops on its [Willard's] right or left, and the brigade soon became engaged."[5]

The brigade formed for their countercharge with the 125th and 126th in front and the Thirty-ninth back and to the left, along with the 111th. This would change quickly, however, as Colonel Clinton D. MacDougall, commanding the 111th, reported:

The brigade commander ordered me to remain at the left in reserve about 200 yards in the rear, when general Hancock came riding up shortly, and ordered me with my regiment to the right in great haste, to charge the rebel advance, which had broken though our lines on the right of the Third Brigade, and had advanced between 20 and 30 rods [330–495 feet] beyond our lines, and was in the act of turning the right flank of our brigade. The rebels were driven back by me beyond our brigade line and almost into the mouth of their own batteries, which they had advanced upon us.[6]

Days later, while fighting for his life and smarting from wounds he incurred on 3 July, Hancock issued the following:

Circular   Philadelphia, Pa.,
                                                                                          July 7 1863

Major-General Hancock desires to know the designation of a certain regiment, and the name of its commander, belonging to the First, Second, or Twelfth Corps, which, at the instance of General Hancock, charged a rebel regiment which had passed through our lines on Thursday evening, 2d instant. The conduct of this regiment and its commander were so marked in this as in the subsequent advance in the line of battle, that General Hancock desires properly to notice the subject.

By order of Major-General Hancock:

W.G. MITCHELL,
Aide-de-Camp and Assistant Adjutant-General.[7]

To this MacDougall responded, "I have every reason to suppose the general referred to my regiment."[8]

Barksdale had overrun several Federal artillery pieces. Few things in this age of warfare motivated men to charge like trophies such as these guns. This became a perfect objective for the Thirty-ninth, which went to work on the left flank of the brigade after the 111th moved to the right. It was one of Birney's aides who commandeered the Thirty-ninth to recover the pieces. But he initially received resistance from its commander Major Hugo Hildenbrandt, who objected on the grounds that the regiment was not under Birney's command. When the aide asked him to whose command the regiment belonged, Hildenbrandt said Hancock's. The aide then rephrased his order that the Thirty-ninth recover the guns at the behest of General Hancock. Hildenbrandt then complied.[9] Captain John Bigelow, who commanded a battery in Colonel Freeman McGilvery's First Brigade of the Artillery Reserve, wrote:

After being badly crippled by the fire of Kershaw's skirmishers, Watson's Battery (I, 5th U.S.) on the left of [Union Artillery Reserve Colonel] McGilvery's new line, was charged by the 21st Miss. (Col. afterwards Gov. Humphries). Just as it was captured, and McGilvery's line was about to be attacked on the left flank, thus opened, the 39th N.Y. Reg't was detached from Willard's 3rd Brig., 3rd Div.,

2nd Corps, which came to the support of the artillery at 7:15 p.m. and drove the 21st Miss. back into its own line.[10]

Meanwhile, the main front of Willard's brigade, New York's 125th and 126th, continued its engagement with the Mississippians. Willard's fresh, eager force proved too much for Barksdale's men, who were worn down by hours of hard marching and fighting. Both commanders went down in the hot fight. A rain of Union lead felled Barksdale and mortally wounded him. Captain Charles Richardson of the 126th New York recalled: "In front of the right of the 125th and left of the 126th Gen. Barksdale fell while almost frantic with rage, he was trying to make his fleeing men stand. Numerous shots were fired at him from both regiments."[11]

Willard's death was instant as a Confederate artillery shot struck him in the face.[12]

The Confederate attack was *en echelon*, meaning that each of its brigades charged only after the adjacent unit on its right. They did this with great discipline and order, creating a wave-like impact, crashing from the Union left to right as it progressed. Consequently, after destroying Birney, the wave was rolling back Humphreys. In response to this, Hancock rode to his right as the action progressed in that direction. Eventually, Humphreys' few remaining men were in the rear, as Hancock reported: "I directed General Humphreys to form his command on the ground from which General Caldwell had moved to the support of the Third Corps, which was promptly done. The number of troops collected was, however, very small, scarcely equal to an ordinary battalion, but with many colors, this small command being composed of the fragments of many shattered regiments. Three guns of one of its batteries had been left on the field, owing to the losses of horses and men."[13]

If he was not able to see through the smoke, it must have been the sound of the fight, progressing rightward, that he followed. He was also attempting, in vain, to rally Humphreys' men himself, who were pouring back on his right. He also sent for help:

> I then sent back to General Meade for other troops to fill in the spaces to my right ... which interval the enemy was threatening in a like manner.... This vacant space was attributable to the advance of Sickles on the Peach Orchard earlier in the day, and to General Caldwell's 1st Division ... being sent to Birney later on, to the Wheatfield towards the Round Top, By General Meades order.
>
> Some regiment of Lockwood's Maryland Brigade [Second Brigade, First Division, Twelfth Corps] responded, conducted by my senior aide, Major W. G. Mitchell, who had received them from General Meade.[14]

The next brigade of Confederates charging unchecked in the Union rear consisted of Alabamians under Brigadier General Cadmus Wilcox. His advance

The Minnesota monument stands near the point from which the First Minnesota made its sacrificial charge, at Hancock's behest, on 2 July. Both the figure atop the monument and a relief at its base depict the desperate rush (photograph by William Bretzger).

marked the passing of the wave from Longstreet's corps to that of General A. P. Hill. Hancock staffer and biographer F. A. Walker wrote: "Galloping along the line toward the north, Hancock sees a portion of Wilcox's brigade breaking into the open, from the cover of a clump of bushes. Believing these to be some of his own troops driven in from the front, the general rides forward to halt and post them, but is undeceived by a volley, which brings down his aide, Captain Miller. There are no troops, right or left, to be seen."[15]

This was the moment of greatest peril for the Union at Gettysburg. The following day, a few hundred Confederates penetrated Federal defenses for a fleeting, futile moment. That became known as "the high water mark." At twilight on 2 July, however, Confederates routed an entire corps and one third of another (Caldwell's division). They were about to occupy a large, unguarded length of Cemetery Ridge. This was when the Union most needed a leader of soldierly genius. Walker continues: "as Hancock turns, he beholds a regiment coming from the rear. Dashing up to the colonel, and pointing to the Confederate column he exclaims: 'Do you see those colors? Take them!' Scarcely are the words spoken when the First Minnesota, under Colvill, spring forward, without even waiting to come into line, and precipitate themselves upon the masses of the enemy."[16]

There are several accounts of this dramatic moment. Some claim to be those of eyewitnesses. The quotes vary in detail, but they all agree in tone. Every account reflects the immediate and succinct clarity of Hancock's orders, and their audacity. One such account is by a captain in the First Minnesota, Jasper Searles: "Hancock … in a commanding voice cried out, 'Minnesota, forward!' Colonel Colville repeated it, adding 'double-quick, march!' and the men, at 'right shoulder shift,' with one time and motion, dashed down the slope, their gleaming muskets a perfect line,—a most stirring spectacle of war."[17]

William Lochren was acting adjutant general of the regiment. His version of that moment reads:

> Just then Hancock, with a single aid, rode up at full speed, and for a moment vainly endeavored to rally Sickles' retreating forces. Reserves had been sent for, but were too far away to hope to reach the critical position until it would be occupied by the enemy, unless that enemy were stopped. Quickly leaving the fugitives, Hancock spurred to where we stood, calling out, as he reached us, "What regiment is this?" "First Minnesota," replied Colvill. "Charge those lines!" commanded Hancock. Every man realized in an instant what that order meant,—death or wounds to us all; the sacrifice of the regiment to gain a few minutes' time and save the position, and probably the battlefield,—and every man saw and accepted the necessity for the sacrifice.[18]

Hancock's fast eye and lack of hesitation were of utmost importance at this moment. The rare gallantry of the First Minnesota was necessary to the success of the operation, and one should not diminish it. But the instant, emphatic quality of Hancock's actions must have been a critical motivator at this pivotal moment. While his quotes vary in each account, all describe the bold and decisive tone that burst out of Hancock and affected all those around him. That, combined with his usual commanding presence, image, and reputation, was critical to convincing the First Minnesota to act without hesitation and make a desperate stand and an awful sacrifice. There is little dispute, as well, between the accounts of that sacrifice. Lochren continued:

> Responding to Colvill's rapid orders, the regiment, in perfect line, with arms at "right shoulder shift," was in a moment sweeping down the slope directly upon the enemy's centre. No hesitation, no stopping to fire, though the men fell fast at every stride before the concentrated fire of the whole Confederate force, directed upon us as soon as the movement was observed. Silently, without orders, and, almost from the start, double-quick had changed to utmost speed; for in utmost speed lay the only hope that any of us would pass through that storm of lead and strike the enemy. "Charge!" shouted Colvill, as we neared their first line; and with leveled bayonets, at full speed, we rushed upon it; fortunately, as it was slightly disordered in crossing a dry brook at the foot of a slope. The men were never made who will stand against leveled bayonets coming with such momentum and evident desperation. The first line broke in our front as we reached it, and rushed back through the second line, stopping the whole advance. We then poured in our first fire, and availing ourselves of such shelter as the low banks of the dry brook afforded, held the entire force at bay for a considerable time, and until our reserves appeared on the ridge we had left. Had the enemy rallied quickly to a counter charge, its great numbers would have crushed us in a moment, and we would have made but a slight pause in its advance. But the ferocity of our onset seemed to paralyze them for the time, and although they poured upon us a terrible and continuous fire from the front and enveloping flanks, they kept at a respectful distance from our bayonets, until, before the added fire of our fresh reserves, they began to retire, and we were ordered back. What Hancock had given us to do was done thoroughly.[19]

Hancock agreed: "I cannot speak too highly of this regiment and its commander in its attack, as well as in its subsequent advance against the enemy, in which it lost three-fourths of the officers and men engaged."[20]

Like many great historical moments, however, exaggerations and embellishments have become part of the popularly believed version of the story. There is a popular understanding that the regiment engaged an entire brigade on its own and that it incurred an 82 percent loss in casualties during this action. The Minnesotans deserve legendary status for their sacrifice and success; but one should scrutinize these most extreme assertions about their action. It was, essentially, Wilcox's Brigade that they encountered. However, one should note that the Alabamians had already been through a substantial fight before they met the First Minnesota. Wilcox himself later wrote of his men's exertions: "when the brigade on my right (Barksdale's) advanced, mine moved off rapidly … and in this march crossed two fences, one of stone, then charged by the right flank, rose up the slope of the ridge on which lay the Emmettsburg road; was exposed to terrible artillery fire from the left; crossed two fences before reaching the road, and then engaged the enemy at short range as they lay along that road."[21]

Furthermore, Wilcox noted the disorganization that occurs in victory almost as commonly as it does in defeat: "As they [Humphreys' line on the Emmitsburg Road] gave way, my men and Barksdale's impinged, and mine were made to incline slightly to the left."[22] Hence, it is fair to say that Wilcox's men were having their own difficulties well before they met the First Minnesota. Wilcox's view, from the receiving end of the First Minnesota's charge, was thus: "This stronghold of the enemy, together with his batteries, were almost won, when still another line of infantry descended the slope in our front at a double-quick, to the support of their fleeing comrades and for the defense of the batteries."[23]

One should also consider that the Minnesotans may have had help from the 111th New York. Recall that its commander, Colonel MacDougall, reported engaging an enemy "turning the right flank of our brigade."[24] This was probably part of Wilcox's Brigade. Historian John Quinn Imholte published a book in 1963 that supports this notion:

> Two accounts written by participants in the charge lend support to the thesis that the First was not alone in its effort to halt the advancing Confederates. Charles Muller, Company A, writing in 1921, stated that prior to the charge a brigade of Union troops with full ranks and new uniforms arrived from the direction of Meade's headquarters and took a position on the left of the regiment and twenty yards to the front. This was probably George Willard's brigade, or a portion of it.[25]

Imholte also notes: "Alfred Carpenter, Company K, indicated in a letter written July 30, 1863, that … two regiments on the right of the First faltered and fell back during the charge. Carpenter was probably referring to the 19th Massachusetts and the 42nd New York."[26]

Then there is the question of numbers engaged: "A legend has evolved depicting the unhesitating and determined advance of 262 Minnesota heroes into a Confederate force of two brigades numbering thousands. It eulogizes the loss of 215 of these men."[27]

However, wrote Imholte, "from available records it appears that the number of enlisted men present in the remaining eight companies [several of the regiment's companies served elsewhere on the field] totaled 335. The obvious discrepancy between this total and the traditional figure of 262 participants in the eventual charge is irreconcilable."[28]

None of this is to assert that the First Minnesota's actions, taken upon a spontaneous order by Hancock, were anything less than heroic, self sacrificing and crucial to the Union cause. In fact, Imholte notes, with careful perusal of the records, the regiment suffered a total loss of 224 killed or wounded during *both days* it fought at Gettysburg.[29] The point is, simply, that the number 215 lost out of 262 participating in the charge of 2 July, or 82 percent is incorrect.

Certainly no one was counting in the heat of the moment. More emergencies were developing. Hancock recalled: "I immediately proceeded a little further and to my surprise, found that the battery and the regiment which I had placed there to protect it, had gone—except the guns—and the enemy's straggling shots were falling all over the place."[30]

"I have always been under the impression that the battery was Weir's ... and that the regiment was the 19th Maine," he later recalled.[31] The battery had indeed been through a terrible afternoon. Weir's official report states:

> The enemy being within a few rods of us, I immediately limbered up, and was about to retire when a regiment of infantry took position on my left and rear, and opened fire. I immediately came into battery again, hoping that our infantry would drive the enemy back, as their force seemed to be small and much scattered. The enemy were too close. I endeavored to get my guns off the field; succeeded in getting off but three, as some of the drivers and horses were disabled while in the act of limbering up.
> My horse was shot at this time, and, as I was rising from the ground I was struck with a spent ball, and everything seemed to be very much confused.[32]

But Hancock also remembered that fortune was starting to turn in his favor: "A new brigade (Vermont troops) from the First Corps, lately arrived, and was marching down in that direction."[33] This was, informally, the "Second Vermont Brigade." First Sergeant George H. Scott of the Thirteenth Vermont explained how the brigade had earlier received the call to action while on Cemetery Hill:

> Col. Randall saw that Sickles and Hancock were being worsted and felt that his regiments would soon be needed. He mounted his horse and stood ready for action.
> He soon saw an officer mounted and coming with all speed towards him. On seeing the regiment, he halted and thus addressed Randall. "Colonel what regiment do you command?" "The 13th Vermont, Sir," said Randall. "Where is General Stannard?" Randall replied, pointing to a clump of oaks some 70 rods away. He then said, "Colonel, will your regiment fight"? "I believe they will, sir," said Randall. "Have you ever been in a battle, Colonel?" Randall replied, "I have personally been in most of the engagements of the Army of the Potomac since the

war began, but my regiment being a new organization has seen but little fighting, but I have unbounded confidence in them." The officer then said, "I am General Doubleday. Introduce me to your regiment. I command your corps." Randall rode with him close up to the regiment, and said, "Boys, this is General Doubleday, our Corps commander." He addressed us substantially as follows:

"Men of Vermont: The troops from your state have done nobly and well on the battle fields of this war. The praises of the old Vermont brigade are on every lip. We expect you to sustain the honor of your state. Today will decide whether Jefferson Davis or Abraham Lincoln rules this country. Your Colonel is about to lead you into battle where you will have hard fighting and much will be expected of you."

The Vermont boys gave three cheers for Doubleday. Doubleday then requested Randall to take his regiment out towards Weed's Hill and report to Hancock; at the same time requesting him to make all speed as Hancock was hard pressed and was losing his artillery. This order Randall at once obeyed. Doubleday then directed Stannard to report to Hancock. The 14th Regiment under Col. Nichols led the way under a sharp fire to the rear of a battery, from which our men had been driven in confusion. The enemy fell back as they advanced. The 16th under Col. Veazey also advanced and came on a body of rebels, as they were rushing upon a battery. They fled as the 16th approached and formed behind the battery, which they found without supports, and this the 16th supported until dark. Agreeably to Doubleday's order Randall spoke a few words of cheer to the left wing of his regiment, told them that we had met with a disaster and the 13th must go out and retrieve it. And then at the command "Attention; by the left flank, march!" We started toward the southwest, up the hill at a quick step.

Randall rode on and met Hancock, who was rallying his men and encouraging them to hold on to the last. A few hardy fellows were taking advantage of the ground to contest the advance of a rebel brigade in their front. As Hancock saw Randall, he said, "Colonel, where is your regiment?" "Close at hand," said Randall. "Good," said Hancock, "the enemy are pressing me hard—they have just captured that battery yonder (a battery about 20 rods in front) and are dragging it from the field. Can you retake it?" "I can, and damn quick too, if you will let me."

At that moment they both observed a rebel brigade deploying from the woods from the left and making for the guns. It proved to be Wright's brigade. "Dare you take the chance, Colonel," said Hancock. "I do, sir," said Randall. "Then go in." In a moment Randall was at the head of his regiment.[34]

Randall's official report covers these events more succinctly:

A heavy fight was going on … in which the Second and Third Corps were engaged, and we received some injury from the artillery fire of the rebels without being able to engage in the fight. At this time an officer, whom I did not know at the moment, but who proved to be General Doubleday, came galloping over the hill from General Hancock's position, and approached my regiment. After having found what regiment we were, and making a few inspiriting remarks to my men, he directed me to take my regiment in the direction from which he had come, and to report to General Hancock, whom I would find there, and hard pressed, and he said he feared he would lose his artillery or some of it before I could get there. I started, riding in advance of my regiment to meet General Hancock and find where I was needed, so as to be able to place my men in position without exposing them too long under fire. As I reached the ridge of highest ground between the cemetery and Little Round Top Mountain, I met General Hancock, who was encouraging and rallying his men to hold on to the position.[35]

Hancock wanted the Vermonters to recover some lost artillery. But according to Randall, he had taken a more negotiable and less strident approach than he had with the First Minnesota: "He told me the rebels had captured a battery he had had there, and pointed out to me the way they had gone with it, and asked me if I could retake it. I told him I thought I could, and that I was willing to try. He said it would be a hazardous job, and he would not order it, but, if I thought I could do it, I might try."[36]

This Vermont brigade was near the end of a mere ninety-day enlistment. It had not yet seen substantial action and the prestige such experience bestowed. Colonel Randall, however, was a veteran and an unapologetic self-promoter. His detailed report provides an unusual view into the complexity of maneuvering hundreds of men in an organized manner: "By this time my regiment had come up and I moved them to the front far enough so that when I deployed them in line of battle they would leave Hancock's men in their rear. They were now in columns by divisions, and I gave the order to deploy in line, instructing each captain as to what they were to do as they came on to the line, and, taking my position to lead them, gave the order to advance."[37]

Sergeant Scott's narrative continues:

We had not gone ten rods ere Randall's horse fell shot through the neck. His regiment faltered. Randall cried, at the same time pulling vigorously at his foot which had got caught in the stirrup, between the horse and the ground,—"go on boys I'll be at your head as soon as I get out of this damned saddle." Several boys stepped up and rolled off his horse. Soon he came running around the side of the regiment to the front, on foot, limping badly, his hat off, his sword swinging in the air, saying, "I am all right. Come on boys, follow me." He led us into the gap.[38]

When Randall recounts the moment his horse went down, he also notes what may well be an encounter with the left side of Wilcox's Brigade: "At this time my horse was killed, and I fell to the ground with him. While on the ground, I discovered a rebel line debouching from the woods on our left, and forming substantially across about 40 rods in our front. We received one volley from them, which did us very little injury, when my men sprang forward with the bayonet with so much precipitancy that they appeared to be taken wholly by surprise, and threw themselves in the grass, surrendering, and we passed over them."[39]

According to Randall, Hancock was available to assist the Vermonters though beset with several emergencies along his line: "General Hancock followed up the movement, and told me to press on for the guns and he would take care of the prisoners, which he did, and we continued our pursuit of the guns, which we undertook about half way to the Emmitsburg road, and recaptured them with some prisoners. These guns, I am told, belong to the Fifth U.S. Regulars, Lieutenant Weir. There were four of them."[40]

One of Scott's accounts incorporates a quote by Hancock otherwise unknown to this author: "Hancock says, 'I recollect of telling the officers and men where to leave the pieces or how far back to take them and remained with them for a few moments. I was anxious that they should not delay too long by carrying pieces too far, so that they would not be delayed in advance.'"[41]

If one is to believe Scott, Hancock need not have worried about how far these men could carry their expedition: "After leaving the guns, we turned about and pursued the enemy a half mile.... We drove the enemy down into the peach orchard until we reached a farm house on the Emmittsburg road, where we halted and fired some 15 rounds into the enemy."[42]

That was only the beginning of Scott's tale of triumph and adventure: "In the meantime Capt. Lonergan, in command of Company 'A' approached a house and found it full of rebels. He informed Randall of the fact, who went up and ordered them to throw their guns out the window and surrender, which they did. At which time Col. Randall, ever mindful of his laurels, remarked to them 'remember you were captured by Col. Randall of the 13th Vermont.'"[43]

"Col. Randall was not the most modest man in the world," explained Scott. "He was fond of his regiment and was determined that the world should recognize every laurel it won."[44] Night was surely falling as his regiment, along with the rest of the brigade, was returning to Cemetery Ridge. But Sergeant Scott explained that Randall was not yet done:

> So on getting within twenty rods of our main lines he ordered us to halt and lie down to rest. Soon an aide from the General came riding down to us whom the Colonel addressed as follows:
> "Captain, report to your General what we have done. We have recaptured six guns, taken two from the enemy, driven him half a mile and taken a hundred prisoners. Also tell him we propose staying here until he acknowledges our achievements."[45]

While waiting for acknowledgment that he was the God of War himself, however, discretion finally got the better part of Randall: "Randall soon discovered the enemy were trying to flank us and take us prisoners, and preferring to lose his laurels than spend the Fall in Libby Prison, he led us back to our original lines."[46]

But Randall would get his praise anyway, according to Scott:

> As the 13th approached our troops, cheer after cheer, long and loud, rang along our lines for the gallant Vermont boys in their first action.... Gen. Doubleday sent his aides to compliment and thank the 13th for their gallantry. Randall says, "It was dark by this time, and on getting back to our lines my first point was to find the Brigade. I soon met one of Gen. Stannard's aides. On seeing me he said, 'Where in Hell have you been? The General has been looking all over the field for your Regiment.' I inquired where the General was, and he showed me, and I approached the General and he rebuked me for wandering off without orders. I told him I followed General Doubleday's orders and I supposed that to be right. By this time a half dozen aides from Hancock, Doubleday, and others surrounded me with congratulations from their chiefs."[47]

The Vermonters had made their charge at a time and place that essentially ended the Confederate assault on the Union left and left center. The *en echelon* wave had reached the ground where Gibbon's Second Corps division stood ready and waiting.

But many of the units placed in preparation for the Confederate breakthroughs had a difficult afternoon. Hancock reported: "The two regiments sent from the Second Division to General Humphreys' assistance (Nineteenth Massachusetts, Colonel Devereux, and Forty-second New York, Colonel Mallon, both under command of Colonel Mallon) ... observing that General Humphreys' command was rapidly retiring, they formed line of battle, delivered a few volleys at the advancing enemy, and themselves retired in good order to their position in line in the Second Corps, having suffered a heavy loss."[48]

Regarding Brown's Battery B, First Rhode Island, and the Fifteenth Massachusetts and Eighty-Second New York, Hancock reported: "The two regiments and battery ... advanced by General Gibbon to the vicinity of the brick house did excellent service in protecting the flank of General Humphreys' command and in preventing it from being cut off from the line of battle. The enemy's attack being on their flank, the two regiments were, however, forced to retire, having met with heavy losses, Colonels Ward and Huston both being killed."[49]

The Nineteenth Maine had its own difficulties, as well. Though it was able to weather the storm, and turn adversity into its own tale of triumph to rival that of the Thirteenth Vermont. First, it had to dodge the refugees of Humphreys' division and, reportedly, tangle with Humphreys himself. By Sergeant Silas Adams' account:

> It was past six p.m. when the broken column of General Humphreys' division came pouring back toward, and finally over the regiment as they lay on their faces. The timely caution given by Colonel Heath had the desired effect and not a man left the ranks. In the tumult of the retreat of that division, General Humphreys rode up to Colonel Heath and ordered him to stop his routed troops at the point of the bayonet. I will give you Colonel Heath's own version of the affair: "When

they had gotten within some two hundred yards of my lines, an officer that I supposed to be General Humphreys rode up to me and ordered me to get my men up, as they were all lying down, and stop his men. I refused to do so, as I feared the regiment would be carried away with the deserting troops. I told Humphreys to get his men out of the way and we would stop the pursuers. He did not seem to appear satisfied with that arrangement, but rode down the rear of my lines, ordering the men up. I followed him and countermanded his orders, he finally going off, his men with him."[50]

Adams' account continued with the inevitable passing of Humphreys' men: "On they came like a great billow, rushing with an irresistible force that no troops could check in flight. They swept over us, they stepped on or between the men and even tumbled over us, having no regard to dignity or military order, or to pick out reasonable paths to walk in, as their only object seemed to be to get to the rear, out of the reach of their relentless pursuers."[51]

According to Adams, not all of the refugees were completely defeated: "there were many brave spirits among the routed troops, and some would call out to us "to hang on and they would form in our rear.... Some of the Excelsior Brigade tried to reform in our rear and perhaps collected one hundred men together, but they were soon swept away in the torrent of whipped and routed troops."[52]

The moment to stand up and strike the charging Confederates came soon enough: "As soon as the last of these men got out of our way, we found the rebels closely following, giving the retreating men good and sufficient reason for being in a hurry. The 'rebs' were about thirty-five yards from our lines, when Colonel Heath gave the order to fire. The regiment arose and delivered a deadly fire into the ranks of the enemy that surprised and staggered them and finally stopped their advance."[53]

The regiment got help from some of the batteries that Hancock had placed between the Second and Third Corps: "The batteries which joined us upon our left commenced firing the moment their front was clear of our own troops and they were doing prodigious work, the men with their coats off and their sleeves rolled up, were hurling grape and canister into their solid ranks with a vengeance, making terrible havoc and confusion in their lines."[54]

Unlike the Vermonters, the Nineteenth Maine faced substantial enemy opposition before it could think of surging forward to collect ground and trophies. Adams noted: "Colonel Heath received a report that the enemy was on his right flank. Then he ordered the regiment to fall back, and in perfect order it did so, and resumed firing."[55]

Adams was boastful of his regiment and the importance of the work it did: "Every man was sensible of the fact that the regiment was in a precarious situation and they alone could stem the current and throw back the surging hosts closely pursuing our retreating comrades."[56]

Adams even proposes a counter-factual scenario to illustrate what he believes was the importance of his unit's performance: "We will suppose that the Nineteenth Maine had given away and was swept with the current back into, yes, across Tannytown road, and the enemy followed, then what? Our army would have been cut in two."[57]

Adams noted that the time had come to revert from the defensive to the offensive:

> After firing several rounds and resuming our original front, we had orders to fix bayonets, and then came the ringing order from Colonel Heath to "charge bayonets." Heath leaped to the front, and off the regiment started like a tornado let loose, down around the field at the heels of the enemy, yelling all the time at the top of our voices, until we nearly reached the Emmitsburg road where we halted, capturing many prisoners, two stands of colors, three pieces of artillery and four caissons. The cannon and caissons were among the captures of the enemy from the Third Corps.[58]

Eventually, said Adams, the Nineteenth advanced beyond the protection of the main lines on Cemetery Ridge: "The regiment did not stop at the guns, but kept right on, and when nearly to the road we were overtaken by an aide whom we supposed to be from General Hancock's staff, who demanded of Colonel Heath where he was going. Colonel Heath replied, 'We are chasing the "rebs."' The aide cautioned him to go no further as he would be captured."[59]

Humphreys' division provided a final annoyance to the Nineteenth by collecting a trophy that, according to Adams, the Maine men had rightfully won: "In looking to the rear, we saw our honors all go in the twinkling of an eye. Those men of Humphrey's division that passed back to our rear and waved flags and cheered us on in that contest, now followed us and came out, a few hundred, nearly a third of the distance from the Union lines to where we lay and picked up the colors of the Eighth Florida Regiment and returned to their lines, waving the flag and cheering so that they were heard all over the field. And they got the credit of capturing that flag!"[60]

Like the Vermont brigade the Nineteenth Maine enjoyed a congratulatory reception upon arriving back on Cemetery Ridge. "When the regiment appeared on the scene with the three guns and four caissons, the whole line went wild with cheers and enthusiasm for the Nineteenth Maine, for their brilliant charge and capture, and congratulations poured in thick and fast, complimenting the regiment on its brilliant work."[61]

Another unit Hancock placed had acquitted itself beautifully. But Corporal Smith reminded his readers that war exacts a terrible toll, even in the height of triumph:

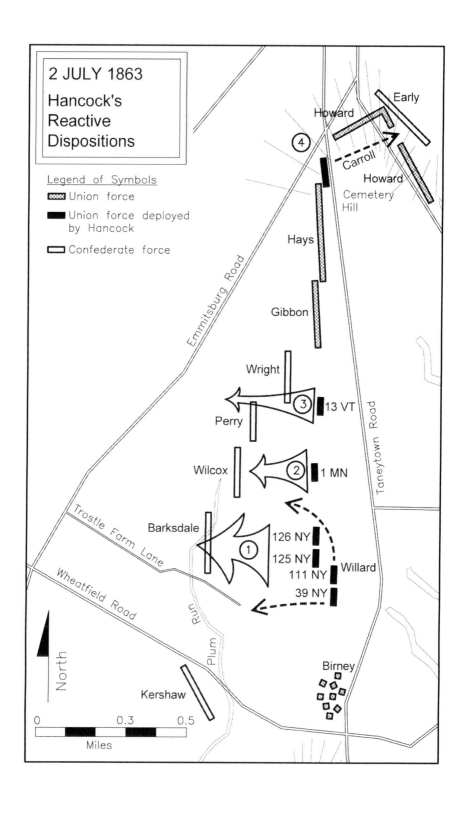

2 JULY 1863
Hancock's
Reactive
Dispositions

Legend of Symbols
▨ Union force
■ Union force deployed
   by Hancock
▭ Confederate force

Early

Howard

④

Carroll

Howard
Cemetery
Hill

Hays

Gibbon

Wright

Perry

③ ■ 13 VT

Wilcox

② ■ 1 MN

Emmitsburg Road

Taneytown Road

Barksdale

① 126 NY ■
   125 NY ■
   111 NY ■   Willard
   39 NY ■

Trostle Farm Lane

Wheatfield Road

Run

Plum

Birney

North

Kershaw

0   0.3   0.5

Miles

While elated in our success in repulsing the enemy, it was a very sad night to the most of the boys of the Regiment. When the roll was called, many a brave boy for the first time failed to respond to his name. The answers made by the living for their dead or wounded comrades were pathetic. As the names of the missing would be called, such answers as these would be returned: "John was killed before we fired a shot." "I saw Frank throw up his arms and fall just after we fired the first volley." "Jim was shot through the head." "Charley was killed while we were charging across the plain this side of the brick house." "I saw Joe lying on the ground, his face covered with blood, but he was not dead." "George was killed by a piece of shell, while we were firing." "Ed is lying dead some distance this side of the Emmitsburg road." Strong men sobbed as the heroic dead were named.[62]

The toll on the Confederates was, of course, also heavy; but their *en echelon* advance was supposed to continue. However, their wave now reached the point where it faced the Second Corps' proper position, or what Gibbon called "our main line."[63] That is, the attackers now confronted that part of Gibbon's division which had stood fast on the favorable ground of Cemetery Ridge, and had not gone piecemeal into the hazardous gap between the Second and Third Corps. The left of this line was just south of what became known as "The" Copse of Trees. On top of the inherent strength of the Cemetery Ridge line, Gibbon noted that still more reinforcements arrived (some of which were responding to Hancock's earlier calls for help): "As they [the Confederates] fell back and the fire slackened, I met, just in the rear of my line, Gen. Meade coming forward with some troops (a part, I think, of Lockwood's brigade) and I assured him that the fight in our front was over."[64]

Gibbon explained that the attack had simply lost its momentum: "By the time the enemy's troops were well under the fire of our main line their propulsive force was pretty well spent, and they made no sensible impression upon it."[65]

But his account is incomplete and unsatisfying. It fails to explain why the Confederate assault, which had been so impetuous and tenacious, seems to have just dissipated. Unfortunately, Confederate recollections of the cessation of their assault also fall flat. Anderson's Division of A. P. Hill's Third (Confederate) Army Corps holds the distinction of having made the deepest penetration into the main Union line as well as having quit the attack. The brigades of

Opposite: **1. Hancock halts the southward movement of Willard's brigade and dispatches it to stop the charging Barksdale. The Thirty-Ninth New York stays left to retake some captured artillery pieces. Hancock, meanwhile, sends the 111th New York to stop a Confederate contingent (possibly Wilcox) which had gotten past the brigade's right. 2. Riding north, Hancock sends the First Minnesota against Wilcox's Brigade in a desperate attempt to gain some time. 3. Continuing north, Hancock dispatches the Thirteenth Vermont to turn back Wright's Brigade and recover some lost artillery. 4. As night falls, Hancock hears fighting on Howard's front and sends Carroll's brigade to assist. Carroll is instrumental in repelling the assailants, who were in Howard's batteries. Maps by the author.**

Wilcox, Perry, Wright, Posey and Mahone comprised the infantry component of this division. Wilcox claimed in his official report that he would have achieved greater success had his comrades better supported them: "Seeing this contest so unequal, I dispatched my adjutant-general to the division commander, to ask that support be sent to my men, but no support came.... With a second supporting line, the heights could have been carried. Without support on either my right or left, my men were withdrawn, to prevent their entire destruction or capture."[66]

But Colonel David Lang, commanding Perry's Brigade, claimed he was on Wilcox's flank the whole time, and that it was Wilcox who broke first:

> About 5 p.m. I received an order from General Anderson to the effect that General Longstreet was driving back the enemy's left, and that Wilcox would advance whenever General Longstreet's left advanced beyond him. I was ordered to throw forward a strong line of skirmishers, and advance with General Wilcox, holding all the ground the enemy yielded.
>
> At 6 p.m., General Wilcox having begun to advance, I moved forward, being met at the crest of the first hill with a murderous fire of grape, canister, and musketry. Moving forward at the double-quick, the enemy fell back beyond their artillery, where they were attempting to rally when we reached the crest of the second hill. Seeing this, the men opened a galling fire upon them, thickly strewing the ground with their killed and wounded. This threw them into confusion, when we charged them, with a yell, and they broke and fled in confusion into the woods and breastworks beyond, leaving four or five pieces of cannon in my front, carrying off, however, most of the horses and limbers. Following them rapidly, I arrived behind a small eminence at the foot of the heights, where, the brigade having become much scattered, I halted for the purpose of reforming, and allowing the men to catch breath before the final assault upon the heights.
>
> While engaged in reforming here, an aide from the right informed me that a heavy force had advanced upon General Wilcox's brigade, and was forcing it back. At the same time a heavy fire of musketry was poured upon my brigade from the woods 50 yards immediately in front, which was gallantly met and handsomely replied to by my men. A few moments later, another messenger from my right informed me that General Wilcox had fallen back, and the enemy was then some distance in rear of my flank. Going to the right, I discovered that the enemy had passed me more than 100 yards and were attempting to surround me. I immediately ordered my men back to the road, some 300 yards to the rear. Arriving here, I found there was no cover under which to rally, and continued to fall back, rallying and reforming upon the line from which we started.[67]

Brigadier General Ambrose Ransom Wright, who charged on the left flank of Perry's Brigade, also reported a lack of support:

> Posey's Brigade, on my left, had not advanced, and fearing that, if I proceeded much farther with my left flank entirely unprotected, I might become involved in serious difficulties, I dispatched my aide-de-camp, Capt. R. H. Bell, with a message to

Major-General Anderson, informing him of my own advance and its extent, and that General Posey had not advanced with his brigade on my left.... Unfortunately, just as we had carried the enemy's last and strongest position, it was discovered that the brigade on our right had not only not advanced across the turnpike, but had actually given way, and was rapidly falling back to the rear, while on our left we were entirely unprotected, the brigade ordered to our support having failed to advance.[68]

Wright added: "I have not the slightest doubt but that I should have been able to have maintained my position on the heights, and secured the captured artillery, if there had been a protecting force on my left, or if the brigade on my right had not been forced to retire."[69]

Brigadier General Carnot Posey's brigade had four Mississippi regiments. He reported receiving orders which divided his command: "In the afternoon, I received an order to advance after Brigadier-General Wright, who was posted on my right in a woods before the advance was made. I received an order from the major-general ... to advance but two of my regiments and deploy them closely as skirmishers. I ... at once sent out the Forty-eighth and Nineteenth Regiments, Colonel Jayne and Colonel Harris commanding. These regiments advanced some 200 or 300 yards beyond the barn and house.[70]

That "barn and house" had to be the Bliss property. Perhaps Union tenacity there, which Chapter 5 herein describes, had a material effect on the main battle. Posey went on to state that his brigade became even more fragmented when "later in the day, I sent out the Sixteenth, and receiving information that the enemy were threatening their right and left flanks, I took out the Twelfth Regiment."[71] Then Posey himself sought support: "[I] requested Brigadier-General Mahone, who was on my left, in the rear of another division, to send me a regiment to support my left. He being at this time ordered to the right, could not comply."[72]

The report of Brigadier General William Mahone, in turn, not only failed to acknowledge the request that Posey claimed to have made; it neglected to mention receipt of any order sending him "to the right." Most peculiar was Mahone's abrupt description of what he seemed to believe was his brigade's lack of action:

> The operations of this brigade in the battle of Gettysburg, Pa., may be summed up in a few brief remarks.
> The brigade took no special or active part in the actions, of that battle beyond that which fell to the lot of its line of skirmishers.[73]

In fairness to General Mahone: he did report his casualties ("Killed, 8 men; wounded, 2 officers and 53 men; missing, 39 men") and recalled that his "skirmishers were quite constantly engaged."[74] But Mahone's brevity, and the lack of consistency between the reports of these brigadiers in Anderson's Division, do little to explain why the great attack of 2 July ceased with them.

Even historian Harry Pfanz, in his detailed and exhaustive analysis *Gettysburg: The Second Day,* could say little more than "something was wrong in Anderson's division that evening."[75] However, Pfanz did conclude that "Hancock, as usual, conducted himself magnificently. It was through Hancock's efforts in great part that the Federals were able to reestablish their position on Cemetery Ridge."[76]

In summary, those efforts began after Hancock dispatched his First Division to the left, leaving it in the hands of its commander, General Caldwell. Shortly thereafter Hancock led Willard's brigade to the left. He sent it into the fight against Barksdale's Confederates while deftly holding the 111th New York in reserve. When a threat appeared to Willard's right (which was probably Wilcox), he dispatched the 111th to meet it.

Following threats as they moved rightward, he then found the First Minnesota with no time to spare, and sacrificed them to stall the approach of Wilcox's Brigade. Then, after Wright's Confederates overran some of his advanced artillery and reached Cemetery Ridge, Hancock found the Vermonters. He issued them into the fray to recover the artillery and repulse Wright (and maybe Perry). Upon reaching the right half of his corps, the one that had maintained its place on Cemetery Ridge, he had accomplished the initial objective of saving the mile long gap in the Union line.

He appears to have erred at the latter end of his flurry of outstanding work. He noticed that Willard's brigade, now under the command of Colonel Eliakim Sherrill, was pulling out of its advanced position. Their work done, they were simply returning to their original location at Ziegler's Grove. But the general did not see it that way. He approached the brigade and addressed it with some indignation. The 111th's Colonel Clinton MacDougall remembered: "He asked where the commanding officer was. I stepped out and said I was in command of my Reg't and that I was commanded by the brigade commander to move in that direction. Sherrill was then placed in arrest by Hancock.... I remonstrated that Col. Willard had ordered that movement just before he was killed."[77]

Months later, General Hays visited Hancock in Norristown while Hancock was recovering from his 3 July wound. Hancock admitted he needed to apologize to Sherrill, but Hays admonished: "That's just like all your d_____d apologies Hancock.... They come too late. He's dead."[78]

Back to the night of 2 July: Other leaders might have rested as survivors cheered and congratulated each other. But while darkness gathered, a new Confederate assault made its way up East Cemetery Hill. Sergeant Scott noted, "As the day closed in upon the left, the contest commenced upon the right center, north of the cemetery."[79]

Hancock's report described the events in his typical clear manner: "It was nearly dark. Proceeding to the right of the Second Corps, near Cemetery Hill, and hearing a heavy engagement on General Howard's front, the firing seeming to come nearer and nearer, I directed General Gibbon to send Colonel Carroll's brigade, Third Division, to that point, to report to General Howard at once."[80]

Just as he brought the episode on his own front to a successful conclusion, Hancock had sensed a new peril emerging on Howard's line.

10

A Night Fight

At last this fire became so heavy and threatening that Hancock, who, in the meantime had rejoined me on the hill, said, "We ought to send some help over there." "Send a brigade, send Carroll!" Carroll, one of the most gallant of officers, was soon in motion, hurrying his brigade forward to the sound of the guns and I afterward learned that his arrival was most opportune and that his brigade performed most important services in restoring the broken lines of the 11th Corps where the rebels, after driving the infantry away, were actually in our batteries fighting over the guns; the cannoneers defending them with rammer staves and handspikes.[1]

—John Gibbon

Hancock had surely gained useful knowledge of East Cemetery Hill as he toiled there the previous afternoon. His dispatch of Carroll to that point now, the evening of 2 July, proved timely. While it points to his tactical awareness, it also raises questions about Howard's lack thereof. Hancock seems to have noticed the crisis no later than Howard, whose own corps was the target of the assault. Howard himself, without apology or explanation, later admitted not noticing the attack until Confederates were almost in his batteries: "It was after seven o'clock when the first cry, shrill and ominous, was heard in front of Ames' division. The Louisiana men, well named 'Louisiana Tigers,' came on with a rush, broke through the front of Von Gilsa's brigade and other points on my curved front, and almost before I could tell where the assault was made, our men and the Confederates came tumbling back together. Quickly they were in front of the entrenched batteries of Major Osborn, whose fire was intended strongly to support that bastioned front of the cemetery. Schurz and I were standing near, side by side."[2]

Schurz echoed this strange surprise: "General Howard and I were standing together in conversation when the uproar surprised us. There could be no doubt of its meaning. The enemy was attacking the batteries on our right."[3]

Although the time of its occurrence, dusk, was unusual, it was by no means a sneak attack. A witness to the attack, Lieutenant Edward Whittier of Battery E, Fifth Maine Light, wrote that it had been particularly slow in developing:

> Delayed by the twilight obscuring the ground to their front; by the difficult passage over rolling farm lands and fields shut in by stone walls which broke up their alignments; by loading and firing as they advanced; delayed perhaps by the fire of sixteen guns directly in their front, on the plateau of East Cemetery Hill, and the fire of the six light twelves on Culp's Hill on their flank, nearly an hour was consumed in passing over the seven hundred yards between their starting point and the short range of our infantry posted behind the walls at the base of East Cemetery Hill.[4]

Regardless of whether or not Whittier was accurate about how slowly the charge developed, it is hard to explain how Howard and Schurz failed to notice it before it reached Union guns on top of East Cemetery Hill. But when Howard and Schurz seemed to have focused their eyes elsewhere, however, Hancock, several hundred yards away on the west slope of Cemetery Hill, detected the threat with his ears.

But first, there is another crucial element of the night fight that is exemplary of Hancock's tactical genius: the placement of guns on what we now call "Stevens' Knoll." Chapter 4 discusses this, as it occurred on the afternoon of 1 July. But it is worth reviewing here. Despite its fortress-like quality, which remains apparent to visitors today, East Cemetery Hill's steep eastern slope poses a problem to the artillerists assigned to defend the eminence. The sharp incline shields an approaching enemy from the guns perched on its top. And even if there was a line of sight, the guns' muzzles could not be lowered enough to cover it. As Whittier put it: "These batteries had absolutely no point blank, and were prevented by the sharp descent of the eastern face of the hill, from exerting any control over that portion of his front which an artillerist holds as his dearest possession, leaving in its place a 'dead angle,' large and of terrible significance, in the place of ground where guns can vex and tear assaulting columns with canister."[5]

But on the previous evening, as Chapter 4 describes, Hancock had noticed this weakness and placed a battery to alleviate the problem. It was Stevens' Battery E, Fifth Maine Light, which Whittier was commanding on the night of 2 July. He explained, "but on a small knoll half way along the northern face of Culp's Hill, which projects at this point like a salient from our lines, and about three hundred and fifty to four hundred yards to the right and somewhat advanced from the plateau of East Cemetery Hill, General Hancock had placed a battery of 12-pounders, the 5th Maine."[6]

In other words, on the previous evening, when forces were retreating from

On 2 July Hancock's men faced assaults by, among others: the brigade of Brigadier General William Barksdale (top left), the brigade of Brigadier General Cadmus Wilcox (top right), the brigade of Brigadier General Ambrose Ransom Wright (bottom left), and the Division of Major General Jubal Early (bottom right) (Library of Congress reproduction numbers LC-DIG-ppmsca–26720, LC-DIG-cwpb–06356, LC-USZ62–84344, LC-DIG-ds–01484).

The Fourth Ohio's monument on East Cemetery Hill highlights the name of the brigade it belonged to. Hancock, who sent them to that location, rides in the background. The regiment has another monument near the Emmitsburg Road (photograph by author).

town, and Hancock was rallying them and establishing the Union line, he placed the battery. And he astutely did so in a way that covers the "dead angle." It was, as Whittier described, on the right flank of East Cemetery Hill. But it was also low enough and forward enough to enable guns on it to rake the steep eastern slope of the hill. Whittier later opined: "we could enfilade any line advancing to the assault of that crest [East Cemetery Hill], and could cover with our canister the sharp acclivity of the hill and its immediate foreground, searching their advance with the most demoralizing and destructive of all that is possible from artillery, an enfilading fire of double canister."[7]

Hence, Hancock had transformed what was potentially a place of refuge for attackers into a deadly field of fire.

Considering the details of the attack plan, this was especially unfortunate for the attackers. Hays' and Hoke's brigades of Early's Division were to form southeast of town and attack the hill, which rose south of town. This meant marching south first and then, when their right flank reached the base of East Cemetery Hill, wheeling right to swing the whole force up the steep eastern slope. This would be a difficult maneuver for two full brigades to perform on a parade ground. With the Fifth Maine Light commanding the base of the hill from its slightly elevated perch, the maneuver was almost suicidal. From the knoll, Whittier might have had the best possible view of the grand Confederate maneuvers, obscured only by the gathering darkness. Their initial southward march had been directly at his battery, but was now swinging across his front toward East Cemetery Hill on his left:

> Early's movements up to within a very short time of his final repulse, were guided by the movement and position of his right flank; the initial command, "right half wheel guide right," having been, as accurately as could be in the rapidly increasing darkness, strictly complied with; but, when Hoke's brigade, having the left of the line constantly increasing in the tendency to "refuse" as it came more and more under the influence of the 5th Maine's guns, had reached the low bottom of the valley separating Culp's from East Cemetery Hill, Colonel Avery (in command since Hoke's severe wound at Chancellorsville), finding his men too far to the left of the position they had been ordered to assault, ordered a change of front and wheeled his brigade to the right, a movement which none but the steadiest veterans could execute under such circumstances.[8]

The attackers' right turn precipitated adjustments by Whittier's battery, made to optimize its ability to inflict as much mortal destruction among the Confederates as possible:

> It was in this movement that the enemy swept past the left flank of my guns within short canister range; shutting out the right half battery so that these guns could not be brought to bear on those troops which were hastening to gain a new position and to re-form on ground from which they could, with better hope, to charge the crest of East Cemetery Hill. The trails of the left half battery were swung sharp and hard to the right, the right half battery was hastily "limbered to the rear," and in the darkness, hurried to a new position on the left of the guns remaining in the works, so that the whole battery was once more effective, and this time with double canister, pouring a most destructive, enfilading, demoralizing, fire into a confused mass of the enemy, struggling in the uncertain shadows at the base of the hill.[9]

It seems to have been a surreal scene exclusive to that age in warfare. Over a thousand Confederates performed a choreographed sweeping maneuver. Individuals tried to ignore the indescribable horror around them, as canister shot tore through the mass of men, so that the line as a whole might face its objective. By Whittier's description, "Avery's change of front brought his men in a body, tangled and confused, among the men of Hays' command, with which, up to the time of this to them most unfortunate change of front, they had made some semblance of alignment."[10]

But Whittier agreed with his enemies that the carnage might have been more severe had the gathering darkness not given them some protection: "General Hays, in his report to General Early, writes, 'The enemy's artillery, now within canister range, opened upon us, but owing to the darkness of the evening verging into the night, and the deep obscurity afforded by the smoke of the firing, our exact locality could not be discovered by the enemy's gunners, and thus we escaped what, in the full light of day, could have been nothing else but horrible slaughter.'"[11]

The steepness of the slope was not the only factor that hindered artillery atop the fortress-like eminence. As Whittier noted, the presence of friendly infantry near the base of the slope also caused the guns to pause. But his battery was well placed to disrupt the enemy lines without harming Union defenders: "Meanwhile our batteries on the crest of East Cemetery Hill were powerless. Breck's (Reynolds') four guns on the southern slope, did not use canister, for fear of our men at that time thought to be behind the walls in his front; while the 'dead angle' made by the abrupt slopes of Cemetery Hill had been changed, by the act of General Hancock, who placed the 5th Maine light twelves on the side of salient created by the north face of Culp's Hill, into a most deadly angle."[12]

Regarding the infantry opposing the Confederate brigades, it is not the intent here to evaluate its performance. But as usual, Eleventh Corps units containing large German contingents attracted severe criticism. Whittier's statement was mild compared to others: "Von Gilsa's brigade, Eleventh Corps, behind the stone walls at the base of East Cemetery Hill, broke and left its front open."[13] So with determination and discipline, surviving attackers made it to the hilltop where Howard's batteries were. Whittier's narrative continues: "Weidrich's and Ricketts' batteries were overrun and the guns seized, the left piece of Ricketts' was spiked, but the cannoneers fought the enemy hand to hand with trail handspikes, rammers, and what few pistols they had, and succeeded in checking them for a moment."[14]

This is when Hancock's intuition paid off, according to Whittier: "Carroll's brigade, sent unasked, by General Hancock's happy inspiration, advancing by front of a single regiment, charged across the small space, drove the enemy from our guns and down the slopes. The position was saved."[15]

But it had not been that simple. William Kepler was a private in the Fourth Regiment Ohio, First Brigade, Third Division, Second Corps. Colonel Samuel S. Carroll commanded the brigade. Kepler later recalled details of the brigade's expedition through darkness to the latest point of crisis. "Word was received that part of the Eleventh Corps, being taken in front and flank, was compelled to fall back from their support of two batteries on Cemetery Hill [there were actually three batteries in danger]. 'Attention! Right face—Double Quick—March!' was instantly obeyed ... we hurried by gravestones struck by the spiteful minie ball—toward the cannon's vivid flash and thundering roar; Baltimore Turnpike was crossed, the position of the rebels determined only by their fire."[16]

There is very little space on the plateau of East Cemetery Hill between its steep east slope and the gatehouse of the Evergreen Cemetery. The fact that it is a salient, whose defense requires guns facing both its north and east sides, along with their horse teams, caissons and other supporting elements, made it a very crowded place. Navigating a brigade across it in broad daylight without enemy fire would have been difficult enough. But the darkness of night and chaos of combat must have required a highly skilled leader. Carroll's report echoed Kepler's description and explained more of the difficulties: "Owing to the artillery fire from our own guns, it was impossible to advance by a longer front than that of a regiment, and it being perfectly dark, and with no guide, I had to find the enemy's line entirely by their fire."[17]

Not restricted by the conventions of an official report, Kepler's description is vastly more dramatic than Carroll's, though not to the point of seeming inaccurate: "hastening toward them, now by the left flank of the brigade, through tanglements of retreating men, caissons and horses, up and along a slope, where maddened gunners of captured batteries raved and swore, or cried in very madness, vowing death to meet rather than give up their guns, striking the rebels with fist, rammer ammunition and stones."[18]

There are many descriptions about this spectacle of artillerists struggling in their batteries against rampaging infantry. General Schurz wrote: "In Weidrich's battery, manned by Germans from Buffalo, a rebel officer, brandishing his sword, cried out: 'This battery is ours!' Whereupon a sturdy artilleryman responded: 'No dis battery is **unser**,' and felled him to the ground with a sponge-staff."[19]

Harry Pfanz includes, in *Gettysburg—Culp's Hill and Cemetery Hill* (1993), the account of a more deadly, though less likely, exchange. In it, a Confederate leaps to the mouth of a gun, and declares himself in control of the piece. Lanyard in hand, a German gunner replies, "Du sollst sie haben!" (You shall have it!) and fires the gun, annihilating the intruder.[20] Though deadly donnybrooks between German artillerists and southern infantrymen make colorful anecdotes, it was Carroll's mission to end them. And he had more than just crowded confusion, darkness, and brawls to contend with. By his report, there was some measure of organized Confederate resistance: "For the first few minutes they had a cross-fire upon us from a stone wall on the right of the road, but, by changing the front of the Seventh West Virginia, they were soon driven from there."[21]

Kepler boasted that when the brigade reached the batteries:

> Bayonets and butts of guns at once joined the efforts of the heroic gunners, then infantry and gunner in a general melee, with flanks of regiments overlaping [sic] and every-man-in-as-you-can sort of way, drove the enemy from unhitching horses and spiking guns, down over the hill, under the cross-fire of Stevens' battery on our right, and captured a number of prisoners. Weiderick's [sic] and Rickett's batteries were recaptured. Company G of our Seventh West Virginia made sad havoc with their old rebel neighbors.[22]

Major William Houghton recalled: "Being in the center of the 14th Indiana, I recollect I passed to the left of the cemetery gate; the most of the brigade passed to the right. We met Ricketts, who was frantically imploring us to save his guns. The musketry was very heavy, and the blaze seemed to be almost in our faces. It was middling hot for a minute, but it couldn't last. We came in good style; a cheer, a volley, a charge, and the hill was ours, the guns retaken and the rebels whooped across the stone wall below."[23]

Carroll's charge had been decisive. But it was not the only reinforcement of East Cemetery Hill. Schurz explained what happened when he and Howard finally recognized the attack:

> With the consent of General Howard I took the two regiments nearest to me, ordered them to fix bayonets, and, headed by Colonel Kryzanowski, they hurried to the threatened point at a double-quick. I accompanied them with my whole staff. Soon we found ourselves surrounded by a rushing crowd of stragglers from the already broken lines. We did our best, sword in hand, to drive them back as we went. Arrived at the batteries, we found an indescribable scene of melee.... Our infantry made a vigorous rush on the invaders, and after a short but spirited hand-to-hand scuffle tumbled them down the embankment.[24]

While Schurz's push had come from behind and left of the batteries, Carroll's had come from behind and the right. As Schurz explained: "Our line to the right, having been reinforced by Carroll's brigade of the Second Corps, which had hurried on in good time, also succeeded in driving back the assailants with a rapid fire, and the dangerous crisis happily ended."[25]

Then, Carroll explained, they solidified the lines: "The firing continued until about 10.20, when they fell back out of range, and skirmishers were advanced in our front. General Ames' division then made connections with me on our right and left."[26]

There Carroll's brigade stayed for the rest of the battle. Yet, while fighting against the Confederates on East Cemetery Hill had essentially ended, it appears that arguing among Union officers began. Whittier explained: "All firing ceased, but rumor has it that a new fight was on. The fiery spirit of the gallant Carroll 'flamed to its height.' Bent on maintaining the safety of this key to our position, conquered, as he believed, from a victorious foe by the high valor of the force he had led, he was ready to fight with his three small regiments the whole of Ames' division, Eleventh Corps, for possession of the lines it had failed to defend, and for whose failure his headstrong, indomitable courage knew no excuse."[27]

Apparently, wrote Whittier, Carroll made his disgust with the Eleventh Corps very clear: "His anger found utterance in words which these pages may not venture to chronicle; his warlike rage found no vent in the language of the schools, but rather of that of the barracks, and with memory of Chancelorsville rankling in his breast, he emptied the vials of his wrath on the devoted heads of the Eleventh Corps officers, high in rank, sparing none of those gathered about him."[28]

A witness, who mistakenly believed Carroll was a general at the time, reported:

> There was a group of officers under a tree. It was so dark I could not distinguish their faces, but one of them was General Carroll which I know from having another officer call him by name. The other, I suppose, was a staff officer. They were evidently very much in earnest. I heard one say: "Well, I can hold this line to-night as long as necessary; but why in the name of ____ don't he get his men into shape again and get them down here? He's got all night to do it in." The other replied: "General Carroll, our troops are very much demoralized. The General does not feel he can depend on them."
>
>   The one who had been addressed as Carroll replied: "____ such a speech as that. Don't talk to me that way. Tell him to bring his men back here and align them on this grass. They will then be in support of my brigade-line. If he can't inspire them, by ____ I can. Get them back here. Don't let them cower like a flock of sheep up there behind the upper batteries" (referring to Stevens and Reynolds on the brow of the hill).
>
>   The officer addressed replied in a low tone which could not be made out, to which Carroll replied with great wrath: "Hancock sent me over here to restore this line. I have done it. But I can't be responsible for the whole left center of the army with my little brigade unsupported. ____ ____ a commander who says he has no confidence in his troops. He had better go and shoot himself. Probably your troops reciprocate your General's lack of confidence. Tell him to either get them back here on this line or relinquish the command."
>
>   Then Carroll went on to say that he himself occupied a peculiar position; that

Hancock had ordered him over there to restore the line, but had not told him to report to anybody, nor had he given him any authority in that position. So he said his brigade was isolated from them. He had no authority to assume command on that part of the line. "If I had such authority," he said, with great vehemence, "I'd resurrect things here quicker than _____ could scorch a feather."[29]

Captain Ricketts himself wrote: "I am particularly anxious to give in my testimony with regard to the conduct of the Eleventh (11th) Corps as ... I am very much afraid, that history will give that corps credit for, what it never did at Gettysburg, fighting."[30]

Referring to Brigadier General Ames, commanding the First Division of the Eleventh Corps at the time, Ricketts wrote, "He also said that in case of emergency he could not depend on his men."[31] Furthermore, said Ricketts, "When the charge was made on my position, their conduct on that occasion was cowardly and disgraceful in the extreme. As soon as the charge commenced, they, although they had a stone-wall in their front, commenced running in the greatest confusion to the rear, hardly a shot was fired, certainly not a volley, and so panic stricken were they that several ran into the canister fire of my guns and were knocked over."[32]

Finally, he contended: "All the credit due to the infantry in that affair is due to Carroll's brigade alone. None of the Eleventh Corps were rallied in time to assist in repulsing the charge."[33]

Regardless of what Eleventh Corps infantry unit or leader failed or under-performed, the Confederate attack ultimately failed. Hancock was a crucial part of its repulse even though he was not present to see it. General Henry Hunt, Chief of Artillery of the Army of the Republic, called his move "a happy inspiration."[34] It speaks volumes of Hancock's genius for tactical analysis and deft handling of resources. His official report boasted: "I was gratified to hear subsequently, from General Howard in person, that it arrived at a very critical time, and that this unexpected re-enforcement materially assisted him in driving the enemy from his front."[35]

As for Carroll, he and his westerners acquitted themselves beautifully in a dark, unfamiliar and crowded place to work.

11

Council of War

Hancock, in giving his vote, said the Army of the Potomac had retreated too often, and he was in favor of remaining now to fight it out.[1]

—Abner Doubleday

A break in major combat would eventually occur on the night of the 2nd, but Hancock's dispatch of Carroll to East Cemetery Hill was not his last major order of the evening. Culp's Hill, to the right of East Cemetery Hill, had also been under serious attack. Some of Slocum's Twelfth Corps had abandoned its trenches to address the crisis on the Hancock / Sickles front, and the Confederates were exploiting their absence. Hancock, in yet another instance of tactical awareness and initiative, recognized this and responded. He reported: "Hearing firing farther to the right, and believing it to be on General Slocum's front, and fearing that the troops he had sent to me had left him without sufficient force, I directed General Gibbon to send two regiments to that point."[2]

But the onset of darkness had become complete, making navigating the already crowded and wooded section of the field nearly impossible. Hancock's final effort to assist on the right would not have the same decisive effect that his dispatch of Carroll had. His report, continuing, stated: "The Seventy-first Pennsylvania, Col. R. Penn Smith, and the One hundred and sixth Pennsylvania, Lieut. Col. W. L. Curry, were dispatched, but they also reported to Major-General Howard. The one hundred and sixth Pennsylvania Volunteers remained until relieved the next day, doing good service. The Seventy-first returned to its command about midnight, without having received orders to do so, after suffering some loss."[3]

Gibbon recalled, "With the end of Carroll's fight the fire died down, to rise again several times later on some parts of the field."[4] Statements about the precise hour that events occurred during this period of history are notoriously unreliable. Clocks were poorly synchronized and human memory from any period is faulty. However, it is notable that Whittier wrote, "Carroll had swept the plateau clean of Confederates" when the time "was now sharp nine."[5] So General Meade found the situation stable enough to call a council of war. Gibbon remembered, "Soon after the firing had ceased, a staff officer from Army Headquarters met Gen. Hancock and myself and summoned us **both** to Gen. Meade's Headquarters where a council was being held."[6]

The reason Gibbon emphasized "both" is that he was surprised to be summoned to such an august event. He later wrote, "I had never been a member of a council of war before (nor have I since) and did not feel confident I was properly a member of this one"[7]; Once Gibbon got to the meeting, he realized, "two corps were doubly represented, the 2nd Corps by Hancock and myself and the 12th by Slocum and Williams."[8]

Meade was still claiming the discretion Secretary of War Stanton had granted him when he appointed him to command the Army of the Potomac. Meade had been using this authorization since the first day when he ordered Hancock to supersede Howard in the absence of General Slocum. He also had Gibbon supersede his senior, General Caldwell, to act as Second Corps com-

Meade made the Leister house his headquarters throughout the battle. Its tiny east room hosted the council of war held on the evening of 2 July (photograph by author).

mander when Hancock proceeded ahead of the corps to Gettysburg. Gibbon went on to describe the scene at Meade's headquarters: "All the corps commanders were assembled in the little front room of the Leister House; Newton, who had been assigned to the command of the 1st Corps over Doubleday, his senior, Hancock of the 2nd, Birney of the 3rd, Sykes of the 5th, Sedgwick who had arrived during the day with the 6th after a long march from Manchester, Howard, 11th, and Slocum, 12th, besides Gen. Meade, Gen. Butterfield, chief of staff, Warren, Chief of Engineers, A.S. Williams, 12th Corps, and myself, 2nd Corps."[9]

He noted the cramped conditions of the tiny Gettysburg farmhouse: "These twelve were all assembled in a little room not more than 10 or 12 ft. square with a bed in one corner, a small table on one side and a chair or two. Of course all could not sit down. Some did, some lounged on the bed, some stood whilst Warren, tired out and suffering from a wound in the neck, where a piece of shell had struck him, lay down in the corner of the room and went sound asleep and I don't think heard any of the proceedings."[10]

Despite this, Warren was later able to render some description of the event: "There was not held what I would call a council of war. The officers met together, but merely for the purpose of explaining to each other how things stood."[11]

Gibbon's recollection echoed Warren: "The discussion was at first very informal and in the shape of a conversation during which each one made comments on the fight and told what he knew of the condition of affairs."[12]

The Army of the Potomac's position was not particularly difficult, especially compared to its opponent and in relation to the fact that it was in the largest battle of the war. It had come to a good defensive position to make a defensive stand. It had suffered badly but that happens in battle. It still had its position, line of supply and morale. And according to Gibbon, the group of generals agreed: "the prevailing impression seemed to be that the place of battle had been in a measure selected for us. Here we are; now what is the best thing to do? It soon became evident that everybody was in favor of remaining where we were and in favor of giving battle there."[13]

Eventually General Butterfield suggested they put various issues to a vote and make them official. Meade had inherited him from Hooker as a Chief of Staff. He was serving as a recording secretary. Perhaps he was weary of the ongoing banter and wanted to conclude the gathering to get some sleep. Regardless

Opposite: **Brigadier General John Gibbon's statue stands on Cemetery Ridge. He attended the 2 July council of war, though he feared his rank did not qualify him (photograph by William Bretzger).**

of Butterfield's motivation, Gibbon remembered: "After the discussion had lasted some time, Butterfield suggested that it would, perhaps, be well to formulate the question to be asked, and General Meade assenting he took a piece of paper, on which he had been making some memoranda and wrote down a question; when he had done he read it off and formally proposed it to the council."[14]

According to Gibbon, the questions put to the council, as Butterfield recorded them, were:

> 1. Under existing circumstances is it advisable for this army to remain in its present position or to retire to another nearer its base of supplies?
> 2. It being determined to remain in present position, shall the army await attack or attack the enemy?
> 3. If we await attack, how long?[15]

And the responses were:

> GIBBON: 1. Correct position of the army, but would not retreat. 2. In no condition to attack, in his opinion. 3. Until he moves.
> WILLIAMS: 1. Stay. 2. Wait attack. 3. One day.
> BIRNEY: 1. Same as General Williams.
> SYKES: "   "   "
> NEWTON: 1. Correct position of the army, but would not retreat. 2. By all means not attack. 3. If we wait it will give them a chance to cut our line.
> HOWARD: 1. Remain. 2. Wait attack until 4 p.m. tomorrow. 3. If don't attack, attack them.
> HANCOCK: 1. Rectify position without moving so as to give up field. 2. Not attack unless our communications are cut. 3. Can't wait long; can't be idle.
> SEDGWICK: 1. Remain. [2.] and wait attack. [3.] At least one day.
> SLOCUM: Stay and fight it out.[16]

Hence, Butterfield had his official tally, Meade had a formal endorsement of what was the obvious course of action. So the council broke up. Gibbon reported a few minor discussions: "It was nearly midnight before we separated and before we left the house I saw Gen. Meade in conversation with Gen. Birney and overheard the former say in a rather curt way, 'Gen. Hancock is your superior and I claim the right to issue the order.' From which I inferred that Birney had made some comments on the assignment of Hancock to command the 3rd Corps."[17]

Gibbon also got assurance from Meade that Gibbon was welcome at the council: "I took occasion before leaving to say to Gen. Meade that his staff officer had regularly summoned me as a corps commander to the council, although I had some doubts about being present. He answered pleasantly, 'That is all right, I wanted you here.'"[18]

Finally, Gibbon recalled Meade predicting the next day's events:

Meade said to me, "If Lee attacks tomorrow, it will be in your front." I asked him why he thought so and he replied, "Because he has made attacks on both our flanks and failed and if he concludes to try it again, it will be on our centre." I expressed a hope that he would and told Gen. Meade with confidence that if he did, we would defeat him. Meade's reliance on the doctrine of chances, that having tried each of our wings, Lee would, if he made a third trial, make it upon our centre, struck me as somewhat remarkable. But he was right.[19]

The end of the meeting was as apt a time as there would be for most of these generals to steal some sleep. But Hancock, a master quartermaster as well as tactician, recalled how some replenishment of his artillery's supplies took place that evening: "During the night of the 2d, the batteries were supplied with ammunition as far as practicable. Having brought but half the ammunition train of the corps, we were dependent somewhat on others. The battery ammunition was supplied by the train of the Artillery Reserve, though not to the full extent required."[20]

There was never any real *quiet* during the battle of Gettysburg. Sporadic musketry, the rumbling of wagons and the hauntingly unnerving cries of wounded filled even the most still night hours. Samuel Hurst of the Seventy-Third Ohio wrote:

> During the night, we could hear the cries of hundreds of wounded and dying men on the field, in our left front, where Hancock repulsed the foe. It was the most distressful wail we ever listened to. Thousands of sufferers upon the field, and hundreds lying between the two skirmish lines, who could not be cared for, through the night were groaning and wailing and crying out in their depth of suffering and pain. They were the mingled cries of friend and foe that were borne to us on the night-breeze, as a sad, wailing, painful cry for help.[21]

Amid these sounds and the thick rural darkness the generals retired for the evening. Gibbon later wrote: "it was near on to midnight when the council broke up and then Hancock, Newton and I repaired to a yard near the next house south of Meade's Headquarters (Brown's) and all three crawling into my Headquarters ambulance, slept."[22]

12

Morning of Uncertainty

A stillness that seemed oppressive had settled over the bat-
tlefield of Gettysburg. It was like the hush in nature elements
which so often precedes the bursting into fury of the gathering
storm.[1]

—Richard S. Thompson

The silence was ominous.[2]
—Charles H. Morgan

The long day of suspense was terrible.[3]
—Ralph Orson Sturtevant

Haskell was enjoying some rare and all too brief sleep when, "at four o'clock in the morning of the 3d I was awakened by General Gibbon pulling me by the foot, and saying 'Come, don't you hear that?' I sprang to my feet. Where was I? A moment and my dead senses and memory were alive again, and the sound of brisk firing of musketry to the front and right of the Second Corps, and over at the extreme right of our line, where we heard it last in the night, brought all back to my memory."[4]

There was a full battle happening on the far right, Slocum's front, where the Confederate's had taken breastworks abandoned to assist in Sickles' sector. But the fighting on the 'front and right of the Second Corps' was probably the continued struggle for possession of the Bliss farm buildings. Haskell explains that if Gibbon was alarmed, most of the soldiers were not: "At the commence-ment of the war such firing would have awakened the whole army, and roused it to its feet and to arms; not so now. The men on the crest lay snoring in their blankets, even though some of the enemy's bullets dropped among them, as if bullets were harmless as the drops of dew around them."[5]

Nevertheless, Haskell explained, it was time to get the men up:

The men were roused early, in order that their morning meal might be out of the way in time for whatever should occur. Then ensued the hum of an army, not in ranks, chatting in low tones, and running about and jostling among each other, rolling and packing their blankets and tents. They looked like an army of rag-gatherers while shaking these very useful articles of the soldier's outfit.... But one could not have told by the appearance of the men that they were in battle yesterday and were likely to be again to-day.[6]

The Bliss farm situation began as the preceding evening had ended: Confederates held the buildings but the Federals were closely upon them, threatening to assault the position at any moment. Lieutenant Brady of the First Delaware described the development:

About 7 o'clock a.m. I received an order from General Alexander Hays, commanding the division, and by whom I was recognized as being in command of the 1st Delaware to "Take and hold the barn at all hazards." For this service volunteers were called and was responded to by twenty seven men from the 1st Delaware, and wither three or four from the 12th N.J. all of whom were under my immediate command.[7]

Brady's claim to command of the regiment was dubious, but his continued description of events seems credible: "We formed in the lane, and after divesting ourselves of all superfluous articles, as haversacks, swords, scabbards &c. we proceeded at a full run to within fifty feet of the barn, where we were checked by a withering fire from the various vents or air holes in its walls, and compelled to retire; not however until the brave heroic Corporal John B. Sheets and private William J. Dorsey of Co. 'D' had been killed, and all the expedition with possibly three or four exceptions, were more or less wounded."[8]

After some artillery action and more exchanges of Bliss farm possession, Hancock had become wary of the struggle. According to Bingham:

General Hancock, who had been quietly watching the matter, now sent an aide to Hays to say to him that he might bring on a general engagement (which was not at the moment desired by General Meade) by holding on to the barn within the enemy's skirmish line & that he would therefore please burn the building and retire his skirmishers to the line originally held by them. These were very unwelcome orders to Hays, who was then in his element, and delighted with the manner in which he had been bagging the Rebs. Turning to an aide, he said, "Major please return to General Hancock and say to him that the old barn is my "Reb" trap. I have caught more than one hundred & fifty in it this morning and if he will only allow me to withdraw my line so that they will come into it and then let me take one more dash at it, I will willingly burn it as he directs."[9]

Hays did not prevail on Hancock to rescind the order; the barn burnt. But there developed post-battle disagreements as to how the razing of the Bliss farm came about. A description in the Papers of the Historical Society of Delaware reads, in part:

> The Fourteenth Connecticut Volunteers was now ordered to dislodge the enemy and keep them out, which service they bravely executed.
>
> While this detachment was charging on the buildings, and the fire from the enemy's line was exceedingly hot, General Hays called for a volunteer to carry an order to the commanding officer to burn the house and out-buildings. Captain J. Parke Postles, of the 1st Delaware, acting assistant inspector-general of the brigade, sprang on his horse, saying "I will go, general! and bending forward, he rode in the face of that storm of lead, delivered the order, and, to the astonishment of all, returned unhurt.[10]

Captain Postles received the Medal of Honor in 1892 for this. But Second Lieutenant Charles A. Hitchcock of the 111th New York had a very different view:

> I carried the order to those who were in the Bliss buildings, I never claimed anything else, but others have told all sorts of stories about it, in fact I have never had occasion but three or four times to give any particulars of the affair. I had just come from the skirmish line, as Gen. Hayes [sic] and staff rode up to our line of battle. I was sitting on the ground eating hard-tack, and heard the Gen. say to McDougall, he would like a volunteer to burn those buildings (a house and barn) I looked around to see if anyone was going. As McDougall repeated the order or request in a loud voice, as no one appeared to volunteer I got up and told the Gen. I would go, and made a request for matches, which was given to me; then Gen. Hayes specified the order to me which I was to carry to the officers in command of the men in the buildings, which was, that he should withdraw his men in the buildings and assemble them at a certain point, and to cease firing and then burn the buildings.
>
> I gathered up some paper which came from cartridge boxes and started on my mission at a double quick, and kept it up till I reached the buildings, there was some hard fighting going on around there, I saw the officer there in command and repeated Gen. Hayes order to him, which was acted upon immediately, by getting the dead and wounded from the buildings. When that was accomplished, we fired the buildings, having accomplished my mission I started for my regiment; when most there I met Gen. Hayes and said to him, "General I have executed your order." He said, "I see you have Sergeant" (for the buildings were then on fire).[11]

Finally, there is Brady's take on the matter:

> The 14th Conn. Was called upon by General Hays, and by him personally ordered to not only take the barn, but burn it. The above regiment formed in the lane and accompanied by a few volunteers from the 1st Delaware, myself included … set forward, under command of Major Theodore G. Ellis, of the 14th Connecticut, with the above object in view. But I am happy to be able to relate, that ere the command had covered two thirds the intervening distance between our line

of the fence and the object of its mission, flames were seen issuing from its roof, and the barn, as all hands agreed, was providentially ignited by a shell from one of the batteries, possibly Woodruff's in our (then) rear. Owing to the then dry weather and well seasoned condition of the roofing material, the fire spread with great rapidity and falling into the hay and straw stored beneath, the barn was soon enveloped in one vast sheet of flames.[12]

Regardless of exactly how, the Bliss buildings burned in the late morning. The loss of the minor "citadel" contributed to a general battlefield lull. Still, the mayhem of the previous day left no shortage of realignment to be done, especially at the left of the corps. According to Haskell: "As early as practicable the lines all along the left are revised and reformed, this having been rendered necessary by yesterday's battle, and also by what is anticipated today."[13]

That anticipation was the source of disagreement and anxiety, as Haskell explained:

It is the opinion of many of our generals that the rebel will not give us battle to-day, that he had enough yesterday; that he will be heading towards the Potomac at the earliest practicable moment if he has not already done so. But the better and controlling judgment is, that he will make another grand effort to pierce or turn our lines; that he will either mass and attack the left again, as yesterday, or direct his operations against the left of our centre, the position of the Second Corps, and try to sever our line.[14]

The lull also fomented anxiety for Richard Thompson, commanding the Twelfth New Jersey:

The artillery firing had ceased; the firing on the skirmish line had quieted down, and a stillness that seemed oppressive had settled over the battlefield of Gettysburg. It was like the hush in nature's elements which so often precedes the bursting into fury of the storm. Like the ominous gathering of clouds, the enemy were moving great masses of troops and artillery. We waited. An hour passed, and still we waited. Another hour passed, and still we waited. Another hour passed, and yet we waited. Even the occasional report of a rifle on the skirmish line seemed rather to emphasize than break the stillness.[15]

But Meade himself, according to Haskell, was not worried: "He was early on horseback this morning, and rode along the whole line, looking to it himself, and with glass in hand sweeping the woods and fields in the direction of the enemy, to see if aught of him could be discovered. His manner was calm and serious, but earnest. There was no arrogance of hope, or timidity of fear, discernible in his face; but you would have supposed he would do his duty conscientiously and well, and would be willing to abide the result. You would have seen this in his face."[16]

When Haskell wrote, "He [Meade] was well pleased with the left of the line today," he was criticizing Sickles' perversion of the line Hancock had designed from Cemetery Hill on the afternoon of the first day.[17] And Haskell continued his praise of the army's position when he recalled that Meade

> had no apprehension for the right where the fight was now going on, on account of the admirable position of our forces there. He was not of the opinion that the enemy would attack the centre, our artillery had such sweep there, and this was not a favorite point of attack with the rebel; besides, should he attack the centre, the general thought he could reinforce it in good season. I heard General Meade speak of these matters to Hancock and some others, at about nine o'clock in the morning, while they were up by the line, near the Second Corps.[18]

The Second Corps did not dig in to the great extent that their Twelfth Corps comrades had on Culp's Hill. But Haskell noted that they did not completely neglect their defenses, either: "The most of the way along this line upon the crest was a stone fence, constructed from small rough stones, a good deal of the way badly fallen down; but the men had improved it and patched it with rails from the neighboring fences and with earth, so as to render it in many places a very passable breastwork against musketry and flying fragments of shell."[19]

The Vermonters who were so successful the previous day had stayed to become part of Hancock's line. They apparently decided to take an opportunity to create their own somewhat forward line and fortify it with makeshift breastworks, according to Ralph Orson Sturtevant:

> While waiting and soon after the noise of battle ceased on our extreme right, Lieutenant Albert Clark in command of Company G saw that a nearby rail fence might be readily converted into a low breastwork and placed considerably in advance of the stone wall that then protected us, and be of great advantage in repelling any charge against us and called for volunteers to go out and do the work of building a breastwork with the fence rails.
>
> Sergeant George H. Scott was the first to volunteer and then others followed until some twenty or more of our regiment largely of Company G as I recall, led by Sergeant Scott charged the rail fence, carried the rails about one hundred yards in advance and further down the slope and laid up a temporary bulwark of rails perhaps two feet high parallel to the battle line then occupied by the 13th regiment.[20]

Sturtevant continued: "The work was quickly and well done and timely, and the protection it gave us later was complimentary to the rare foresight and cool calculation of Lieutenant Albert Clarke of Company G. General Stannard saw the boys at this work and approved it with a nod and a smile, while Colonel Randall and the regiment encouraged the enterprise with cheers and congratulated the boys on their safe return."[21]

Hancock claimed the forward position was no spontaneous decision by the Vermonters themselves. In the margins of a published article by Abner Doubleday, he scribbled "The Vermont Brigade was in front of the main line.

A bronze likeness of Brigadier General George Stannard stands atop the Vermont monument on Cemetery Ridge, near the spot at which his Second Vermont Brigade fought on 2 and 3 July. It shows the general without his right arm to symbolize sacrifice, even though he did not lose the arm until later in the war (photograph by William Bretzger).

The other command was close behind it. I ordered it."[22] These Vermonters, one will realize, were proud and not shy about touting their accomplishments at Gettysburg. Said Sturtevant:

> This was the first real battle of these Vermont regiments, and their conduct in the baptism of fire on the previous day under the direction and eye of General

Hancock gave promise and assurance to him, that they were the boys to occupy and hold the front battle lines in the impending charge and final struggle.

This was indeed a flattering compliment from so distinguished and able a fighter as General Hancock to General Stannard and his command.[23]

The advanced placement of a small group may seem unusual and undesirable. But the Vermonters, protruding from the left flank of the Second Corps line, were not as prone as those advanced on the right flank, the Eighth Ohio. Lieutenant Thomas F. Galwey of the regiment wrote:

The position of the 8th Ohio Vol. Infantry (Carroll's brigade, Hays' division, Hancock's corps) was so singular a one that it seems worthy of special notice....

The isolated and advanced position of the regiment was taken up early in the afternoon of the 2d, during the fight on the left.... Just before the great charge on the 3d we were absolutely alone out there.[24]

Their position was so audaciously advanced that historian John Bachelder did not believe their claims about it. Their commander, Lieutenant Colonel Franklin Sawyer wrote a scathing rebuttal to remarks Bachelder had made: "You said we could not have been there, and would have been of no use there, and that 'Col. Sawyer was reeling drunk and did not know where he was' &c. Now every word of that is false, which I can prove by every surviving member of my regiment who was there."[25]

As his argument continued, he added specifics to explain why he and his men were out there for so long:

I think about eleven o'clock [in the morning of 3 July], Col. Carroll sent one of his staff officers, Capt. Gregg (also of the 8th) to see how we were getting along. While he was still there the artillery duel opened, and he remained until it ceased. When he returned to his brigade, I asked him to have Carroll relieve me; but the charge of the enemy on Gen. Hancock's front followed so quickly that this could not be done, and we remained until after the battle....

Now Colonel, this is a brief but true account of the matter, I am not responsible for being there or staying there. My corps, divisions and Brigadier Generals all knew I was there and did not see fit to recall me.[26]

In fact, the advanced position of the Eighth Ohio, especially in conjunction with that of the Thirteenth, Fourteenth, and Sixteenth Vermont at the other end of the Second Corps,[27] proved invaluable to Hancock in the ensuing Confederate charge, detailed later.

Most were pleased with the Second Corps line; others saw dangerous weaknesses in the details. Captain Dave Shields of Hays' division later wrote: "Between the right of the Third Division in Ziegler's Grove and the left of the Eleventh Corps line, Coster's brigade of Steinwehr's Division, posted along the cemetery wall on the Taneytown Road, there was a gap which later was filled with Robinson's Division of the First Corps."[28]

But previous to that was the lull. While it brought anticipation and anxiety for some, for others it was a welcome opportunity. If one is to believe Hancock's wife, Almira, he found the time and resources to telegraph her: "On the morning of July 3 General Hancock telegraphed me from the battle-field (as was his custom each day while the action lasted), 'I am all right, so far.'"[29] The claim that the necessary facilities would be available for the general to make such a transmission is dubious. But why would she lie about such a matter? Haskell remembered that the quiet around 11:00 a.m. presented the chance for an unlikely picnic: "Now it so happened that just about this time of day a very original and interesting thought occurred to General Gibbon and several of his staff; that it would be a very good thing, and a very good time, to have something to eat. When I announce to you that I had not tasted a mouthful of food since yesterday noon, to have something to eat."[30]

Among those who attended the opportunistic meal besides Gibbon and his staff were Meade, Hancock, Newton of the First Corps and Cavalry Corps Commander Major General Alfred Pleasonton.[31] But Haskell says the menu items were extremely difficult to procure:

> We had nothing but some potatoes and sugar and coffee in the world. And I may as well say here, that of such, in scant proportions, would have been our repast, had it not been for the riding of miles by two persons, one an officer, to procure supplies; and they only succeeded in getting some few chickens, some butter, and one huge loaf bread, which last was bought of a soldier, because he had grown faint in carrying it, and was afterwards rescued with much difficulty, after a long race, from a four-footed hog which had got hold of and had actually eaten part of it.[32]

The rare battlefield break must have been a welcome relief to the participants; but, not surprisingly, enemy action abruptly cut it short. Morgan remembers: "General Hancock was dictating an order to one of his staff concerning fresh beef for the men, when the first shell fell into the group. An attempt was made to finish the order in deliberation, but the shells came thicker and faster; several of the horses broke loose and ran wildly about; the horses of the ambulance containing the lunch broke away, the driver, an old veteran of the regular service, being killed—altogether creating a scene of confusion such is seldom seen, even on the field of battle."[33]

It is fitting that Hancock, the logistician and quartermaster, was ordering food for his men when the rude and deadly interruption occurred. The real work of the day had only just begun.

13

Cannonade

I can almost fancy I see Hancock again as he rode past the front of his command, just previous to the assault, followed by a single orderly displaying his corps flag, while the missiles from a hundred pieces of artillery tore up the ground around him.[1]

—Abner Doubleday

There is a duality to the cannonade. While it was the largest of the war and horrific to experience, its ultimate tactical effect was minimal, at best. Anecdotes of the cannonade vary from the terrifying and tragic to the almost comical. If one assumes the plausible number of one hundred fifty Confederate guns deployed against Cemetery Ridge and Hill, each firing twice per minute, there were five missiles per second arriving at their targets. Or as Hancock noted in his official report, "The air was filled with projectiles, there being scarcely an instant but that several were seen bursting at once."[2] He also later testified: "It was a most terrific and appalling cannonade—one possibly hardly even paralleled.... I doubt whether there has ever been more concentrated [artillery] upon an equal space, and opening at one time."[3]

The noise alone must have been more than sufficient to cause madness, especially if you consider the added effect of the reply of Union guns. Said William Haines of the Twelfth New Jersey: "I almost tremble yet when I think what an awful din it made, the shrieking of shells bursting everywhere and the solid shot tearing through the house and barn on our right.... I believe, in times like this, each individual thinks that every shot he hears coming near him is going to hit him."[4]

Franklin Sawyer recalled the horror thusly:

Nothing more terrific than this storm of artillery can be imagined. The missiles of both armies passed over our heads. The roar of the guns was deafening. The air was soon clouded with smoke, and the shriek and startling crack of exploding shell above, around, and in our midst; the blowing up of our caissons in our rear; the driving through the air of fence-rails, posts, and limbs of trees; the groans of dying men, the neighing of frantic and wounded horses, created a scene of absolute horror.[5]

Oddly, there are accounts of men shrugging off the ordeal. For instance, George R. Stewart's 1959 work *Pickett's Charge: A Microhistory of the Final Attack at Gettysburg, July 3, 1863*, quotes some men as casually reporting, "'Oh this is bully,' or 'We are getting to like it,' or 'Oh, we don't mind this.'"[6]

The generals had more to do than just withstand the storm; they sought to steady their men as well as predict what the barrage was leading to. The barrage even gave professional artillerist Hunt a perverted thrill: "the signal-gun was fired, and the enemy opened with all his guns. From that point the scene was indescribably grand."[7] Said Gibbon: "Whilst standing here and wondering how all this din would terminate, Mitchell, an aide of Gen. Hancock, joined me with a message from Hancock to know what I thought the meaning of this terrific fire. I replied I thought it was the prelude either to a retreat or an assault."[8]

Of the many concerns of generalship that seemed to be regularly on Hancock's mind was the morale of his men. The terror of the horrendous barrage was every bit as much a threat to the will of his corps as a threat to life and limb. Morgan said of the Confederate artillerists, "it is possible they might have stampeded the men and forced them from the ground."[9] Keenly aware of the natural impulse to flee such a terrifying place, Hancock strove to keep his men in place and steel themselves, not just for the cannonade, but for the assault he figured might follow. According to Bingham:

> In the most tumultuous moments of this fire, Hancock, mounted, started at the right of his line of battle and followed by his Staff, his Corps flag flying in the hands of a brave Irishmen of the 6th New York Cavalry, rode slowly along the terrible crest to the left of his position, while the shot and shell roared and crashed around him and every moment tore great gaps in the ranks at his side. It was a gallant deed of heroic valor … for the noble presence and calm demeanor as he passed through his lines during that fiery crisis, encouraging his men set an example before them which an hour later cropped out and served their stout hearts to win the greatest & bloodiest battle ever fought on American soil.[10]

Doubleday was also a witness: "I can almost fancy I see Hancock again as he rode past the front of his command, just previous to the assault, followed by a single orderly displaying his corps flag, while the missiles from a hundred pieces of artillery tore up the ground around him."[11]

Francis A. Walker added: "Only once was the cavalcade interrupted; so furious was the fire, his favorite black charger became unmanageable, and Hancock was obliged to dismount and borrow the horse of an aid to complete the circuit of his line."[12]

Hancock's ride was both courageous and dangerous; and one can presume it accomplished the object of inspiring his men. There is an irony, however, in that the Confederate missiles were largely carrying to the rear of Hancock's line. Given this, the farther behind the Union line the more severe was the pounding. One can reason that his demonstration, made in front of his line, was at the safest area of the Union position. Nevertheless, Hancock's demonstration of courage and tenacity shows the importance he placed on not just the material aspects of tactics, but the moral and psychological as well.

It is precisely Hancock's interest in maintaining infantry morale during the cannonade that led to conflict with a fellow leader, General Henry Hunt, Chief of Artillery. Hancock's official report stated: "The artillery of the corps, imperfectly supplied with ammunition, replied to the enemy most gallantly, maintaining the unequal contest in a manner that reflected the highest honor on this arm of the service."[13]

His language is tellingly precise: "artillery of the corps," not *all* artillery. This is because, along the Second Corps' line, especially its left end, were interspersed several batteries from the Artillery Reserve. Hunt, who was more concerned about saving ammunition and producing effective fire than making a demonstration for the infantry's morale, claimed command over all artillery. He recalled having predicted that "an assault would be preceded by a heavy cannonade for which we must be prepared, that they (our battery commanders) would not return fire for fifteen or twenty minutes at least, that they must watch closely the effect of the enemy's cannonade; note the most efficient part of his lines, which they would probably find to be the one on which most guns were placed, and to concentrate our fire on that point, firing slowly, deliberately and making target practice of it."[14]

Hunt was a highly learned authority on artillery, and had strong convictions on its use. During the Seven Days campaign he had released the following order: "The firing will be **deliberate**—and the greatest care will be taken to secure accuracy. Under no circumstances will it be so rapid that the effect of each shot and shell can not be noted when the air is clear.... There is no excess of ammunition, what we have must be made the most of."[15]

As the above order states, Hunt was not just trying to save ammunition; he was promoting accuracy and effectiveness: "accuracy requires careful pointing, with close observation of the effect, and these require time. Twelve shots in an hour at an object over 1,000 yards distant, the time being spent in careful loading and pointing, will produce better results than fifty shots will ordinarily produce from the same gun in the same time."[16]

Major General George Gordon Meade (top left) had command of the Army of the Potomac for only three days prior to the battle. With command of the army, he inherited Major General Daniel Butterfield (top right) as his Chief of Staff. The army's Chief of Artillery was Brigadier General Henry Hunt (bottom left), who clashed with Hancock over control of some batteries on 3 July. Its Chief of Engineers was Brigadier General Gouverneur Kemble Warren (bottom right), who was complimentary of Hancock's actions on 1 July (Library of Congress reproduction numbers LC-DIG-ppmsca–19398, LC-DIG-cwpb–05423, LC-DIG-cwpb–05876, LC-DIG-cwpb–05646).

Of those who would operate differently, he reasoned, "An officer who expends ammunition improperly proves his ignorance of the proper use of his arm, and a want of capacity for the command of a battery."[17] 3 July at Gettysburg would, of course, be no different. Hunt explained his desire for a deliberate response thusly: "as the cannonade of the enemy was to precede an assault, it was of vital importance that when his fire ceased, we should have in the chests a sufficient reserve of ammunition to sustain a rapid and effective fire from all our batteries on the advancing Infantry."[18]

But to Hancock, the unprecedented cannonade was no time for restraint. His chief of staff Morgan well summarized his boss's position: "The artillery on the line suffered heavily from the cannonade, several caissons being blown up. General Hancock insisted and properly that the enemy's fire should be stoutly returned on account of the moral effect of the infantry."[19]

General Schurz's, division in the Eleventh Corps also received substantial cannonading. His view on the moral effect of artillery paralleled Hancock's: "How would the men endure this frightful experience? One of the hardest trials of the courage and steadfastness of the soldier is to stand still and be shot at without being able to reply. This ordeal is especially severe when the soldier is under a heavy artillery fire which, although less dangerous than that of musketry, is more impressive on the nerves."[20]

The opposing views between Hancock and Hunt collided when, as Hancock described:

> During the last day of the battle, when I commanded the left centre of our army composed of three corps, there was a portion of my line on which there was no infantry, and while the enemy's great cannonade was in progress, just previous to their grand assault, I rode to that point and found that the guns of a battery posted there were silent, although other batteries on the line were firing slowly. I sent orders by my chief of artillery to the commander of the battery, which happened to belong to the reserve artillery of the army, (and had been sent up to strengthen that part of the line during the assault then impending) to open fire at once.... This order was not obeyed, and I was informed that the battery commander had orders not to fire, from the chief of artillery of the Army of the Potomac. I then rode to the battery myself, and was actually compelled to threaten force, on my own line of battle before I could cause the battery to fire upon the enemy.[21]

He reasoned: "I would have been held responsible in the event of the loss of the line, while the Chief of Artillery of the Army would have had no responsibility in that event."[22]

Captain Patrick Hart, commanding an Artillery Reserve battery, described a similar or the same incident:

General Hunt rode up to me and ordered me to reserve my fire when the enemies arty opened … and to reserve all my effective ammunition to meet the great charge he expected the enemy would make that day.…

The enemy opened fire with their arty. I did not open fire and some considerable time after the enemy opened fire General Hancock rode up to me and not in a very mild manner wanted to know why I did not open fire. I informed him that I had received my orders from General Hunt Chief of arty and would obey them. He ordered me to open fire that I was in his line. I replied that should he give me a written order that I would open fire under protest.[23]

Captain Charles Phillips headed the Fifth Massachusetts Battery, also attached to the Artillery Reserve. He recalled, in a letter to his brigade commander, Lieutenant Colonel Freeman McGilvery: "Having received orders from General Hunt and from you, not to reply to their batteries, I remained silent for the first half hour, when General Hancock ordered us to open. We then opened fire on the enemy's batteries, but in the thick smoke probably did very little damage. By your orders we soon ceased firing."[24]

According to Hunt: "I ordered, myself, as I believe I state in the report, the cessation of our fire, gradually from right to left, to induce the enemy to believe he had silenced us, and to precipitate his assault."[25]

He continues: "General Hancock, as soon as the enemy opened fire, ordered all his own (2d Corps) and other batteries near him to open in reply, that on my orders being repeated to him, he said his troops would not stand unless the reply was made, and that he would be responsible to me for the disregard of my instructions."[26]

The end result being:

the batteries attached to his corps obeyed his orders, those of the Artillery Reserve under Col. McGilvery refused to do so. These latter were accordingly fully prepared for the assault which followed, but unfortunately [those who obeyed Hancock] had fired away all their ammunition except their canister and could not be brought into effective action, until the enemy were comparatively close up. I attribute the failure of the Artillery alone, to repel their assault to the interference I have spoken of.[27]

The essential conflict between Hunt and Hancock involves three questions. First: Is it necessary to, or worth, expending materially useful ammunition just to maintain infantry morale? Second: Did the use of ammunition before the infantry assault substantially retard the defense against said assault? And finally: Who has command over artillery that is physically on the line of a corps, but is not otherwise belonging to that corps?

One cannot answer the first question with certainty; there are too many variables and conditions specific to the time and place of the cannonade. Is it possible that the men would have given up the position were it not for knowledge that their own guns were returning fire? One may argue that the infantry was enduring an ordeal regardless of what the Union artillery did; but few of us have experienced a similar bombardment and none of us experienced that one in particular. In favor of Hancock, it is clear that he was excellent in maintaining esprit de corps, and knew very well what was best in such matters. Walker later argued that both generals were expert in their fields, but Hunt lacked the experience with infantry to decide what it would stand:

> Would the advantage so obtained [by withholding artillery fire] have compensated for the loss of **morale** in the infantry which might have resulted from allowing them to be scourged, at will, by the hostile artillery? Every soldier knows how trying and often how demoralizing it is to endure artillery fire without reply…. Certainly a service almost wholly in the artillery could not yield that intimate knowledge of the temper of the troops which should qualify him, equally with Hancock, to judge what was required to keep them in heart and courage under the Confederate cannonade at Gettysburg, and to bring them up to the final struggle, prepared in spirit to meet the fearful ordeal of Longstreet's charge.[28]

The Hancock contingent's emphasis on psychology and morale was in stark contrast to Hunt's concentration on material effect. Despite decades of arguing (and it went on until all parties were dead), in the actual event, the Union defense against the grand assault was successful. One cannot prove Hunt's claim that "Artillery alone" would have repulsed the infantry assault were it not for Hancock's "interference." Conversely, there is no assurance that Hancock's men would have performed less well were it not for a robust artillery response, as Hancock claimed. Walker concluded: "Hancock had full authority over that line of battle; he used that authority according to his own best judgment, and he beat off the enemy. That is the substance of it."[29]

Regarding the question of how the artillery reply made against his wishes affected the battle, Hunt seemed sure about the answer: "Had McGilvray also exhausted his ammunition before the assault, the enemy would in all probability have succeeded in carrying the position. Had Hazard been able to cross his fire with McGilvray at the commencement of the enemy's advance we would not have been in serious danger. As it was, the escape was a very narrow one."[30]

But again, no one will ever prove or disprove this. Also the eventual repulse of the grand assault was hardly a "very narrow one."

Turning to the question of authority over the batteries, Hunt's claim depended partly on precedent set at the battle of Antietam. He argued: "I exercised all the duties of commander of the artillery, as recognized in modern armies, in the same way as at Antietam, where General McClellan told me on the field that he held me responsible for everything in connexion with the artillery, and that I might make every use of his name if I came across anybody that ranked me; that is, I took full control of the artillery where, by the regulations and necessities of the service, it was not under the exclusive command of others."[31]

In other words General McClellan, then commanding the army, gave Hunt wide authority and discretion as Chief of Artillery. Hunt continued in that role under Burnside at Fredericksburg. But when General Joseph Hooker took command of the Army of the Potomac in January 1863, he reduced Hunt's responsibilities. According to Hunt himself, he was limited to "administrative duties."[32] After the stunning defeat at the battle of Chancellorsville, Hunt opined about his newly limited position in a note to Hooker: "The command of the artillery, which I held under Generals McClellan and Burnside ... was withdrawn from me when you assumed command of the army, and my duties made purely administrative.... It is not, therefore, to be wondered at that confusion and mismanagement ensued."[33]

Hunt also testified to the Joint Congressional Committee on the Conduct of the War: "I do not know that any person commanded the artillery, in the proper sense of the word, from the time General Hooker deprived me, of the command down to the time he was relieved from the command of the army."[34]

Hence, Hunt recognized that he no longer held the comprehensive authority McClellan granted him and Burnside maintained. However, on 28 June, George Meade relieved Hooker as commander of the army. Then, in the pre-dawn hours of 2 July at Gettysburg, Hunt claimed that Meade "directed me ... to see that the artillery of the corps was properly placed, and to make the best disposition as to the Reserve Artillery, on its arrival."[35] It was at that point that Hunt reclaimed all the extensive authority McClellan gave to him: "These orders recognized, in fact necessarily vested in me all the powers of a commander-in-chief of the artillery in their plentitude [*sic*], as assigned to me specifically by Gen. McClellan on the battlefield of Antietam."[36]

Hence, a few verbal instructions from Meade, with no discussion about the extent or duration of Hunt's authority, and nothing in writing, were enough for Hunt to conclude that his former authorities were restored. Or, as he stated, Meade had "thus recognized my 'command' of the artillery; indeed, he did not know it had been suspended."[37] In front of the congressional committee, he also seemed to stake a claim to all artillery in the army, not just that of the Reserve Artillery: "It was in discharge of my duties as commander of the artillery of the army that I went to every point of attack, where it was frequently necessary to use the artillery of adjoining corps, together with portions of the reserve artillery brought up."[38]

Of the many claims to authority Hunt made, this one was the most specious. If he wished, he could have taken a few seconds to verify with Meade the extent of his authority under Meade. Instead, he quietly assumed himself to be commander-in-chief of all weapons pulled by horses. This is not to say he did not have good points about restraining fire, or that he was not an excellent soldier.

Hancock's argument was more about simple practicality than the formality of what orders were given, and when, and by whom. For instance, Carroll's brigade spent the evening of 2 July and all day on 3 July in the Eleventh Corps' line; yet Hancock, a headstrong, assertive commander did not interfere with its operation. This is just one of many examples at Gettysburg where units became intermingled without major disagreements between high-level commanders. No one would expect Hancock to contradict Howard's directions for Carroll's brigade. Generals cannot be everywhere at once. It is only practical that no one commander should directly control troops along miles of lines. What if other emergencies were taking place in other areas during the cannonade? Would Hunt expect to simultaneously direct artillery on Culp's Hill and the Round Tops as well?

Some other personal friction revealed itself at this time, though much less consequential. The commander of the brigade in Gibbon's division that shared a flank with Hays' division was General Alexander Webb. Shields recollected that Hays was concerned about Webb's brigade during the cannonade:

> Webb's line was plainly weak; enough to warrant General Hays' anxiety. His own lines were weak, too, but he had confidence in his troops and proposed to hold his line come what may....
>
> "Dave," he said to me, "go over to Webb and see how he is standing it."
>
> I rode over at once and found General Webb with his men in the little "copse of trees...." I delivered the general's compliments and asked General Webb how he was faring. He replied that I could see his men were in line and he was doing all that could be expected. His troops were suffering with the rest under heavy fire.
>
> I asked him if he could hold the line if attacked in force, and he replied that he could and would. I rode back and reported to General Hays, who made no comment except to say, "We will soon see."
>
> But the general was not satisfied. "Go and find General Hancock," he commanded, "and tell him how things are here...."[39]

After some ninety minutes (time estimates vary, as usual), the cannonade subsided. Its results were substantial but minimal considering its size and duration. Of the five batteries in the Second Corps, Lieutenant T. Fred Brown's Battery B, First Rhode Island Light was crippled to the point of having to leave the field.[40] However, Captain Andrew Cowan's First New York Independent, of the Sixth Corps, was able to replace it.[41] The barrage also forced Lieutenant Evan Thomas' Battery C, Fourth United States from the field.[42] Major Alonzo Cushing's Battery A, Fourth United States was ultimately able to post three of the four guns it started with, but Cushing himself received severe wounds, and did not survive the ensuing assault after staying at his post.[43]

The Confederate artillery had done about all it could. It was now time for the Confederate infantry to do its part, where it would meet tragic consequences for its valor.

14

"Longstreet's Assault"

No fifteen thousand men ever arranged for battle can take that position.[1]

—James Longstreet

Day Three has become settled in collective memory as the supreme climax of an epic, real life, three-act drama. This should not come as a surprise; not many battles culminate so spectacularly. But at Gettysburg, the largest of all American battles, a grand, cinematic frontal assault was the last major engagement of the battle, as if scripted.

Today, the location of the apex of Pickett's Charge, commonly known as "the high water mark," is bristling with monuments and interpretive markers—obelisks, equestrian statues, heroic figures on stone plinths, cannons, plaques and all manner of Victorian Era sculpture. An array of commemorative statuary comprises "the high water mark of the Rebellion" monument under the shade of the (capitalized) "Copse of Trees," just south of the jog in the stone wall known simply as (capitalized) "The Angle." Gettysburg is by far the most well preserved and marked Civil War battlefield, and "the high water mark" area is the central magnet of all things Gettysburg. Cars and buses, crawling and parked, jam Hancock Avenue along the Second Corps' line. There are busloads of school children and armies of Boy Scouts. There are families, children with costumes and toy weapons, enthusiasts in period dress, and casual observers. "The high water mark" is a Mecca of sorts for Civil War pilgrims. The place is teeming, especially every 3 July.

Its main draw is its status as "the high water mark of the Rebellion" where, supposedly, the Confederates got as close as they ever would to winning the war. But this is a faulty premise. "Pickett's Charge" or "Longstreet's Assault" (and all other monikers it carries) was folly. Its fleeting breakthrough at The Angle was minute, a few hundred intrepid Confederates, at best, pierced Hancock's line only to face a swarm of anxious reserves and annihilation. The charge's lure emanates from its Napoleanic, cinematic spectacle, and the fact that it was the last major action of the battle.

But the Confederates had been much more successful the previous day, when they actually took some ground and effectively destroyed Sickles' Third Corps. Confederate brigadier Ambrose Wright and his men had gained Cemetery Ridge just south of the Copse on the 2nd without being annihilated. While his account exaggerated his success, it is worth considering:

> My men, by a well directed fire, soon drove the cannoneers from their guns, and, leaping over the fence, charged up to the top of the crest....
>
> We were now complete masters of the field, having gained the key, as it were, of the enemy's whole line ... we had carried the enemy's last and strongest position.[2]

Wright had gained Cemetery Ridge, unopposed until Stannard drove him off. Yet the small, short-lived and ineffective breakthrough that Pickett's Charge achieved, on almost the same spot, is what ultimately received credit as the Confederacy's "high water mark." In actuality the dismal failure of Pickett's Charge best demonstrated, besides the valor of its participants, the utter superiority of the Union position. When the Joint Committee asked General Humphreys to compare the advanced position of July 2 to the July 3 position, he replied: "We were driven from this advanced position which we took up, and were not driven the next day from Round Top ridge [Cemetery Ridge], although we had a reduced force then."[3]

Brigadier General Albion Howe (Second Division, Sixth Corps) was blasé about how beneficial the Union position was: "Our position did the work for us ... it was the most orderly fight I have ever been in, growing out of the position. In a military point of view it was not much of a battle; it was a very ordinary affair as a battle."[4]

The cannonade was hardly "ordinary" to the men who endured it, however. Private William Haines of the Twelfth New Jersey recalled its long sought cessation: "This battle lasted about an hour and a half; it stopped as suddenly as it started. What a relief to be able to get on our feet and stretch ourselves."[5]

Also of the Twelfth New Jersey, Captain Richard Thompson remembered how even the appearance of his enemy was preferable to the rain of artillery: "A soldier cried out, 'Thank God! There comes the infantry!' He voiced the feelings of his comrades. Anything that promised action was better than inaction under the horrors of that cannonade."[6]

Sturtevant of the Thirteenth Vermont agreed: "The Union army was intently watching and waiting the expected charge. The dread spell of silence suddenly gave way to excitement and activity, from Cemetery Hill to Round Top and like the rush of a mighty wind came the word down our lines, 'See they are coming.'"[7]

On Hancock's right, his irrepressible friend was in his glory; as Private Haines reported: "General Hays (I can see him yet) rode along in front of our line shouting, 'They are coming boys; we must whip them, and you with the buck and ball, don't fire until they get to that fence'; pointing to the fence along the Emmittsburg road."[8]

The scene on Hancock's left was similar, according to Benedict: "The shout 'There they come' comes from our watchful general, brought every man's arms into his hands, and many a man's heart to his mouth. Two long and heavy lines came over the opposite ridge and advanced upon us."[9]

Some 12,000 Confederates gathered and commenced their assault. As Hunt had predicted, the Union guns were essentially ineffective due to the lack of long-range ammunition. Hancock, in his official report, was not afraid to admit this: "No attempt was made to check the advance of the enemy until the first line had arrived within about 700 yards of our position, when a feeble fire of artillery was opened upon it, but with no material effect, and without delaying for a moment its determined advance."[10]

The assailants moved obliquely toward Hancock's right. This exposed their flank to the Vermonters perched left of the Second Corps. His report explains: "Two regiments of Stannard's Vermont Brigade (of the First Corps), which had been posted in a little grove in front of and at a considerable angle to the main line, first opened with an oblique fire upon the right of the enemy's column, which had the effect to make the troops on that flank double in a little toward their left. They still pressed on, however, without halting to return fire."[11]

The Eighth Ohio delivered similar flanking fire from in front of Hancock's other flank, creating a double envelopment. Walker touted their work:

> Among the most remarkable features of this famous assault was the conduct of the 8th Ohio. This regiment, under Lieutenant Franklin Sawyer, had been for nearly twenty-four hours on skirmish in front of Hays' division, across the Emmettsburg road. When the great charge took place, instead of retiring to the division line, Colonel Sawyer collected his regiment at a point just far enough outside the path of Pettigrew's advance to escape the Confederate column.... So audacious was the action of this regiment as to give rise to an absurd report among those who witnessed it, but did not know the Eighth Ohio, that its commander was intoxicated. Those who did know the Eighth Ohio, however, were well aware that this was the very sort of thing which it was most likely to do in such a case.[12]

Lieutenant Thomas Galwey commented on the extraordinarily exposed quality of his regiment's position: "By the way, the position of the 8th Ohio Vol. Infantry (Carroll's brigade, Hays' division, Hancock's corps) was so singular a one that it seems to me worthy of special notice.... Just before the great charge on the 3d we were absolutely alone out there, and to the best of my recollection remained alone from early in the afternoon of the 2nd."[13]

So what was a single regiment doing in such a forward and vulnerable position? According to Sawyer, it started on 2 July:

> The rebels held this point and annoyed our artillery and shot one of Gen. Hancock's staff. Hancock ordered Col. Carroll to send a regiment and clean them out and hold the place. Carroll sent me with the 8th, we cleaned them out. In an hour or so they rallied from towards town, and attacked us with great fury. We repulsed them. We were not again molested until day light the next morning, [3 July] when we were again attacked and again repulsed, but were constantly under fire by sharpshooters.[14]

Then why did they *stay* out there? Sawyer continues: "I think about eleven o'clock, Col. Carroll sent one of his staff officers, Capt. Gregg (also of the 8th) to see how we were getting along. While he was still there the artillery duel opened, and he remained until it ceased. When he returned to his brigade, I asked him to have Carroll relieve me; but the charge of the enemy on Gen Hancock's front followed so quickly that this could not be done, and we remained until after the battle."[15]

Later, in a letter to Bachelder, Sawyer addressed some accusations:

> You said we could not have been there, and would have been of no use there, and that "Col. Sawyer was reeling drunk and did not know where he was" &c. Now every word of that is false, which I can prove by every surviving member of my regiment who was there. I was amazed at such a statement. Your own series of maps gives me the position as I claim it....
>
> Now Colonel, this is a brief but true account of the matter, I am not responsible for being there or staying there. My corps, division and Brigadier Generals all knew I was there and did not see fit to recall me. My loss was severe. There were, including three who died after being taken to the rear, 23 killed, and there were about 70 wounded, and this is out of 209.... As for being drunk the charge is wholly untrue. I drank no liquor nor do I believe I ate a mouthful while we were at that point, and I must say Colonel that I think you did me a great wrong in making the charge. I beg you will pardon me this letter, but I believed it a duty to say what I have said.[16]

As for what his regiment did when the fighting started, Sawyer detailed:

> Soon we saw the long line of rebel infantry emerge from the woods along the rebel front, that had hitherto concealed them.
>
> These troops were the division of PICKETT followed by that of PETTIGREW. They moved up splendidly, deploying into column as they crossed the long, sloping interval between the Second Corps and their base. At first it looked as if their line of march would sweep our position, but as they advanced their direction lay considerably to our left, but soon a strong line, with flags, directed its march immediately upon us.
>
> I formed the few remaining braves in a single line, and as the rebels came within a short range of our skirmish line, charged them. Some fell, some run back, most of them, however, threw down their arms and were made prisoners.[17]

But the main body of Confederates continued up Cemetery Ridge. Sawyer continued: "We changed our front, and taking position by a fence, facing the left flank of the advancing column of rebels, the men were ordered to fire into their flank at will."[18]

Galwey wrote:

> When the charge did come we went forward on the run, from the ditch where we had kept close under cover during the cannonade, to the fence beyond, that I have spoken of above, and held that position to the last. Pender's lines coming so close toward us that I could readily distinguish the features of their men, but breaking soon under our fire and the fire of the artillery on the ridge behind us. When Pender's line fell back, which happened before Pickett's rout, we wheeled to the left in an irregular mass, without orders from anyone so far as I heard or understood, and began to pepper the left flank and rear of Pickett's column.[19]

As the assailants passed the Eighth Ohio, the rest of Hays' division's made something of an enveloping maneuver of their own. Lieutenant L.E. Bicknell of the Massachusetts Sharpshooters (Andrew's Sharpshooters) recalled:

> While the enemy were advancing to the Emmittsburg Road, General Hays drilled the line in the manual of arms, allowing them to fire left oblique while the enemy were closing with our line to the left of the Bryan house, then swung them down by a left wheel to the lane which then ran from the house to the Emmittsburg Road; across the lane they then fired. The moment chosen for the left wheel or flanking movement was just as the last division of the enemy's charging column was crossing the Emmittsburg Road, moving directly for Ziegler's Grove. As the entire front of the Second Corps to the left of the Bryan house was already covered and in many places penetrated, this fresh [Confederate] division would probably have forced our line back and gained the shelter of the grove had it not been subjected to our flank fire, which destroyed its formation and sent its shattered and disordered masses along the other side of the lane and in front of the Third Division of the Second Corps.[20]

Bicknell exaggerated the Confederate threat, but some intrepid Confederates did famously penetrate the main Union line. As Hancock described in his official report, the double envelopment (Stannard on the Union left with Sawyer and Hays on the right) funneled the most determined attackers toward Hancock's center:

> Those of the enemy's troops who did not fall into disorder in front of the Third Division were moved to the right, and re-enforced the line attacking Gibbon's division. The right of the attacking line having been repulsed by Hall's and Harrow's brigades ... assisted by the fire of the Vermont regiments before referred to, doubled to its left and also re-enforced the center, and thus the attack was in its fullest strength opposite the brigade of General Webb.[21]

That is, the Confederate attack was massing toward the center because of Union fire on both its flanks. This precipitated a small and brief break in the center of Hancock's line. He recalled:

> Two regiments of the brigade, the Sixty-ninth and Seventy-first Pennsylvania Volunteers, were behind a low stone wall and a slight breastwork hastily constructed by them, the remainder of the brigade being behind the crest some 60 paces to the rear, and so disposed as to fire over the heads of those in front. When the enemy's line had nearly reached the stone wall, led by General Armistead, the most of that part of Webb's brigade posted there abandoned their position, but fortunately did not retreat entirely.[22]

The retreat by men in his division alarmed General Gibbon "to my amazement, the men commenced to break to the rear, though there was no fire whatever to amount to anything on their front."[23] Hays' suspicions of Webb's brigade began to seem well-founded. Webb himself was horrified: "When my men fell back I almost wished to get killed, I was almost disgraced."[24] Haskell also found the situation dire: "Great heaven! were my senses mad? The larger portion of Webb's brigade—my God, it was true—there by the group of trees and the angles of the wall, was breaking from the cover of their works, and without orders or reason, with no hand lifted to check them, was falling back, a fear-stricken flock of confusion! The fate of Gettysburg hung upon a spider's single thread!"[25]

But Haskell did not panic and, like a good soldier, became more determined in the crisis:

> A great, magnificent passion came on me at the instant; not one that overpowers and confounds, but one that blanches the face and sublimes every sense and faculty.... I ordered these men to "halt," and "face about," and "fire," and they heard my voice, and gathered my meaning, and obeyed my commands. On some unpatriotic backs, of those not quick of comprehension, the flat of my saber fell, not lightly; and at its touch their love of country returned, and with a look at me as if I were the destroying angel, as I might have become theirs, they again faced the enemy.[26]

Colonel Arthur Devereux's Nineteenth Massachusetts was behind the front line and to the left. He recounted:

> We see that Webb cannot firmly hold his men against the shock of that fierce charge though he may throw himself with reckless courage in front to face the storm and beg, threaten, and command....
>
> A great gap yawns, immediately between Webb and Hall.... Every gun on our front is silenced. Woodruff, Cushing, Brown, Rorty and every other commissioned officer, almost without exception, of the respective batteries is dead or disabled and Gibbon badly wounded.
>
> Was this devoted Second Corps whose proud boast it was that it "Never lost a gun or a color," to succumb at last?[27]

Brigadier General Alexander Webb's bronze likeness appears on Cemetery Ridge, where his actions earned him the Medal of Honor, and at the City College of New York, where he served as president for 33 years (photograph by William Bretzger).

This was the so-called "high water mark of the Rebellion." Devereux's narrative sketches the appearance of his corps commander: "Just then a headlong rush of horse's feet spurred to the utmost, came up the hollow behind me from the direction of the Baltimore Pike. I turned. There looking the very embodiment of the god of war rode Hancock, the 'Superb.'"[28]

Once again, Hancock's quick eye led him to exactly the right place at the right time. Devereux continued:

> "See," I cried "their colors, they have broken through. Let me get in there."
> His characteristic answer fitted time and place and he shot like an arrow past my left toward Hall's struggling lines.[29]

Devereux more explicitly details Hancock's "characteristic answer" in another document:

> Just then Hancock came riding furiously up. I halted him, pointing out the enemy's colors crossing the stone wall and asked permission to put my men in there. His prompt direction was "To get in G—D—quick."[30]

What followed was a veritable stampede to the breach by eager units from the Union second line and those on the front who were not pressed. Hancock described the great rush:

> Colonel Devereux, commanding the Nineteenth Massachusetts Volunteers, anxious to be in the right place, applied to me for permission to move his regiment to the right and to the front, where the line had been broken. I granted it, and his regiment and Colonel Mallon's (Forty-second New York Volunteers on his right) proceeded there at once; but the enemy having left Colonel Hall's front, as described before, this officer promptly moved his command by the right flank to still further re-enforce the position of General Webb, and was immediately followed by Harrow's brigade.[31]

Their enthusiasm overpowered military discipline:

> The movement was executed, but not without confusion, owing to the many men leaving their ranks to fire at the enemy from the breastwork. The situation was now very peculiar. The men of all brigades had in some measure lost their regimental organization, but individually they were firm. The ambition of individual commanders to promptly cover the point penetrated by the enemy, the smoke of battle, and the intensity of the close engagement, caused the confusion. The point, however, was now covered. In regular formation our line would have stood four ranks deep.[32]

"The high water mark of the Rebellion" had come and gone in minutes if not seconds. Hancock's men had annihilated it with a terrible enthusiasm and an abundance of resources. But there was more, according to Hancock: "after a few moments of desperate fighting the enemy's troops were repulsed, threw down their arms, and sought safety in flight or by throwing themselves on the ground to escape our fire. The battle flags were ours and the victory was won."[33]

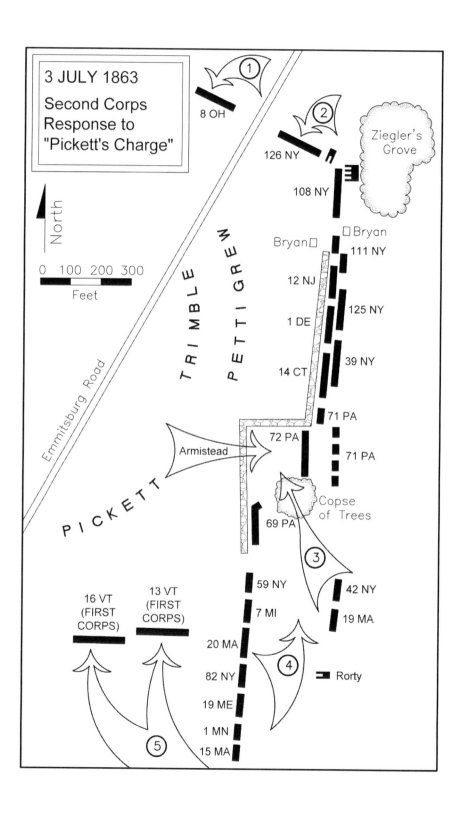

3 JULY 1863
Second Corps
Response to
"Pickett's Charge"

North

0 100 200 300
Feet

1
8 OH

2
126 NY

108 NY

Ziegler's
Grove

TRIMBLE

PETTIGREW

Bryan☐ ☐ Bryan
111 NY
12 NJ
125 NY
1 DE
39 NY
14 CT

71 PA
72 PA
71 PA

Armistead

PICKETT

69 PA

Copse
of Trees

3
59 NY 42 NY
7 MI 19 MA

16 VT
(FIRST
CORPS)

13 VT
(FIRST
CORPS)

20 MA
82 NY
19 ME
1 MN
15 MA

4
Rorty

5

Emmitsburg Road

Silas Adams of the Nineteenth Maine described the mob-like disorder: "The regiment pressed forward without orders or order, firing and stepping back, allowing the rear men to step forward and fire. Soon they found themselves in front of other troops. Not having time to load, the regiment used bayonets, clubbed with their muskets, and hurled stones to break up their charge and to turn back the determined assault."[34]

Still, according to Hancock's report, he was not done: "While the enemy was still in front of Gibbon's division, I directed Colonel [General] Stannard to send two regiments of his Vermont Brigade, First Corps, to a point which would strike the enemy on the right flank."[35]

George Grenville Benedict described the scene from the Vermonters' perspective:

> They had nearly reached the Union bayonets, and it began to be a question how lines of battle but two men deep could stand the onset of a massed column, when a new and unlooked for arrangement changed the appearance of things. The point of attack had no sooner become evident, than General Stannard ordered forward the Thirteenth and Sixteenth regiments to take the enemy on flank. The Vermonters marched a few rods to the right, and then, changing front, swung out at right angles to the main line, close upon the flank of the charging column, and opened fire. This was more than the rebels had counted on. They began to break and scatter from the rear in less than five minutes, and in ten more it was an utter rout. A portion made their way back to their own side; but fully two-thirds, I should think, of their number, dropped their arms and came in as prisoners.[36]

Adding to the tragic futility, Wilcox's Brigade came up behind the right flank of the charge. Their path took them south, or behind, of the pivoted Vermont brigade, rendering them vulnerable to yet another flanking movement. The Vermonters merely needed to turn around to unleash yet another storm of lead into an enemy's fat flank. Benedict continued:

> It was a savage onset and a glorious repulse; but it did not end the fight on the left centre. Veazey and Randall and their men were occupied with the agreeable duty of receiving colonels' and majors' swords, when the order came to "about face" and meet another charge. A body of the enemy, evidently the supporting body of the main rebel column, was coming down to the left of us, apparently

Opposite: **1. The Eighth Ohio's advanced position forces the Confederate left flank to pinch inward. The Ohioans then push further forward and to their own left. 2. The 126th New York also exploits the Confederate pinching movement and swings around. 3. After the Sixty-Ninth and Seventy-First Pennsylvania partially withdraw in front of Armistead, Hancock appears and orders the Forty-Second New York and Nineteenth Massachusetts into the breach. 4. Several regiments from the center and left of the Second Corps also pour into the breach. 5. Either by Hancock's order or otherwise, the Thirteenth and Sixteenth Vermont (First Corps) wheel right from their already advanced positions. Combined with the Eighth Ohio, they complete a double envelopment of the attacking Confederates. Maps by the author.**

aiming at the position of the Fourteenth. The same mode of treatment was applied to their case, with the happiest result. The Fourteenth met them with a hot fire in front, and Colonel Veazey with the Sixteenth, hurrying back on the double quick, took them on the flank and bagged about a brigade of them.

The Sixteenth took in this charge the colors of the Second Florida, a beautiful silk flag inscribed with "Williamsburg" and "Seven Pines"—the colors of the Eighth Virginia, and the battle flag of another regiment, which was foolishly thrown away by the sergeant to whom it was given to carry, who pitched it into the bushes, declaring that he could not fight with that flag in his hands.

With these repulses of the enemy the big fight in effect closed.[37]

Of this late flanking movement by the Vermonters, Sturtevant wrote:

At this juncture the unheard of happened, namely, those standing in the rear rank of the 13th and 16th regiments who had been firing into General Pickett's right flank causing fearful slaughter, because of good aim and short range, the rear ranks of the 13th and 16th regiments at the same time were facing in an opposite direction and with steady aim firing as rapidly into the charging left flank of the belated columns that had come in support of General Pickett's right flank with equal effect. For a time the 13th and 16th stood in line in double ranks across Plum Run valley extending from near the base of Cemetery Ridge to within a few rods of the Emmitsburg Road, the front rank facing northerly towards Gettysburg village and firing into Pickett's huddled struggling ranks and the rear rank facing southerly towards Peach Orchard, Devil's Den, Big Round Top deliberately and steadily firing into the left flank of what proved to be General Wilcox's brigade and command. This was an accidental situation, but who unless inborn fighters would have so suddenly taken advantage of so good an opportunity and made use of it as an expected duty.[38]

During the annihilation on Hancock's left, the adventurous Eighth Ohio continued pulverizing Confederates on Hancock's right. Sawyer recalled how the advanced Ohioans found yet another opportunity when the great charge turned into a rout:

Suddenly the column gave way, the sloping landscape appeared covered, all at once, with the scattered and retreating foe. A withering sheet of missiles swept after them, and they were torn and tossed and prostrated as they ran. It seemed as if no one would escape. Of the mounted officers who rode so grandly in the advance not one was to be seen on the field, all had gone down.

The 8th advanced and cut off three regiments, or remnants of regiments, as they passed us, taking their colors, and capturing many prisoners. The colors captured were those of the Thirty-fourth North Carolina, Thirty Eighth Virginia, and one that was taken from the captor, Serg't Miller, Co. G. by a staff officer, the number of the regiment not being remembered.

The battle was now over.... For nearly two days our little band had stood alone nearly one half mile in advance of the battle line.[39]

In another account, Sawyer recalled: "Now when Pettigrew's men fled from their position they seemed lost and rushed into our lines. We captured three flags and a great many prisoners. After the battle was fairly over, I was relieved and rejoined the brigade with the prisoners and colors."[40]

"When Pickett broke we were of course just where we could do the most good. We got three stands of colors and many prisoners," said Galwey.[41]

Then, at the very climax of victory, Hancock fell wounded.

"Gen. Hancock was shot from his horse while he was talking to Gen. Stannard," wrote Benedict. "I helped the latter to bandage Hancock's wound and his blood stained my hands."[42] He was more detailed in another letter:

> Lieutenant George W. Hooker and myself were standing near the general's side … he uttered an exclamation and I saw that he was reeling in the saddle.
>
> Hooker and I with a common impulse sprang toward him, and caught him as he toppled from his horse into our outstretched arms. General Stannard bent over him as we laid him upon the ground, and opening his clothing where he indicated by a movement of his hand that he was hurt, a ragged hole, an inch or more in diameter, from which the blood was pouring profusely, was disclosed in the upper part and on the inside of his thigh. He was naturally in some alarm for his life. "Don't let me bleed to death," he said. "Get something around it quick."

A stone monument marks the location of Hancock's wounding on 3 July. The trees in the right background are those of the Copse of Trees and Ziegler's Grove (photograph by William Bretzger).

Stannard had whipped out his handkerchief, and as I helped to pass it around Hancock's leg, I saw that the blood, being of dark color and not coming in jets, could not be from an artery, and I said to him: "This is not arterial blood, General, you will not bleed to death." From my use of the surgical term he took me for a surgeon, and replied, with a sigh of relief: "That's good; thank you for that, Doctor." We tightened the ligature by twisting it with the barrel of a pistol, and soon stopped the flow of blood. Major Mitchell of Hancock's staff rode up as we were at work over the general, and uttering an exclamation of pain as he saw the condition of his chief, turned and darted away after a surgeon. One came in fifteen minutes, and removing the handkerchief thrust his forefinger to the knuckle into the wound and brought out from it an iron nail bent double. "This is what hit you, General," he said, holding up the nail, "and you are not so badly hurt as you think."[43]

Sturtevant recalled, "There he lay during Pickett's charge watching and giving orders to General Stannard and other Generals in the Second and Third Corps then under his command."[44] Hancock was able to issue orders while wounded and lying on the field. According to Major Mitchell, Hancock said to him: "Tell General Meade that the troops under my command have repulsed the enemy's assault and that we have gained a great victory. The enemy is now flying in all directions on my front."[45]

In an 1866 letter to Hancock, Mitchell described his ensuing actions: "I delivered the message to General Meade on the field (as he was riding up toward the crest of Cemetery Hill) a few moments after I received it, and also informed

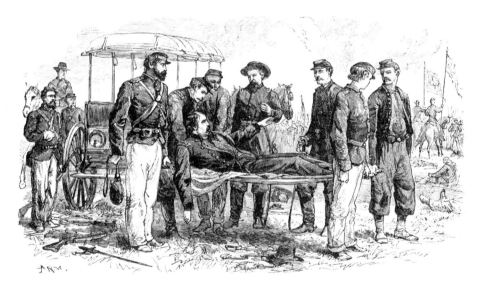

Soldiers carry the stricken Hancock from the field. In this depiction, the general appears distressed but is still attempting to sit up and gesture, issuing orders or other dispatches (from the collection of the Historical Society of Montgomery County).

him that you were dangerously wounded. He replied as follows: 'Say to General Hancock that I regret exceedingly that he is wounded and that I thank him for the Country and for myself for the service he has rendered today.'"[46]

To stress the accuracy of his statements, Mitchell added: "P.S. The message from General Hancock, and the reply of General Meade above given, are taken from a written memorandum made by me on the evening of the 3d July 1863."[47]

Charles Morgan recalled that the stricken general was still full of fight: "General Hancock remained on the field long enough to witness the total repulse and to dictate a dispatch to General Meade, that if he would advance the 5th and 6th Corps we would win a glorious victory."[48]

Bingham, in a post-war letter to Hancock, remembered:

When I found you, you were on the ground wounded. I rode up to you in company with General Mitchell whom I met as I was riding over the field towards the left of our line.... After Mitchell and myself expressed to you our sympathy and regret for your severe wound and suffering, Mitchell went off for an ambulance and you ordered me to see that several regiments, afterwards ascertained to be the Vermont Brigade (Stannard's I think) should change front and attack in flank a body of the enemy's troops during their flank attack, after its accomplishment I rode to Gen. Caldwell and informed him that yourself and Gen. Gibbon had been wounded and therefore he was the ranking officer in command of the corps.[49]

There is also a written record of a dispatch Hancock issued through his corps' medical director:

I have never seen a more formidable attack, and if the Sixth and Fifth Corps have pressed up, the enemy will be destroyed. The enemy must be short on ammunition, as I was shot with a tenpenny nail. I did not leave the field until the victory was entirely secured and the enemy no longer in sight. I am badly wounded, though I trust not seriously. I had to break the line to attack the enemy in flank on my right, where the enemy was most persistent after the front attack was repelled. Not a rebel was in sight upright when I left. The line should be immediately restored and perfected. General Caldwell is in command of the corps, and I have directed him to restore the line.
Your obedient servant,

> WINF'D S. HANCOCK,
> Major-General,
> By A. N. Dougherty,
> Surgeon, and Medical Director Second Corps[50]

"Thus ended General Hancock's connection with the memorable battle of Gettysburg," wrote Morgan. "He was taken first to the field hospital, thence that night to Westminster, arriving in Baltimore the following morning, and in Philadelphia at noon."[51]

15

Aftermath

We've enfiladed them — d—n them![1]
—Winfield Scott Hancock

Long used to scenes of mass death and gore, the soldiers of Hancock's line began a grand celebration amid the dead and mutilated bodies. A soldier writing for a Buffalo, New York, newspaper, observed:

> Then enters Alexander Hays, brigadier general, United States Volunteers, the brave American soldier. Six feet or more in height, erect and smiling, lightly holding in his hand his horse, the third within an hour- a noble animal, his flanks bespattered with blood, tied to his streaming tail a Rebel flag that drags ignominiously in the mud, he dashes along our lines, now rushing out into the open field, a mark for a hundred sharpshooters, but never touched, now quietly cantering back to our lines to be welcomed with a storm of cheers. I reckon him the grandest view of my life. I bar not Niagra.[2]

Shields recalled:

> When the enemy were retreating in disorder and confusion, the general exclaimed, "Boys, give me a flag." The Rebel color was handed him. He then commanded his adjutant general, Capt. George P. Corts, and myself, saying, "Get a flag, Corts; get a flag, 'Dave' and come on." We each took a flag and the general immediately dropped his flag behind his horse and trailed it in the dust and blood of the battlefield. Capt. Corts and I did likewise, and we started on the grandest ride men ever took....
>
> We rode in the rear of our division line to the right flank of the 111th New York, then down the whole front of the division, turning at the left of the 14th Connecticut to the place of the beginning, the men of the Third Division throwing their caps high in the air as we rode along, cheering lustily in their exuberance, showing their admiration for their glorious division commander, some men dancing in their delirium of their joy, others hugging their comrades in close embrace, wild with the exultation of victory.
>
> There were times when we had to weave in and out in our course to avoid riding over wounded Rebels and even prisoners still coming in and going to the rear.[3]

Later, Hays would write, "My defenses were stone walls, and since Jackson is dead I think I have a claim to his title."[4] The chief of ambulances of the corps was Thomas L. Livermore. He helped move Hancock to a field hospital and left the following anecdote:

> Soon after the charge had been made, I met an ambulance between the Taneytown road and our line of battle coming off the field with General Hancock wounded, and this was the first I knew of that misfortune, I think. I at once made my presence known to the general, and escorted him to the hospital. When we had reached the vicinity of the Taneytown road, the general, who was somewhat excited, insisted upon halting for some purpose—I think, indeed, it was just as I met him—I think to write a dispatch. At this time the rebels had a piece of artillery posted in the vicinity of the town of Gettysburg with which, at intervals of three or four minutes, through shot or shell down the Taneytown road which must have gone as far as Weed's Hill, and it was directly in range of these shots that the general caused the ambulance to halt. I suggested to him that he had better move on a little, as the rebels were enfilading our line with their shots and we were directly in their range. To this his reply was: "We've enfiladed them — d—n them!"—and added that we had so completely beaten them that if other troops were only now sent in, we could rout them. Fortunately the shots did not hit the ambulance, and I got him safely to the hospital.[5]

There arose a polite disagreement over who ordered the devastating flanking of Pickett's Charge by the Vermont regiments. Here is how Morgan saw it: "It is proper to notice a controversy which has arisen since the battle, with reference to the part taken by Stannard's troops. In a monograph by Lieutenant Benedict, entitled 'Gettysburg, and the Part Taken Therein by Vermont Troops,' it is stated that the flank attack was ordered by General Stannard before General Hancock arrived."[6]

However, argues Morgan, Hancock clearly states in a "memorandum": "I had seen the importance of it myself, and probably General Stannard had also, and may have given similar directions. It is quite probable, for General Stannard was a cool and reliable officer, in whom I had great confidence from earlier associations. Yet with the exception of the small detachment of troops already firing on the enemy's flank ... no flank attack was made until that directed by me."[7]

According to Morgan, the memorandum continued: "While I was on my back I recollect of ordering General Stannard to attack the enemy in flank; a regiment marched past me by the flank to do so. I ordered another regiment. Lieutenant Mitchell, not knowing that I was wounded, came there about the time I was shot, and also gave an order in my name for the attack of the enemy's flank, he seeing that the troops were well placed for that purpose."[8]

Yet Benedict, as late as 1893, seemed certain that Stannard initiated the movement, without any prompting by Hancock or anyone else:

Gen. Stannard, in his report, written on the field the day after the battle, says in substance that he alone gave the order. Gen. Doubleday, commanding the division, in his report of later date, gives the credit for the movement to Stannard. When, at a still later date, Gen. Hancock's official report appeared, to the astonishment of Gen. Stannard and others familiar with the facts it was found to contain this paragraph: "While the enemy was in front of Gibbon's division I directed Col. Stannard to send two regiments of his Vermont brigade, to a point which would strike the enemy on the right flank. I cannot report on the execution of this order as Col. Stannard's report has not passed through my hands; but from the good conduct of those troops during the action, I have no doubt that the service was promptly performed." Hancock and Stannard were personal friends and neither of them would have been the man to intentionally appropriate any glory belonging to the other. Stannard certainly knew what he was talking about. How came Gen. Hancock to state that he ordered him to make the flank attack, when Stannard says he received no such order?[9]

Benedict goes on to claim prevailing upon the general with reason:

Happening to meet Gen. Hancock, still feeble from the effect of his wound, in Washington four months after the battle, I took the liberty of putting this question to him. He frankly admitted that his impressions of what happened at that time were so confused by his wound that he could not say of his own knowledge how it was. His staff officers had told him that he gave the order; and as he remembered that when he rode down to Stannard's side he had the idea in his mind that there was a good chance to make such a flank attack, he supposed his staff had got it straight. I ventured to cross question him a little. How long did he think he had been speaking to Stannard when he (Hancock) was hit? "Less than a minute," he said. Did he remember how things looked right in front of him, just before he fell? "Yes, he remembered there was a line of troops a few feet in front of him." Were they lying down? "No, they were on their feet and moving; he guessed they were forming in column of fours." What troops must they have been? "One of Stannard's regiments, of course." I said no more, and he saw at once what followed from his own replies. "Well," said he, after a moment's silence: "That regiment must have had an order to move before I spoke to Stannard." Before we parted, he said it was plain to him that his own report was wrong in that particular, and that he would put on file at the War Department a correction of it. This however he never he did, being probably persuaded that he was not called on to do anything of the kind.[10]

What is specious about Benedict's claim is Hancock's failure to recall details. Hancock's official report was characteristically clear, lucid and detailed. If his memory was ever unclear, his collection of facts in the process of writing his report would have filled any gaps in his memory. But Benedict seemed certain of his position. Of his brigade's commander, Benedict held: "Gen. Stannard never qualified his own statement. He persisted up to his death, in the assertion that he received no order from Gen. Hancock, or from any officer of Gen. Hancock's staff, at any time during the third day of battle."[11]

Ralph Orson Sturtevant, also a Vermont man, proclaimed: "As General Stannard looked over the field his quick eye discovered the salient angle, and like a flash of lightning came the inspired thought that evolved the famous and now historic order (unique in maneuvering in the midst of battle) 'Change front, forward on first company.'"[12]

Also, added Sturtevant, "General Stannard had given the order to move out on Pickett's flank only a moment before the arrival of General Hancock."[13] Finally, there was the contention of yet another Vermont soldier which conflicts with that of Hancock. But George H. Scott of the Thirteenth Vermont does not credit Stannard. Instead, he attributes the initiative of the flanking movement to his regiment's commander, Colonel Francis Randall:

> Randall found Hancock's line was not stout enough to resist the shock. He saw his opportunity to help Hancock by attacking the enemy upon his right flank. It was no sooner thought than executed without waiting for orders. To do this Randall moved his regiment by the right flank until his left cleared a clump of trees. And then he orders his regiment to change "front forward on first company."
>
> This brings the regiment at right angles with its original position, and at right angles with the rebel line and on its flank. Here the Thirteenth pour a murderous fire into the flank of the advancing enemy at short range.[14]

If there is one event that proves the contention "Victory has a hundred fathers" it is the battle of Gettysburg. There was even a fight of sorts around the matter of who informed General Meade of the repulse of Pickett's Charge. Haskell recalled:

> General Meade rode up, accompanied alone by his son, who is his aide-de-camp…. As he arrived near me, coming up the hill, he asked in a sharp, eager voice, "How is it going here?" "I believe, General, the army is repulsed," I answered. Still approaching, and a new light began to come upon his face, of gratified surprise, with a touch of incredulity, of which his voice was also the medium, he further asked, "What! Is the assault entirely repulsed?" his voice quicker and more eager than before. "It is, sir," I replied. By this time he was on the crest, and when his eye had for an instant swept over the field, taking in just a glance of the whole,–the masses of prisoners, the numerous captured flags, which the men were derisively flaunting about, the fugitives of the routed enemy disappearing with the speed of terror in the woods,—partly at what I had told him, partly at what he saw, he said impressively, and his face was lighted, "Thank God."[15]

Morgan made a couple of references to the matter. First:

> While his wound was being dressed he [Hancock] sent Major Mitchell to report to General Meade that he was wounded, that the troops under his command had repulsed the enemy's assault, that we had gained a great victory and that the enemy was flying in all directions in his front. The message was delivered to General Meade as he was riding to the crest of Cemetery Hill, and he replied, "Say to

General Hancock that I regret exceedingly that he is wounded, and that I thank him, for the country and for myself, for the service he has rendered to-day."[16]

Second:

In Rothermel's great historical picture illustrating the battle of Gettysburg, painted for the state of Pennsylvania, the artist has depicted Lieutenant Hascall [*sic*] of General Gibbon's staff, announcing to General Meade the discomfiture of the enemy. This is a perversion of historical truth in one respect, and an injustice to General Hancock's senior aide, Major Mitchell, who carried to General Meade General Hancock's announcement of the victory, the instant General Hancock, raising himself on his hands, saw the enemy's line break. It is true that the incident of which the artist has taken advantage occurred at a later period, when General Meade rode on to the line, but there is a manifest impropriety in making General Meade receive the intelligence of the rout of the enemy from the staff-officer of a subordinate commander to General Hancock. Lieutenant Hascall was a brilliant young officer, but he surpassed Major Mitchell neither in conspicuous gallantry nor in the most intelligent and faithful discharge of duty. Justice might have equally been done, by giving Lieutenant Hascall the place he really had, which was between the lines, urging our men to follow, and leaving to Major Mitchell the delivery of General Hancock's message.[17]

The "Friend to Friend Masonic Memorial" illustrates the meeting between Captain Henry H. Bingham and Confederate Brigadier General Lewis Armistead, after Armistead fell mortally wounded on 3 July. The memorial is adjacent the intersection of Taneytown Road and Steinwehr Avenue in the National Cemetery Annex, on the north side of the cemetery itself (photograph by William Bretzger).

Hancock and Armistead

The friendship of Hancock and Confederate General Lewis Armistead is the foundation of legend and myth. Henry Bingham is the best witness of what transpired between them upon their both falling wounded (Armistead mortally) at the apex of Pickett's Charge. In an 1869 letter to Hancock, Bingham wrote:

> I saw Armistead first at the high point of the enemy's repulse. I was on the right and alongside of Webb's brigade, second line, just at the crest, when Webb's front line was driven back. I was wounded and did all I could to rally the troops, my horse was wounded but not seriously. I met Armistead just under the crest of the hill, being carried to the rear by several privates. I ordered them back, they replied that they had with them an important prisoner and designated him as General Longstreet. By this time I saw from the ornaments on his dress that he was an officer of rank, and, impressed with the importance of carefully attending to the security of a Commander holding the rank of Longstreet, and observing the great suffering the prisoner was in, I dismounted from my horse and inquired of the

A four and a half foot tall granite scroll marks the location of Armistead's wounding (photograph by William Bretzger).

prisoner his name, he replied General Armistead of the Confederate Army. Observing that his suffering was very great I said to him, General I am Captain Bingham of General Hancock's Staff, and if you have anything valuable in your possession which you desire taken care of, I will take care of it for you. He then asked me if it was General Winfield Scott Hancock and upon my replying in the affirmative he informed me that you were an old and valued friend of his, and that he desired me to say to you "Tell Gen. Hancock for me that I have done him and done you all an injury which I shall regret or repent (I forget the exact word) the longest day I live." I then obtained his spurs, watch, chain, seal and pocketbook. I told the men to take him to the rear to one of the Hospitals.... I think I found you in about 15 minutes after I got Armistead's message and effects.[18]

Bingham did not immediately address to Hancock the matter of Armistead. Instead, he rode about taking care of Hancock's more pressing and official matters. But finally, he writes, "Shortly after this I rode back to where you were, (a temporary Hospital in the woods) and gave you the message and effects Armistead entrusted to me."[19]

The next day, Saturday, 4 July, the two great armies were quiet save some skirmishing, cautiously wary of one another. By the fifth, Meade found Lee had evacuated west toward the relative safety of the mountains. On 14 July, Lee crossed the Potomac River back into Virginia; and the Gettysburg campaign was over.

16

Lost Opportunity?

> *My dear general, I do not believe you appreciate the magni-*
> *tude of the misfortune involved in Lee's escape. He was*
> *within your easy grasp, and to have closed upon him would,*
> *in connection with our other late successes, have ended the*
> *war. As it is, the war will be prolonged indefinitely.*[1]
>
> —Abraham Lincoln to George Meade,
> from a letter never sent

There was controversy in the Union army and the northern political class after Lee's army re-crossed the Potomac River, on 14 July 1863, to the relative safety of Virginia. There were accusations that Meade had lost a great opportunity to destroy the Army of Northern Virginia. A leader in this school of thought was President Lincoln himself. The president's son, Robert, recalled: "I went to my father's office ... and found him in distress, his head leaning upon the desk in from of him, and when he raised his head there was evidence of tears upon his face. Upon my asking the cause of his distress he told me that he had just received the information that Gen. Lee had succeeded in escaping across the Potomac river at Williamsport [Maryland] without serious molestation by Gen. Meade's army."[2]

When Lee had reached the river some days before his eventual crossing on the 14th, he had found it flooded before he could organize a crossing for his army. Conditions forced him to dig in and await attack until the river receded. According to Robert Lincoln, the president had even offered to take all the blame in the event of a failed attack and none of the credit should it succeed: "He at once sent at order to Gen. Meade ... directing him to attack Lee's army with all his force immediately, and that if he was successful in the attack he might destroy the order, but if he was unsuccessful he might preserve it for his vindication. My father then told me that instead of attacking upon the receipt of the order, a council of war had been held, as he understood, with the result that no attack was made, and Lee got across the river without serious molestation."[3]

Meade's critics cited this moment as the one at which Meade should have advanced, attacked, and destroyed Lee. Today, some believe that Lee's position, though backed against the swollen Potomac, was naturally strong and very well fortified, and that Union forces had little or no chance of success against it. Perhaps, however, there was an opportunity to destroy or more severely damage the southern army during the Gettysburg campaign, and that opportunity was the moment immediately after the repulse of the Confederate assault of 3 July. Hancock later testified to Congress's Joint Committee on the Conduct of the War: "I think it was probably an unfortunate thing that I was wounded at the time I was, and equally unfortunate that General Gibbon was also wounded, because the absence of a prominent commander, who knew the circumstances thoroughly, at such a moment as that, was a great disadvantage. I think that our lines should have advanced immediately, and I believe we should have won a great victory."[4]

This was Hancock the tactician espousing an ancient and widely held tenet of military theory: follow victory by pursuing the enemy; do not give them a chance to recover and regroup. He added: "We should have pushed the enemy there, for we do not often catch them in that position; and the rule is, and it is natural, that when you repulse or defeat an enemy you should pursue him, and I think it is a rare thing that one party beats another and does not pursue him, and I think on that occasion it only required an order and prompt execution."[5]

Adding to his assessment that the Confederates were unusually vulnerable at the instant of Pickett's and Pettigrew's repulse, Hancock told the committee "and there was a gap in their line of one mile that their assault had left."[6] When a member of the committee asked him to clarify that there was in fact a gap so large as a mile, Hancock replied, "There must have been practically a gap to that extent, because it took a mile of troops in position to have made that attack in column as it was made."[7]

It seems a reasonable deduction. To advance the large numbers the Confederates did, they had to leave behind a large gap. Also, one thing Hancock did not note but was surely aware of, was the overall layout of the opposing battle lines. The curve of the Union position was a classic interior line, making the Confederate exterior line a much longer (and thinner) one. Only those Confederates immediately adjacent the point in question could have reinforced it in a defensive emergency. Meade could have, theoretically, drawn from almost any point in his line to contribute to a counterattack. Meanwhile, much of Lee's army, particularly Ewell's entire corps, was simply miles away from the gap Pickett's Charge had left, and wholly out of play regarding the contingency of a Union counterattack on that point. Hancock was not the only one who seemed to think it "natural" to make a counterattack. Private William Kepler of the Fourth Ohio noted, "Everybody was jubilant, and there was many an expressed wish to follow the Confederates in a general charge and put an end to Lee's army."[8] In their testimony to the Joint Committee, several top leaders also claimed to have favored a swift counterattack and that the army was ready, at least in spirit, to make one. General Hunt, commanding the Artillery Reserve, in an uncharacteristically succinct and unqualified moment of testimony, simply stated "Our troops were in very good spirits."[9]

The committee asked General Doubleday: "After the repulse of the enemy, were our troops so much exhausted by the three days' fighting, that it was impossible to for them to follow up the enemy vigorously?"

He responded: "I think not, our troops for two days had been lying down a great deal in a defensive position."[10] Brigadier General Albion P. Howe echoed Doubleday's assessment of their army's condition:

> But I did not consider that the fighting on our side was such as taxed us to the utmost, because our position was naturally a very strong one; and, as it seemed to me, a large portion of the strength of our army was not brought to bear. Our position did the work for us. The enemy worked at great disadvantage ... and after the fight of the 3d of July, I considered that our army had plenty of fight in it, if I may so express myself. Our army was badly cut up; we had had quite a number of disabled men, for sure, but it was an orderly fight. We were in a position where there was no straggling or demoralization; we had some pretty sharp cuts from that cannonading, but it was the most orderly fight I have ever been in, growing out of the position. In a military point of view it was not much of a battle; it was a very ordinary affair as a battle.[11]

Most of those in of the First, Second, Third, Eleventh and Twelfth Corps might have taken issue with Howe's statement. His was the vantage from the Sixth Corps, whose condition General Hunt accurately assessed: "They were fresh so far as fighting, but not so far as marching was concerned, for they had done very hard marching."[12] But even Humphreys, whose Third Corps division had suffered severely the previous day, testified:

> I can only say that the spirit of my men was just as fine after the battle as at any time. I know that on the afternoon of the 3d of July, when I moved up, the greatest difficulty I had was to keep my men (a part of them) from jumping over the little breastwork in front of the artillery, and advancing against the enemy without any orders. They were full of fight, and felt angry at the way they had been cut up the day before. So far as my division was concerned, they were in fine spirits after the battle; they were not in the least disheartened.[13]

And General Wadsworth, who had commanded the First Division of the First Corps, contended: "The slaughter had been terrible; but the spirit of the troops was unimpaired, and, in my opinion, our troops were in good condition to have taken the offensive, and they would have taken it with alacrity."[14]

General Warren stated to the committee: "They were in splendid spirits; they were not fatigued then. Those three days had been days of rest for the most of them; but we had lost a great many of our most spirited officers. General Reynolds was dead, and General Hancock was wounded and carried to the rear."[15]

The instant of the Confederate repulse did not go completely without an attempted counterattack, according to Hancock: "I was very confident that the advance would be made. General Meade told me before the fight that if the enemy attacked me he intended to put the 5th and 6th corps on the enemy's flank; I therefore, when I was wounded, and lying down in my ambulance and about leaving the field, dictated a note to General Meade, and told him if he would put in the 5th and 6th corps I believed he would win a great victory."[16]

He was referring to the statement he issued through A. N. Dougherty, medical director of the Second Corps, just after the repulse of Pickett's Charge: "if the Sixth and Fifth Corps have pressed up, the enemy will be destroyed."[17] Whether he received Hancock's note or not, Meade claimed to have made an effort to seize the moment: "As soon as the assault was repulsed, I went immediately to the extreme left of my line, with the determination of advancing the left and making an assault upon the enemy's lines. So soon as I arrived at the left I gave the necessary orders for the pickets and skirmishers in front to be thrown forward to feel the enemy, and for all the preparations to be made for the assault."[18]

But according to Meade, the complexities of the operation caused it to lose impetus before it fully developed: "The great length of the line, and the time required to carry these orders to the front, and the movement subsequently made, before the report given to me of the condition of the forces in the front and left, caused it to be so late in the evening as to induce me to abandon the assault which I had contemplated."[19]

Meade was a competent general. And the Army of the Potomac was a formidable army. But the above disclosure is not that of a masterful leader of a fully adept fighting force. Lacking was initiative and flexibility. The repulse of a great exertion by the enemy, especially an enemy as adaptive and resilient as the Army of Northern Virginia, is a fleeting instance and a time for swiftness and audacity. It is not the time for "pickets and skirmishers in front to be thrown forward to feel the enemy" or to await "the report given to me of the condition of the forces in the front and left." As Hancock contended: "Unless the very moment is seized it passes away, because the troops on both sides have become so inured to war, that if you give them time to collect again they are ready for another fight. They know the advantage of collecting together as soon as possible, and if you allow them time to do it you lose all the benefits of your victory, or at least of that condition of things which immediately follows a victory."[20]

And Doubleday added: "Meade, it is true, recognized in some sort the good effects of a counter-blow; but to be effective the movement should have been prepared beforehand. It was too late to commence making preparations for an advance when some time had elapsed and when Lee had rallied his troops and had made all his arrangements to resist an assault."[21]

But Hancock testifies that he *had* planned and acted, in advance, to exploit an eventual repulse: "When this assault first commenced I was on the extreme left of our line. As soon as I saw the skirmishers coming over the hill I knew the assault was coming, and I followed it up to see where it was going to strike, and as I passed General Caldwell, who commanded the left division of the 2d corps, I told him this: 'If the enemy's attack strikes further to your right I want you to attack on their flank; why I say so is this—you will find the 5th and 6th corps on your left, and they will help you.'"[22]

But as his testimony continues, Hancock regrets that his plans simply did not come to fruition: "He did not attack on their flank; why, I do not know. Perhaps it would not have been wise for him to do so, because the 5th and 6th corps did not make the movement."[23]

The failure to convert a successful defensive action into an offensive victory was not for want of a tactical opportunity. It was for a failure to seize a fleeting moment. It is easy to blame Meade and his lack of imagination on the failure of his army to spring forth from a defensive position like a coiled snake. He did not possess the inspiring presence of a Hancock, who had the ability to change the spirit of an entire battlefield as he had on the first day. Then there was Meade's cautiousness. He was not one to take chances; and, as General Hunt testified: "We must risk to win."[24] And the mindset of the Army of the Potomac was simply not one to leap to the offensive at that moment. That mindset had been long in the making. And although Meade did little, if anything, to change that mindset, he was by no means its creator. His army had never been a quick, nimble and responsive machine. And the consecutive humiliations of Fredericksburg and Chancellorsville, followed by the change in roles from invader to defender, imbued the army with desperation for a simple battlefield victory—any kind of victory. The Army of the Potomac was, at the moment, like that of a losing team with its back against the goal line. It was looking to make a stop—a goal line stand. It needed the ball back before it could think about scoring itself. And when the opponent fumbled, it fell on the ball conservatively instead of trying to pick it up on the run and score at the other end of the field; and it was happy to do so.

No one, to that moment, had mandated Meade to destroy Lee's army in Pennsylvania. An excerpt from General-in-Chief Henry W. Halleck's first written order to Meade reads:

> GENERAL: You will receive with this the order of the President placing you in command of the Army of the Potomac....
>
> You will not be hampered by any minute instructions from these headquarters. Your army is free to act as you may deem proper under the circumstances as they arise. You will, however, keep in view the important fact that the Army of the Potomac is the covering army of Washington as well as the army of operation against the invading forces of the rebels. You will, therefore, maneuver and fight in such a manner as to cover the capital and also Baltimore, as far as circumstances will admit. Should General Lee move upon either of these places, it is expected that you will either anticipate him or arrive with him so as to give him battle.[25]

The only strategic orders Meade knew, from the moment he succeeded Hooker in the predawn of 28 June, was to *defend* the capital against Lee. Furthermore, Hooker himself had left Meade virtually nothing to run with. Meade testified: "My predecessor, General Hooker, left the camp in a very few hours after I relieved him. I received from him no intimation of any plan, or any views that he may have had up to that moment."[26]

And during the battle, Meade's immediate subordinates did not press him to take the offensive, though he gave them ample opportunity. Even Hancock, who Warren described as one of "our more spirited officers"[27] did not begin to prepare a counterattack until Pickett's Charge was well under way. When Meade held a council of war on the evening of the 2nd, the overwhelming consensus was to hold the existing strong defensive line.

Yes, there was a tactical opportunity for a successful counterattack on the heels of Pickett's Charge's reverse. There was even indication of a substantial appetite for a counterattack in the army. But there was no preparation for one. Yes, Hancock had said to Caldwell: "If the enemy's attack strikes further to your right I want you to attack on their flank; why I say so is this—you will find the 5th and 6th corps on your left, and they will help you."[28]

But Hancock became absorbed in repelling the attack, and did not develop or follow up on those orders until he was severely wounded. If Lincoln wanted more than a successful defensive fight, he should have first appointed a more aggressive commander than Meade and second given him more ambitious orders.

17

The Hancock Factor

He had no opportunity to conduct large operations independently, but the skill and promptitude with which he marshaled the Union forces on the field at Gettysburg showed the eye and instinct of the commander.[1]
—Major-General John F. Hartranft

As his ambulance trundled away from Gettysburg on 3 July 1863, Hancock left behind a series of historic events that bore his stamp. His regular job was that of a junior corps commander; several generals on the field had outranked him. But on the first day he commanded the entire field, and it was not preordained that he would elect to try to rally the troops present. Nor was it predetermined that he would report to Meade that conditions were "not unfavorable" for a general concentration. These were aggressive and optimistic decisions. He could just as well have determined that it would be easier to continue falling back and rally around the Pipe Creek line, where Meade had already prepared to fight.

His placement of troops on Culp's Hill may seem like an obvious tactical move in hindsight, but no one else had done it. The same goes for the placement of Steven's battery on what we now call "Steven's Knoll."

But it was Hancock's placement of Geary's division which was his most prescient tactical disposition of the first day. He had only seen Little Round Top from the Taneytown Road and maps he studied en route to Gettysburg. At the time he sent troops there, it was difficult to conceive it as part of the battlefield. All the fighting had been on the other side of town, and all available Union arms were grouped on and around Cemetery Hill, almost two miles north of Little Round Top. Yet one should note that he recognized the eminence as a key position to occupy. After all, it was not a mere company or regiment he sent there; it was a full, fresh division.

Hancock was the architect of the famous "fish hook" line. He established points along which the army could develop a very strong position. All the army had to do was file into line between these points. When Sickles abandoned the line, it required Chief Engineer General Warren, General Sykes' Fifth Corps and Hancock's Second Corps to save the day for the Union cause. Sickles' corps, for its part, had to fall back in disarray. More evidence to the wisdom of Hancock's early layout occurred on the third day. Implementing the original design intent—a line anchored on the Round Tops—Union arms held relatively easily against the hugely formidable Pickett's Charge. Had he received his disabling wound just after the dispositions on 1 July, Hancock would still have been a great hero of the battle. But he had two afternoons of fighting before he actually did fall. His actions on 2 July were particularly brilliant. On the third, the location he helped select and the line he helped design did most of the work. But he was extraordinary under fire once again. Reinforcing his already stellar reputation, he continued to be exactly on the spot of crisis or place where he might exploit an advantage.

The Union army had most of the advantages at Gettysburg. It had more men, more guns, more supplies, a shorter supply line, and it was on its own turf. In hindsight, a defensive victory seems to have been likely. Only General Lee's stunning string of victories coming into Gettysburg made a Confederate triumph seem possible. It would be hyperbolic to posit that the Army of the Potomac required Hancock's heroics to achieve the victory that it did. But it is also true that were it not for Hancock and his skill and hard work that the battle might not even have been fought. It is also true that when the Confederates did get to the verge of breaking the Union line on 2 July, Hancock's extraordinary abilities prevented them from achieving it.

Gettysburg was bigger than any one person, but Hancock arguably had greater effect on the battle than any other single person on the Union side.

18

After Gettysburg

When Grant set the two armies in a death grapple, with the determination never to break or loosen it until one or the other was exhausted and subdued, a soldier like Hancock was invaluable to him.[1]

—Major-General John F. Hartranft

Hancock went on to a long, distinguished career, which this chapter outlines. But immediately following Gettysburg, the matter of his survival was in considerable doubt. His condition did not improve and he suffered intensely for weeks. The nail that the surgeon pulled from his wound likely came from the pommel of his saddle. The bullet, which had carried the nail into his body, remained there. Doctors made multiple attempts to locate and extract the bullet, but succeeded only in inflicting more suffering on the general. They eventually moved him from Philadelphia to his childhood home in Norristown. The head of McKim United States Hospital in Baltimore was also a Norristown man, Dr. Louis Wernwag Read.[2] He recalled paying the ailing general a visit in late August:

> I found him much disheartened. He had grown thin, and looked pale and emaciated. He said he felt as if he was going to die, and that he had been probed and tortured to such an extent that death would be a relief. I endeavored to cheer him up, and as I was about bidding him farewell he said: "Goodbye, Doctor: I may never see you again."
>
> I had my hand on the door knob of his chamber when he said: "See here, Doctor, why don't you try to get this ball out. I have had all the reputation in the country at it; now let's have some of the practical."[3]

It turned out that the local physician did have a clever insight. The "practical" aspect that Read brought was the idea of positioning Hancock to straddle a chair, simulating the position he was in when shot, perched in the saddle.[4] This enabled the doctor to locate and, the next day, remove the minie ball that lodged

This minie ball was in Hancock's body for weeks despite multiple attempts to extract it. Dr. Wernwag Read was finally able to find a straight path to it by having the general straddle a chair, recreating the position he was in when the bullet hit him, atop his horse. The standard minie ball is approximately 1¼ inches in length (from the collection of the Historical Society of Montgomery County).

"in the sharp bone which you sit upon."[5] The patient began to improve immediately, though he would never fully recover.[6] He gained a great deal of weight during his recovery, permanently transforming his physique to a more portly one; though he maintained his proud and commanding presence.

He was still in recovery when, on 28 January 1864, Congress passed a joint resolution of thanks, singling out Generals Hooker, Meade and Howard for the success of the Gettysburg campaign.[7] Predictably, the act proved controversial. Colonel Carroll, writing under the pseudonym "Truth," published a response in the *Army and Navy Journal* which read, in part:

> The passage of the resolution of Congress thanking Major Generals Meade, Hooker and Howard, for their services with the Army of the Potomac, is certainly a matter of great surprise to persons familiar with that Army. As far as Generals Meade and Hooker are concerned, there will not be much difference of opinion. The former commanded the Army and was successful, in the most momentous

battle of the war; and the latter commanded the army during most of the maneu-vering preceding the battle. But by what process of reasoning or distortion of facts is the name of Major General Howard placed in the resolution? On what ground is he alone of all the corps commanders selected for this high honor?[8]

Carroll added that Hancock "was, next to the Commanding General, the promi-nent man at Gettysburg. The Army gave to him the credit which Congress has given to Major General Howard."[9]

The Overland Campaign

In March 1864, Ulysses S. Grant ascended to the rank of Lieutenant Gen-eral and command of all Union armies. He made his headquarters with the Army of the Potomac, but retained Meade as its official commander. That army, which had consisted of seven corps at the battle of Gettysburg, consolidated itself into three corps: the Second, Fifth, and Sixth.[10] These three corps absorbed the units of the old First and Third Corps.[11] Hancock returned to command of the Second Corps, while Warren became commander of the Fifth, and General Sedgwick continued in command of the Sixth.[12] The Eleventh and Twelfth had previously left the eastern theater.[13]

The Second Corps left winter camp on the evening of May 3. When it pitched into the battle of The Wilderness on 5 May it comprised some 27,000 men.[14] It lost over 5,000 in the two day affair.[15] And of those losses, perhaps the worst for Hancock was the life of his old friend at West Point and hero of Get-tysburg, Alexander Hays.[16] The fight was a bloody stalemate; but Grant made it a turning point of sorts when he continued south after the fight instead of withdrawing to lick his wounds.

On the morning of 12 May, the Second Corps faced a salient of Confed-erate trenches at Spotsylvania Court House, Virginia. There Hancock was to lead a great assault; his preparations were characteristically thorough, com-mencing the action at 4:30 a.m. It was an immediate success, capturing almost a mile of trenches and close to 4,000 prisoners.[17] But the Confederate coun-terattack was formidable, as well. According to Walker:

> The contest had become beyond all comparison the closest and fiercest of the war. The Confederates were determined to recover their entrenchments at what-ever cost. For the distance of a mile, in a cold drenching rain, the combatants were literally struggling across the breastworks. They fired directly into each other's faces; men even grappled their antagonists across the piles of logs. Han-cock had brought some of his guns up to within three hundred yards of the cap-tured works, and these were firing solid shot and shell over the heads of our troops

into the space now crowded with Confederate brigades. Two sections were even run up to the very breastworks; and, though the muzzles protruded into the faces of the charging Confederates, the begrimed cannoneers continued to pour canister.[18]

Walker described how Hancock helped sustain the awful spectacle with deft tenacity:

> Over that desperate and protracted contest Hancock presided, stern, strong, and masterful, withdrawing the shattered brigades as their ammunition became exhausted, supplying their places with fresh troops, feeding the fires of battle all day long and far into the night. It was not until after twelve o'clock—twenty hours after the command "Forward!" had been given the column ... that the firing ceased; and the Confederates, relinquishing their purpose to retake the captured works, began in the darkness to construct a new line, to cut off the Salient, which for them had much better never have been built.[19]

Lee's new entrenchments behind those of the Salient (also known as the "Mule Shoe" for its shape), precipitated another stalemate. That is not to say that the two armies stared idly at each other. For the balance of May, Grant used his forces around the clock to probe for openings or weaknesses in Lee's lines, costing thousands in losses. He was putting the whole army to use, of course, not just the Second Corps. But for his corps' part, Charles Morgan complained: "There is an old adage that it is the willing horse that is worked to death"[20]; Meade's orders to Hancock on the evening of 1 June reinforced Morgan's contention that there were special expectations of the Second Corps: "You must make every exertion to move promptly and reach Cold Harbor as soon as possible.... Every confidence is felt that your gallant corps of veterans will move with vigor and endure the necessary fatigue."[21]

"So much as this is rarely expressed in the formal orders from headquarters," wrote Walker "and General Hancock took it in earnest."[22] But Hancock explained that the march did not go as planned:

> Captain Paine, topographical engineer, was directed to report to me to guide my column.... Every exertion was made, but the night was dark, and the heat and dust oppressive, and the roads unknown. Still, we should have reached Cold Harbor in good season had not Captain Paine unfortunately taken one of my divisions by a short cut where artillery could not follow, and so thrown my command into great confusion. My staff officers are entitled to great credit for reuniting the column and repairing the unfortunate mistake. The head of my column reached Cold Harbor at 6:30 a. m., June 2, but in such an exhausted condition that a little time was required to allow the men to collect and to cook their rations.[23]

Unfortunately, the mishap was just the beginning of a much grimmer episode, as Cold Harbor soon came to symbolize tragic, senseless futility.

"Upon Hancock's representations as to the state of his command, General Meade postponed the attack to 5 p.m.," said Walker, "and then put it off until half past four the next morning."[24] By that time, Lee's men were well entrenched, with the Chickahominy River covering their right flank and "the wooded swamps of the Totopotomoy and the Matadequin" protecting their left.[25] But with the Confederate capital of Richmond only six miles behind Lee's lines, "Grant determined to hazard a grand assault. It was, beyond question, the most unfortunate decision made during that bloody campaign." lamented Walker.[26] Nevertheless, the Second Corps made its charge at dawn on 3 June. It accompanied the Sixth Corps, now under General Horatio Wright, and the Eighteenth Corps, under Baldy Smith, which was part of Major General Benjamin Butler's Army of the James. "Scarcely twenty-two minutes after the signal had been given," wrote Walker, "the repulse of the corps was complete. Three thousand had fallen."[27] Then an order from Meade arrived: "I send you two notes from Wright, who thinks he can carry the enemy's main line if he is relieved by attacks of the Second and Eighteenth Corps; also, that he is under the impression he is in advance of you. It is of the greatest importance no effort should be spared to succeed. Wright and Smith are both going to try again, and unless you consider it hopeless I would like you do the same."[28]

There was just enough discretion in the orders ("unless you consider it hopeless") to allow Hancock to demur, and he did: "General: … An assault can be promptly repeated if desired, but division commanders do not speak encouragingly of the prospect of success since the original attacks failed. Unless success has been gained in other points, I do not advise persistence here."[29]

The Overland Campaign, as it came to be called, had reached another turning point. The fighting had been almost constant for four weeks, and with a horrendous casualty rate. The men had learned what kind of positions they could and could not capture. Winfield Scott Hancock, who had refused to withdraw despite orders at Williamsburg, sacrificed the First Minnesota on the second day at Gettysburg, tried to organize a counterattack on the third day at Gettysburg, and issued countless waves of men into the carnage for twenty hours at Spotsylvania, had finally refused to advance.

Wright and Smith did try a second time and met with equally dismal failure.[30] Grant famously wrote in his memoirs, "I have always regretted that the last assault at Cold Harbor was ever made."[31]

But the men clung to the limited ground they gained, and dug in, precipitating horrendous living conditions. "Through all the day not a man, over large parts of the line, could show his head above the works," wrote Walker, "or go ten yards to the rear without being shot. This continued until the early evening of the 12th."[32] Cold Harbor was the culmination of a gruesome campaign

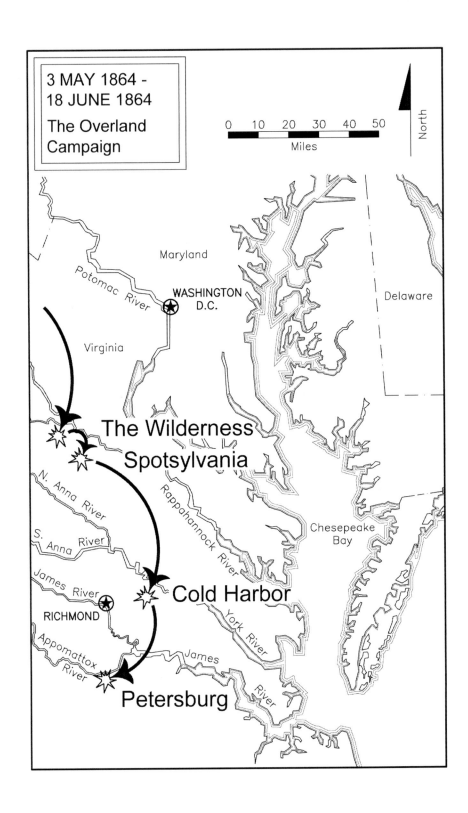

3 MAY 1864 -
18 JUNE 1864

The Overland
Campaign

0   10   20   30   40   50
Miles

North

Maryland

Potomac River

WASHINGTON
D.C.

Delaware

Virginia

The Wilderness

Spotsylvania

N. Anna River

S. Anna River

Rappahannock River

Chesepeake
Bay

James River

RICHMOND

Cold Harbor

Appomattox
River

York River

James River

Petersburg

for the Second Corps, having lost an average of over four hundred per day in about a month.[33] Morale, said Walker, had all but collapsed: "The confidence of the troops in their leaders had been severely shaken. They had again and again been ordered to attacks which the very privates in the ranks knew to be hopeless from the start; they had seen the fatal policy of 'assaults all along the line' persisted in even after the most ghastly failures; and they had almost ceased to expect victory when they went into battle."[33]

But none of this stopped Grant. He realized that Petersburg, a railroad center just south of Richmond, was essential for the capital's survival; and that if Lee blocked the road to Richmond, Petersburg was vulnerable. Just as he seemed little more than a butcher bent on frontal assaults, Grant orchestrated a feat of maneuver that left Lee in the lurch. The Second Corps stealthily backed out of its dreaded trenches in the evening darkness of 12 June, and by early on the fifteenth had crossed both the Chickahominy and the James Rivers.[34] "The Confederates were not only outmarched," Walker raved, "but distinctly outgeneraled."[35] His lament turned to exaltation: "Strategically, the movement from Cold Harbor to the James, between the 12th and 14th of June, 1864, was distinctly the finest thing the Army of the Potomac had ever done."[36]

But no one had captured Petersburg. "What was Hancock to do?" Walker asked. "By what further steps was the movement, thus far so successfully carried on, to be brought to a triumphant conclusion?"[37] The simplest oversight, Walker determined, prevented the army from completing Grant's masterstroke:

> Grant's plan was that Smith's corps ... should on this day, the 15th of June, advance rapidly upon Petersburg and seize the place, which was reported to be slimly held. Hancock, with his still powerful corps from the Army of the Potomac, was to move by a much longer route toward Petersburg, to be in readiness to support Smith, if required. But, by one of the strangest fatalities in the whole history of the war, it came about that Grant omitted to inform Meade of Smith's expedition. So far as Meade knew, Hancock was simply to move toward Petersburg, without any orders to attack the place or to support another force in doing so. Consequently, Hancock's instructions only required him to move toward Petersburg and take up a position "where the City Point Railroad crosses Harrison's Creek." Hancock, having no intimation that he was to do more than accomplish this march, desired to have his troops rationed before setting out, as any good general would have done.... Had Hancock received the slightest intimation that he would be needed to support Smith, he would have marched in the early morning, rations or no rations.[38]

Hancock's official report stated that he did receive intimation, albeit tardily:

Opposite: **The Overland Campaign was one of almost unbroken clashes between the combatants, but major battles punctuated the continuous engagement. This map shows the location of major battles between 5 May and 18 June 1864 (map by author).**

> At 5:30 p.m. ... a dispatch from General Grant, addressed to General Gibbon or any division commander of the Second Corps, reached me. This dispatch directed all haste to be made in getting up to the assistance of General Smith, who it stated had attacked Petersburg and carried the outer works in front of that city. A few moments later a note from General Smith was delivered to me by one of his staff, which informed me that he (General Smith) was authorized by Lieutenant-General Grant to call upon me for assistance and requesting me to come up as rapidly as possible.[39]

Continuing, his report was defensive in tone: "I desire to say here that the messages from Lieutenant-General Grant and from General Smith, which I received between 5 and 6 p.m. on the 15th, were the first and only intimations I had that Petersburg was to be attacked that day. Up to that hour I had not been notified from any source that I was expected to assist General Smith in assaulting that city."[40]

In its role as the leading force, the Eighteenth Corps was fatally tentative. "Smith ... since morning had been reconnoitering the works of Petersburg," said Walker; and "when Hancock at last reached the neighborhood of Petersburg he found that Smith had captured several of the enemy's redoubts ... but was still far from reaching the city itself."[41] Then Hancock, who by then was Baldy Smith's senior, yielded control in a way that seems uncharacteristic, considering his behavior at Williamsburg and on the first day at Gettysburg. Walker explained:

> Hancock was ignorant of the topography of the country, much of which was covered with dense woods. There was no time to make a reconnaissance during the few minutes of daylight remaining. He accordingly deferred to Smith upon the point of deciding whether another attack should be made, offering to put in his two divisions at any point which that officer might indicate. Smith, who believed that Petersburg had been heavily re-enforced during the afternoon, contented himself with asking Hancock to relieve his troops in the front line of captured works. This relief was effected by eleven o'clock at night.[42]

Hindsight determined that Petersburg was indeed "slimly held"; and that day the Union missed a grand opportunity to end the war in 1864. Lee, of course, soon realized Grant's intent and, accordingly, got more troops to the Petersburg front.

The fault for not taking Petersburg that day rests largely with Baldy Smith. A great deal of blame also has to go to the failure of Grant and Meade to communicate more clearly. Hancock did not fail to do his job; he failed to be transformative. And there was a profusion of mitigating conditions: The carnage of the campaign had been oppressive; Cold Harbor exemplified the futility of assaulting well made works. His Gettysburg wound was persistently miserable. And the hour was late.

Regardless of who or what was to blame, the hesitation allowed the Confederates just enough time "to construct a strong interior line of works, against which our troops were vainly to be hurled," wrote Walker, "making the 18th of June one of the bloody days of the Army of the Potomac."[43] Meanwhile, reported Hancock, his physical pain had become more than he could bear: "The night of the 17th of June I was compelled to turn over my command on account of disability from my wound, which during the entire campaign had given me great annoyance, and at times had prevented me from taking that active part in the movement of my troops which I desired to do."[44]

The Siege of Petersburg

He returned to command on 27 June. By this time the armies had transitioned to siege activities.[45] So Grant resumed the practice of probes and marches, seeking to flank Lee, find a weak spot, or cause him to weaken one point in the effort of reinforcing another. Among these projects were two expeditions the Second Corps made to Lee's left flank at Deep Bottom. The first occurred in late July, partly with the purpose of drawing Confederate strength away from the planned explosion of a mine which Burnside's men were digging.[46] The detonation took place on 30 July, but the ensuing battle of The Crater was a fiasco for Union arms. The second Deep Bottom expedition took place in mid–August. Neither of the endeavors had decidedly positive or negative results.

Such was not the case at Reams' Station on 25 August, where things ran afoul for the Second Corps. It was on an expedition tearing up the Weldon Railroad. Nearby was a set of trenches, poorly conceived, which another corps on a previous mission left behind. Among the design flaws of the complex was its sharply angled U shape, so closely arranged that artillery assailing it on one side could also target the rear of the other.[47] But Hancock opted to use it when Lee dispatched elements of A. P. Hill's corps against him. The Confederates attacked and captured the works, handing the Second Corps its only truly humiliating defeat of the war. Its commander had explanations:

> Had my troops behaved as well as heretofore, I would have been able to defeat the enemy on this occasion.... I attribute the bad conduct of some of my troops to their great fatigue, owing to the heavy labor exacted of them and to their enormous losses during the campaign, especially in officers. The lack of the corps in this respect is painfully great and one hardly to be remedied during active operations. The Seventh, Fifty-second, and Thirty-ninth New York are largely made up of recruits and substitutes. The first-named regiment in particular is entirely new, companies being formed in New York and sent down here, some officers being unable to speak English. The material compares very unfavorably with the veterans absent.[48]

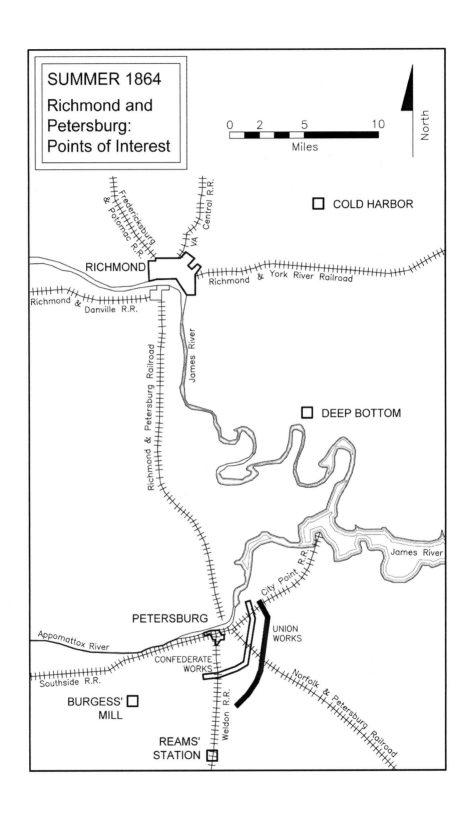

SUMMER 1864
Richmond and
Petersburg:
Points of Interest

0   2   5   10
Miles

North

☐ COLD HARBOR

Fredericksburg & Potomac R.R.

VA Central R.R.

RICHMOND

Richmond & York River Railroad

Richmond & Danville R.R.

Richmond & Petersburg Railroad

James River

☐ DEEP BOTTOM

James River

City Point R.R.

PETERSBURG

Appomattox River

UNION
WORKS

CONFEDERATE
WORKS

Southside R.R.

Norfolk & Petersburg Railroad

BURGESS'
MILL ☐

Weldon R.R.

REAMS'
STATION ☐

Hancock posed with his three division commanders at Petersburg: Brigadier General Francis C. Barlow, Major General David B. Birney, and Gibbon (Library of Congress reproduction number LC-DIG-cwpb–01701).

Opposite: This map shows the major railroads and points of interest for the Second Corps in the vicinity of Richmond and Petersburg. Grant initially assailed Petersburg from the east, but gradually stretched his siege lines clockwise around the town to capture railroads (map by the author).

Morgan described his chief's humiliation: "It is not surprising … that General Hancock was deeply stirred by the situation, for it was the first time he had felt the bitterness of defeat during the war. He had seen his troops fail in their attempts to carry entrenched positions of the enemy, but he had never before had the mortification of seeing them driven and his lines and guns taken, as on this occasion; and never before had he seen his men fail to respond to the utmost when he called upon them personally for a supreme effort."[49]

Meade was quick to console his friend. It was only a few hours after the fighting when he dispatched: "Dear General: No one sympathizes with you more than I do in the misfortunes of this evening…. I am satisfied you and your command have done all in your power, and though you have met with a reverse, the honor and escutcheons of the old Second are as bright as ever, and will on some future occasion prove it is only when enormous odds are brought against them that they can be moved. Don't let this matter worry you, because you have given me every satisfaction."[50]

"Some future occasion" came in late October, after Grant's siege lines had stretched far enough westward to hold the Weldon Railroad. He now sought the Southside Railroad, possession of which would force Lee to abandon Petersburg. He planned one last attempt at this before winter conditions set in.[51] By 27 October, two divisions of the Second Corps had maneuvered well west of the Union siege lines, spearheading the army's movement toward the objective. However, Grant found the Confederate works extended farther than he had assumed, and called the whole thing off. But before it could withdraw, the Second Corps handsomely repelled an attack near Burgess' Mill.[52] The cancellation of the overall mission predictably caused Hancock great disappointment. "Reluctant as I was to leave the field, and by so doing lose some of the fruits of my victory," he complained, "I felt compelled to order a withdrawal rather than risk disaster by awaiting an attack in the morning only partially prepared."[53] Thus, he withdrew that evening from his exposed position.

It was to be the last battle of the war for him, though no one knew it at the time.[54] Walker explained that Hancock had every intention of returning to the campaign in the spring: "But Grant had for some time entertained other views; and Hancock's intimation of a desire for a leave of absence was met with the suggestion that he … with the aid of his military prestige and personal popularity, should raise a new corps, to be composed entirely of veterans, with which he might take the field upon the renewal of hostilities in the spring."[55]

In pursuit of creating and commanding a newly conceived "Veterans Corps," Hancock turned the Second Corps over to General Humphreys on 26 November 1864.[56] But the new corps idea failed. Grant had envisioned a force of 20,000 veterans; Hancock was able to gather just over 4,400.[57] So instead,

Hancock became commander of the Department of West Virginia and the Middle Military Division on 27 February 1865.[58] This entailed relieving Major General Philip Sheridan, which freed him up to lead his cavalry in the actions around Petersburg. On 1 April, before Hancock performed any major combat operations, Grant's men, with help from "Little Phil's" cavalry, broke through the Confederate works at Five Forks; and the chase was on. It is thoroughly anticlimactic that Hancock was not present when Lee surrendered at Appomattox Court House 9 April. "Hancock," said Walker, "who, from Williamsburg to the Boydton road, had been the most conspicuous single figure in the Army of the Potomac—was left out of the final triumph.[59]

But what kept him away from Appomattox put him in the center of action upon the assassination of President Lincoln a few days later. His Middle Military Division included the Department of Washington, a city under the grip of considerable alarm.[60] He returned there under orders, said Almira "to contribute in every manner to allay the alarm that was so widespread, and take measures to meet the peril that every public man felt surrounded him."[61] Also, she said: "His orders directed special attention to the employment of an adequate force in the arrest of persons engaged in the murder of President Lincoln, taking all proper means for their detection, and to report to the Secretary of War daily for instructions."[62]

There was no criticism to speak of when John Wilkes Booth died at the hands of federal soldiers on 26 April. There was a good deal of controversy, however, surrounding the apprehension and conviction of several alleged conspirators. The most dubious case was that of Mary Surratt, who probably did no more than run the boarding house at which Booth and some of the defendants had stayed. She, with three others, received the sentence of death. Her hanging took place, simultaneous with the others, on 7 July 1865. Hancock took criticism about the matter for years, even though he had no culpability in it. In 1880, biographer David Xavier Junkin explained:

> Although General Hancock was in Washington in command of the Middle Military Division, comprising in all about 100,000 men, during the trial and execution of the prisoners charged with the assassination of President Lincoln, he was not a member of the military commission which tried Mrs. Surratt, nor had he anything whatever to do with her trial, nor any responsibility of the finding of the court, nor for the sentence imposed.
>
> The troops that guarded the prisoners, including Mrs. Surratt, were, of course, under General Hancock's command, being a portion of the forces stationed within his division; and when the orders for the execution were issued by the President of the United States, those orders were directed to General Hancock, as the highest officer present in command, according to invariable military usage when military sentences are to be executed.[63]

In fact, he took extraordinary measures to ensure Mrs. Surratt be given every opportunity to avoid the noose. "Not once, but many times," wrote Almira, "did my husband urge upon the President unanswerable reasons for granting a pardon."[64] Furthermore, Junkin observed:

> Indeed, it is in evidence from his very acts that General Hancock did all within his power with a view to saving Mrs. Surratt. Thinking it possible that … a reprieve might be issued, addressed to him, he went to the arsenal where the prisoners were confined, and remained there until the last moment. Not only this, but he stationed couriers at positions along the streets leading from the White House to the arsenal, for the purpose of having conveyed to him instant intelligence if any favorable orders should be issued.[65]

Postbellum Assignments

After the furor of Lincoln's assassination and its aftermath, things seemed to have settled down for the general. Though the work of reuniting the nation carried its own kind of difficulties, it would not be as tempestuous as fighting a full blown civil war. By 21 April 1866, Congress got around to amending its previous statement of thanks regarding the battle of Gettysburg: "Resolved by the Senate and House of Representatives of the United States of America, in Congress assembled, That, in addition to the thanks heretofore voted by joint resolution … the gratitude of the American people and the thanks of their representatives in Congress are likewise due, and are hereby tendered, to Major-General Winfield S. Hancock, for his gallant, meritorious, and conspicuous share in that great and decisive victory."[66]

On 26 July, he received a more tangible reward in the form of promotion to major general in the regular army.[67] This preceded his 6 August appointment to command of the Department of the Missouri.[68] At this station, tangling with various Indian tribes was a major part of the routine.[69] But his assignment on the plains ended after President Andrew Johnson, on 26 August 1867, put him in command of the Fifth Military District, comprising Louisiana and Texas.[70] His brief tenure there became a seminal moment in his future political career when he issued his "General Orders No. 40," which effectively returned the district to civilian rule. Issued on 29 November, the day after he arrived in New Orleans, the act affirmed the principles that his father, the Jacksonian Democratic lawyer, had instilled in him. "In war it is indispensable to repel force by force," the order proclaimed, "but when insurrectionary force has been overthrown and peace established … the military power should cease to lead, and the civil administration resume its natural and rightful dominion."[71] This brought Hancock great popularity, not only in the Fifth District, but throughout the South.[72] Of this action Baldy Smith would later opine: "At a time when military men thirsted for power, when one part of our country was demoralized by poverty and defeat, and when even the people of the North were getting accustomed to the despotism of long-continued military authority, General Hancock clearly proclaimed the fundamental principle of the subordination of the military power ... to the civil, which alone has the interests of mankind and its keeping."[73]

But his popularity, while strong among white southerners, was anything but universal. "Altogether, the controlling powers at Washington were not satisfied with the ... manner in which Hancock was administering the government of the district under his command," wrote Junkin.[74] "General Garfield, the Chairman of the Committee on Military Affairs of the House of Representatives," continued Junkin, "introduced a bill to reduce the number of major generals in the army, with the avowed purpose of ousting General Hancock."[75] The bill failed; but the political environment was too uncomfortable for Hancock. "The President is no longer able to protect me," he wrote, "so that I may expect one humiliation after another until I am forced to resign."[76] Accordingly, he requested reassignment. After being relieved as commander of the Fifth District, he took command of the Division of the Atlantic on 31 March 1868.[77]

His principled policy stances, added to his renown as a soldier, solidified his popularity in the Democratic Party; and he came under serious consideration as a presidential candidate at its convention that summer.[78] But it was not his year; nor was it a Democratic year. Republican nominee Ulysses S. Grant became the eighteenth President of the United States. His inauguration was 4 March 1869. The next day orders went out moving Meade to command the Division of the Atlantic and Hancock to the Department of the Dakota.[79] In 1872, the year of the next presidential election, there was again some spirit in the Democratic Party to nominate General Hancock. "General Hancock's friends were active in their efforts to bring his name before the Convention," Almira recalled. But "this was not to his liking, and he wrote, or caused to be written, hundreds of letters to the effect that he was not a candidate for the Presidency."[80] They eventually nominated Liberal Republican and New York City newspaper man Horace Greeley, who lost badly to Grant. The day after the election, 6 November, George Meade died, and Hancock returned to command the Division of the Atlantic. "The official duties entailed by this command were unlike any others," remembered his wife, "inasmuch as they were not so laborious, requiring vigilance, but without the grave responsibilities that were ever present while serving in the Indian territory."[81]

Despite the relative tranquility of the Atlantic post, more opportunities to assert his views on the subordination of military authority emerged. In 1875,

Hancock served on a military court of inquiry into General Orville Babcock's alleged involvement in the Whiskey Ring scandal.[82] "General Hancock expressed himself in positive terms as to the illegality of the whole proceedings," Almira wrote, "in the calling for a Military Court of Inquiry while an investigation was pending in the Civil courts."[83] His argument prevailed, she claimed, when "the Court of Inquiry immediately adjourned upon the conclusion of this address."[84]

The 1876 presidential election dispute dwarfed the Whiskey Ring matter in terms of gravity and potential disaster; there was talk of war between the parties.[85] The situation prompted a voluminous exchange between Hancock and Sherman. Hancock's long dispatch of 28 December included more declarations on his adherence to the principles of limited military authority:

> The army should have nothing to do with the selection or inauguration of Presidents. The people elect the President. The Congress declares in a joint session who he is. We of the army have only to obey his mandates, and are protected in so doing only so far as they may be lawful.... The people or politicians may institute parades in honor of the event, and public officials may add to the pageant by assembling troops and banners, but all that only comes properly after the inauguration—not before; and it is not a part of it.[86]

Ever mindful of *morale,* Hancock explained that it was not just a matter of legality, but one of practicality, in that overusing the military diminished its credibility: "The army is laboring under disadvantages, and has been unlawfully

at times, in the judgment of the people (in mine certainly), and we have lost a great deal of the kindly feeling which the community at large once felt for us. It is time to stop and unload."[87]

The matter ended peacefully (though controversially) with the inauguration of Republican Rutherford B. Hayes on 4 March 1877. But still more turmoil ensued that year when real, widespread violence erupted in the Great Railroad Strike and sympathetic labor actions. It began with a labor strike against the

Undated portrait (Library of Congress reproduction number LC-USZ62– 100787).

Hancock appears in an 1880 presidential campaign poster with his running mate, William H. English (Library of Congress reproduction number LC-DIG-ds-00846).

Baltimore and Ohio Railroad on 16 July, and spread across the country.[88] "The railroad riots continued until the end of July," Junkin wrote "the losses, chiefly in Pittsburgh Pa., but also in Chicago, Cincinnati, Buffalo, Albany, and at other points have never been fully estimated."[89] The situation was too severe for Hancock to completely withhold intervention, but he used such deft restraint that the involvement of Regulars was bloodless as well as effective.[90]

His skillful management during the crises of 1877 further cemented Hancock's high public reputation.[91] Following this the Democratic Party, at last, nominated him as their presidential candidate. It was 1880, and his Republican opponent was James Garfield. In the general election on 2 November, with about nine million votes cast, Hancock lost the popular vote by the minute margin of 7,018.[92] The electoral college favored Garfield 214–155; but if Hancock had won New York, which he lost narrowly, he would have won 190–179.[93] The general was exceptionally composed and magnanimous. "His defeat Hancock bore with perfect dignity and unimpaired good nature," said Walker.[94] Almira recalled: "At 7 o'clock, P. M., on the day of the election, he yielded to the extreme weariness and prostration that ensued from his five months' labors and went to bed, begging me under no circumstances to disturb him, as the result would be known sooner or later, and to-morrow would be time enough. At 5 o'clock on the following morning he inquired of me the news. I replied, 'It has been a complete Waterloo for you.' 'That is all right,' said he, 'I can stand it,' and in another moment he was again asleep."[95]

"His profession at least remained," Walker mused, "and that profession was one that absolutely suited him."[96] So it is appropriate that he continued at his Governors Island, New York, headquarters for the remainder of his days.

The Final Years

Though the excitement of battle and political dispute had passed, Almira recalled that the general's post was not all quiet: "Governor's Island being so near to New York City, our social requirements had become very irksome and exacting. Few distinguished guests were permitted to leave the metropolis without a full inspection of a 'model United States fort.' These constant social requirements imposed, necessarily, additional labors, which were cheerfully and ably performed."[97]

Almira recalled one of the more immense labors demanded of the Atlantic Division commander:

> In the fall of 1881 General Hancock was called upon to take charge of the Yorktown celebration, entertaining the nation's guests on the occasion of the Centennial celebration of the surrender of Lord Cornwallis. In order to make this interesting event a success, carte-blanche was given him by the authorities at Washington, which enabled him, without fear of disapproval, to make the affair brilliant and a credit to his government.... This Centennial will never be forgotten by those who were privileged to take part in or witness the grand military observances that were marked out for each day, and the other ceremonies equally novel and interesting.[98]

In August 1885, the funeral for Ulysses S. Grant was another grand ceremony Hancock had the obligation of conducting. Allie remembered: "General Hancock was seen for the last time in public, in his official capacity, commanding the pageant that escorted the remains of General Grant to their final resting-

Opposite: Undated portrait of Hancock (from the collection of the Historical Society of Montgomery County).

place, Riverside Park … he was authorized to make 'one of the grandest and most impressive displays that lay within his power.' His soldier-like directness served him faithfully upon this occasion. How well he performed this arduous and difficult duty, his fellow-countrymen well known without further mention."[99]

There was no hint that the grand procession would be his "last time in public, in his official capacity." He was only 61 and there appears no indication that his health was failing. He returned to Gettysburg later that November with John Bachelder. At the time, Bachelder was Superintendent of Tablets and Legends of the Gettysburg Battlefield Memorial Association, and was a key figure in directing the placement of monuments on the field.[100] He was also under government direction to write a history of the battle.[101] It was Hancock's first visit there since 1866.[102] "I am satisfied that the position indicated where I was shot, is incorrect," he wrote to the historian shortly thereafter. "I would be pleased if you would work with a stake or small boulder (in such a way that they cannot be moved again) the spot indicated by General Stannard and to which General Mitchell assented as sufficiently near the true place."[103] He seems to have felt well, inviting Bachelder to come to New York and "stay all night with me … in time for dinner and remaining until we have had a talk after breakfast, the next day."[104]

But the general did not live long enough for these things to come to fruition. At the end of January 1886, he developed a painful boil on the back of his neck.[105] As the days passed, several physicians saw him, but his condition worsened.[106] It was clear he had more than just a skin ailment when he became bedridden and delirious. On 9 February a urine test determined he had diabetes, a disease from which his late father had suffered.[107] That convinced his doctors he would not survive; and he passed away later that day.[108] He was five days short of his sixty-second birthday.

His funeral on 13 February was simple, per Almira's request; though it covered the considerable distance from Trinity Church in New York, to Montgomery Cemetery in Norristown, Pennsylvania.[109] His remains are alongside of his daughter Ada, who predeceased him. Fittingly for a commander who moved mountains on the field of battle, their vault is of his own design.[110]

Opposite: **The vault of Ada Hancock and her father: soon after the general's funeral in 1886 (above) and in 2015 (below) (upper photograph from the collection of the Historical Society of Montgomery County; lower photograph by the author).**

19

Letters and Addresses

*And you, great soldier, commissioned a generation ago to
carry triumphant the flag of your country on this field of
battle—the greatest of the century—well done!*[1]
—Henry H. Bingham at the unveiling of Hancock's
equestrian statue on East Cemetery Hill, 5 June 1896

In 1878, General Hancock helped found the Military Service Institution
of the United States, an organization of officers dedicated to the advancement
of the science and arts of war.[2] Shortly after Hancock's death, the institution
held a meeting to remember and honor him. There were many distinguished
speakers and still more prominent figures that could not attend, but sent tributes in writing.

Many statements touted Hancock's great fame, often declaring, inaccu-
rately, that it would persist through generations to come. "I heard of his magnificent conduct at the battle of Gettysburg, with the fame of which the whole
country rang," said Major General William B. Franklin. "His name will go down
in history as one of the noble products of the Civil War, and of the Army of
the United States."[3] Referring to Hancock's narrow presidential election defeat,
former Hancock staffer Brevet Major William P. Wilson proclaimed: "He
needed no Presidency, nor higher title, to round out the fullness of his fame.
It is enshrined ineffaceably in the hearts of the American people and neither
monuments nor annals of history will be needed to teach the inheritors of free
government that it lost one of its noblest, purest and most heroic supporters
when Winfield Scott Hancock was 'gathered to his fathers.'"[4]

Another staffer, Captain W. D. W. Miller, declared "he has been rewarded
with ... an imperishable name in history."[5] "Imperishable" was also how
Thomas B. Musgrave, Esquire characterized Hancock's fame.[6] Major General
Edward L. Molineux simply stated, "His name will live in history."[7] The battle
of Gettysburg was already a generation previous, but the speakers still remem-

bered Hancock's leadership there. Brevet Major General Nelson A. Miles recalled Hancock's instant assessment of the battlefield: "At this time, when the Southern army was exulting over recent victories and the Confederate cause was at the zenith of its power, the fate of the great cause to which he had devoted his life trembled in the balance; it was then that his genius and patriotism rose to the grandeur of the great crisis. Quickly selecting the strategic crests of Gettysburg, almost as quickly the Union lines were, in the hands of the master, placed in position in advance of the arrival upon the ground of the general-in-chief."[8]

Brevet Lieutenant Colonel John P. Nicholson agreed regarding the fortunate timing of Hancock's arrival on the field:

> It was under these circumstances that I first saw Hancock, a moment after he arrived upon the field to assume command. Not the command of troops in serried ranks bidding defiance to an advancing foe, but the command of troops that had made an heroic fight, and had, nevertheless, been discomfited and were now retiring through the narrow streets of the town, with all the disorganization that such a movement naturally brought with it, coupled with the dispiriting influence wrought by the fact that the field was left in possession of the successful foe. Such were the conditions under which Hancock assumed command. Then it was that his qualities shone forth![9]

He also agreed with Miles about Hancock's quick eye:

> Grasping at once the scene that lay at his feet, as he sat upon his horse, upon the crest of Cemetery Ridge—the bold inviting topography of the surrounding country that had failed to be fully appreciated, or if appreciated, failed to be fully utilized—the surging mass—the momentous issues that still hinged upon the outcome,–all these were taken in. Then, by his personal direction, and bringing to bear that magnetic influence possessed only by those whose actions on fields of battle have won the hearts of the troops whose lives have been entrusted to their keeping, he proved how justly his chief had judged of his fitness when he sent him forward to assume command.[10]

One of Hancock's most commonly-cited trait was his loyalty. Fellow Norristownian Major General Hartranft's written submission touted: "His loyalty was absolute. I do not mean loyalty to the Cause only, but loyalty, as a soldier, to his chief. Whatever opinions of his own he may have had, and undoubtedly he had some very decided ones, his interpretation and obedience of orders were altogether unbiassed [*sic*] and impersonal. To comprehend and carry out the plans of his chief, to subordinate himself to duty, had become second nature to him."[11]

The great William Tecumseh Sherman himself, who testified in writing, agreed with Hartranft: "No matter what his opinions, and they were always strong, he was knightly loyal to his superior officers."[12] Brevet Major General Orlando

B. Willcox also echoed these sentiments: "But I also had some personal knowledge of a trait less known to the world, and that is, his perfect loyalty to every commander-in-chief of that army." "He was incapable," added Willcox, "of infidelity to man, woman or child."[13]

Dan Sickles is hardly one to opine about loyalty, or character in general, for that matter. But his prominence and his appearance at the 25 February proceedings make his comments worth noting here. "No commander ever doubted for a single instant the absolute loyalty of Hancock."[14]

Even though he had been overweight since his recovery from the Gettysburg wound, twenty-three years previous, many continued to speak of his striking appearance. "He was certainly, in his uniform, among the grandest figures that I ever gazed upon," said Brigadier General James Grant Wilson.[15] "But I remember well his tall, slender, and handsome person," said Willcox of Hancock in his later days as a West Point cadet.[16] The Honorable Egbert L. Viele recalled that "Hancock's form and soldierly bearing were known to all."[17]

Several presenters praised Hancock's preference of civil law over martial law. Brevet Major General George W. Cullum touted: "During the reconstruction period Hancock, on his way to his Southern command, penned his famous

order No. 40, saying 'In war it is indispensable to repel force by force, to overthrow and destroy opposition to lawful authority; but when insurrectionary force has been overthrown and peace established, and the civil authorities are ready and willing to perform their duties, the military powers should cease to lead and the civil administration resume its natural and rightful dominion.'"[18]

General Franklin had similar observations: "when the war was ended, and he was, as it were, made the civil autocrat

Undated photograph (from the collection of the Historical Society of Montgomery County).

of sovereign States just devastated by the war, his conduct toward the beaten people, his conciliatory manner, his able civil papers by which he made a reputation as a civilian equal to that which he already had as a soldier, all showed that here was a man equal to any emergency."[19]

General and former Senator John B. Gordon agreed: "this self-imposed restraint of a great soldier, this subjection of himself and all his military powers to the supremacy of the civil law is a spectacle of moral grandeur almost without parallel in history."[20]

Hancock's preference for the civil over the martial, and his reticence to subject the defeated territories to further pain, reflected in his personal life, as well. In fact, there was more testimony to his personal kindness, gentle manner, and generous behavior in the social realm than any other qualities at the Military Service Institution event. "I can distinctly recall my trepidation on entering his office, and how quickly it was dispelled by his cordial greeting," recalled William Wilson. "His considerate kindness won my confidence."[21] "Genial in manner, courteous, and of unswerving loyalty and integrity," said Brigadier General Horatio C. King, "he will ever linger in my memory as one of the first gentlemen of America."[22] To Hancock's softer side, Miles testified:

> He possessed the indomitable and inflexible spirit of a great commander, yet there throbbed within his manly breast a heart as tender as that of a woman.
>
> Always sensitive of the feelings of others, and never allowing himself to do what might seem to be an unkind act, I have known him—when he fancied that he had spoken with undue sharpness—go out of his way to apologize to one of the humblest of his subordinates.
>
> I never knew him to make an ungentlemanly remark or do an unmanly act. There was no place in his great heart to harbor feelings of hatred or revenge, and although he held difficult and exalted stations in different parts of the country— in which the interests of hundreds of thousands of his fellow-countrymen were confided to his care ... his course was so honest, humane, and just, that he left behind him a multitude of friends in every State and Territory of the Union....
>
> In his public and official life he was true and great; yet the highest attributes of his character were most beautifully illustrated in his private and domestic life. A firmer friend, a truer husband, a more devoted father, could not be found in all this land.[23]

Chapter Notes

Introduction

1. Statement of Basil Norris, Military Service Institution, *Letters and Addresses Contributed at a General Meeting of the Military Service Institution Held at Governor's Island, N.Y.H., February 25, 1886, in Memory of Winfield Scott Hancock* (cited hereafter as *Letters and Addresses*) (New York: G. P. Putnam's Sons, 1886), 76.

2. Francis A. Walker, *History of the Second Army Corps* (cited hereafter as Walker, *Second Army Corps*) (New York: Charles Scribner's Sons, 1886), 283. United States War Department, *The War of the Rebellion: A Compilation of the Official Records of Union and Confederate Armies*, Series I, Volume XXVII, Part III, Correspondence, Etc. (cited hereafter as *OR Correspondence*) (Washington, D.C.: Government Printing Office, 1889), 371.

3. David L. Ladd and Audrey J. Ladd, eds., *The Bachelder Papers: Gettysburg in Their Own Words* (cited hereafter as *BP*), Volume I, 5 January 1863 to 27 July 1880. Colonel William Colvill, Jr., to Colonel John B. Bachelder, 9 June 1866, 256.

4. Harry W. Pfanz, *Gettysburg, the Second Day* (cited hereafter as Pfanz, *Second Day*) (Chapel Hill: University of North Carolina Press, 1987), 414. See also William F. Fox, *Regimental Losses in The American Civil War 1861–1865* (Albany: Albany Publishing Company, 1893), 26–27.

5. Statement of Winfield Scott Hancock, *Grand Army Review*, Feb. 1886, clipping in Hancock Papers, Pennsylvania State Library. As cited in Glenn Tucker, *Hancock the Superb* (cited hereafter as *Hancock the Superb*) (Dayton: Morningside, 1980), 144.

6. Statement of Abner Doubleday, *Letters and Addresses*, 21.

7. Statement of William W. Burns, *Letters and Addresses*, 19.

8. Ulysses S. Grant, *Personal Memoirs*, ed. E. B. Long (Cleveland: World Publishing Co., 1952), 582. As cited in David M. Jordan, *Winfield Scott Hancock: A Soldier's Life* (cited hereafter as Jordan) (Bloomington: Indiana University Press, 1988), 3.

9. *New York Evening Post*, 10 Feb. 1886.

10. *New York Herald*, 10 Feb. 1886.

11. Statement of William B. Franklin, *Letters and Addresses*, 15.

12. Samuel S. Carroll, *Army and Navy Journal*, 20 Feb. 1864, 403. As quoted in John Gibbon, *Personal Recollections of the Civil War* (Dayton: Morningside, 1978), 205.

13. Statement of Daniel E. Sickles, *Letters and Addresses*, 17.

14. C. W. Denison and G. B. Herbert, *Hancock "The Superb": The Early Life and Public Career of Winfield S. Hancock, Major–General U.S.A.* (cited hereafter as *Denison and Herbert*) (Cincinnati: Forshee & McMakin, 1880), iii.

15. *Hancock the Superb*, 13.

Chapter 1

1. Francis A. Walker, *Hancock in the War of the Rebellion*, a paper read at a meeting of the New York Commandery, February 4, 1891 (cited hereafter as *Hancock in the War…*), 2.

2. Adjutant General's Office, Military Academy Applications, National Archives. As cited in *Hancock the Superb*, 26.

3. *Hancock the Superb*, 26.

4. Frederick E. Goodrich, *The Life and Public Services of Winfield Scott Hancock, Major–General, U.S.A.* (cited hereafter as Goodrich) (Boston: Lee & Shepard, 1880), 23.

5. *Ibid.*, 26. Jordan, 5–6.

6. Goodrich, 26. Jordan, 5–6.

7. Goodrich, 26.

8. Jordan, 5.

9. Tucker, 26. Jordan, 6.

10. Denison and Herbert, 25. Mentions Hancock engaged in such pursuits at age twelve. Tucker, 23, gives an anecdote that has Hancock leading the marching company at seven, though the source of that information is unclear. See also Goodrich, 28.

11. Tucker, 22.
12. Denison and Herbert, 34.
13. Jordan, 7.
14. Tucker, 26.
15. Denison and Herbert, 63.
16. Tucker, 37.
17. Jordan, 14.
18. *Ibid.*
19. *Ibid.,* 14.
20. *Ibid.,* 15.
21. *Ibid.,* 16.
22. *Ibid.*
23. *Ibid.*
24. Tucker, 41.
25. Jordan, 16.
26. Tucker, 43.
27. Jordan, 18.
28. *Ibid.,* 17.
29. *Ibid.,* 20–21.
30. *Ibid.,* 22.
31. *Ibid.,* 22–23.
32. *Ibid.,* 22.
33. *Ibid.,* 23.
34. *Ibid.,* 24.
35. *Ibid.*
36. *Ibid.*
37. *Ibid.,* 24–25.
38. Almira R. Hancock, *Reminiscences of Winfield Scott Hancock* (cited hereafter as *Reminiscences*) (New York: Charles L. Webster & Co., 1887), 34.
39. Jordan, 25.
40. *Ibid.*
41. *Ibid.,* 25–26.
42. *Ibid.,* 26.
43. *Ibid.*
44. *Ibid.,* 27.
45. *Ibid.,* 28.
46. *Ibid.,* 33.
47. *Ibid.,* 32.
48. *Hancock in the War…,* 2.
49. Jordan, 33.
50. *Ibid.,* 36–37, 38.
51. *Ibid.,* 37.
52. *Ibid.,* 44.
53. *Ibid.,* Tucker, 86–88.
54. Jordan, 44.
55. *Ibid.*
56. *Ibid.,* 48.
57. *Ibid.,* 50.

58. *Ibid.,* 53.
59. *Ibid.,* 53–54. Tucker, 93.
60. Jordan, 60.
61. Jordan, 61. Tucker, 100.
62. Jordan, 64.
63. *Ibid.,* 65.
64. Tucker, 115.
65. Jordan, 66–67.
66. Jordan, 70. Tucker, 120.
67. Jordan, 72–73. Tucker, 121–122.
68. Jordan, 75.
69. *Ibid.,* Tucker, 124.
70. Edwin B. Coddington, *The Gettysburg Campaign: A Study in Command* (cited hereafter as Coddington) (New York: Charles Scribner's Sons, 1984), 209.
71. Statement of George Meade (son of General George Gordon Meade), *Letters and Addresses,* 33.

Chapter 2

1. Statement of William Farrar Smith, *Letters and Addresses,* 3.
2. *Hancock in the War…,* 1.
3. Henry W. Bingham, *Oration at the Unveiling of the Equestrian Statue of Major General Winfield Scott Hancock on the Battlefield of Gettysburg, June 5, 1896* (cited hereafter as Bingham, *Oration*) (Philadelphia, 1899), 5.
4. *Ibid.*
5. *Hancock in the War…,* 2.
6. Francis A. Walker, *Great Commanders: General Hancock* (cited hereafter as Walker, *General Hancock*) (New York: D. Appleton and Company, 1895), 28.
7. Statement of Major–General William B. Franklin, *Letters and Addresses,* 14–15.
8. *Reminiscences,* 92.
9. *Ibid.,* 94–95. Almira provides no date for the letter; but it appears to be from the aftermath of the battle of Chancellorsville.
10. Tucker, 34.
11. *Ibid.,* 55–56.
12. *Reminiscences,* 25. Almira states that Winfield could not turn down a promotion in the Quartermaster's Department, "having been a lieutenant for nearly twelve years," despite the fact that "he very much disliked quartermaster duties."
13. Jordan, 24.
14. *Reminiscences,* 27.
15. Jordan, 25–26.
16. *Ibid.,* 25.
17. *Ibid.,* 26.
18. *Hancock in the War…,* 2.

19. Frank Aretas Haskell, *The Battle of Gettysburg*, a paper published by the Military Order of the Loyal Legion of the United States (cited hereafter as *Haskell*), Commandery of the State of Massachusetts, Boston, 1908. 9.

20. Statement of John F. Hartranft, *Letters and Addresses*, 19.

21. Jordan, 9.

22. Jordan, 10. Tucker, 34.

23. Tucker, 34. Denison and Herbert, 56–57.

24. *Ibid.*

25. Walker, *General Hancock*, 38.

26. *Ibid.*

27. Statement of E. W. Clark, *Letters and Addresses*, 29–30.

28. *Hancock in the War…*, 4.

29. *Ibid.*, 3.

30. Statement of W. D. W. Miller, *Letters and Addresses*, 31.

31. Statement of William Tecumseh Sherman, *Letters and Addresses*, 10.

32. Franklin Sawyer, *A Military History of the 8th Regiment Ohio Volunteer Infantry* (Cleveland: Fairbanks & Co. Printers, 1881), 118.

33. Goodrich, 26. Jordan, 5–6.

34. Tucker, 20–21.

35. *Ibid.*

36. Scrapbook, Hancock Papers, Montgomery County Historical Society. As cited in Tucker, 25.

37. Jordan, 5.

38. *Ibid.*, 8.

39. Tucker, 27.

40. *Ibid.*

41. Winfield Scott Hancock, Letter to Virgie Wentz. As cited in Jordan, 6.

42. Tucker, 27.

43. Jordan, 6.

44. Much of the documentation of Hancock's childhood herein originates from biographies written during his life but some half century after the fact. There are few known verifiable eyewitness accounts of Hancock before he entered West Point. These biographies by Denison and Herbert, Goodrich, and Forney, came out in 1880. They do not typically cite sources and were intended to shed a positive light on the Democratic presidential candidate of that year. However, they are very consistent with the more verifiable traits of Hancock during the Civil War. Furthermore, there are few if any disputes to such positive accounts about Hancock's childhood, despite there being ample anti-Hancock pamphleteering in 1880. Also, twentieth century biographers such as

Glenn Tucker, David Jordan, and Al Gambone frequently cite these biographies as well.

45. Denison and Herbert, 36–37.

46. *Ibid.*, 36.

47. *Ibid.*, 22–23.

48. *Ibid.*, 26–27.

49. *Ibid.*, 26.

50. *Ibid.*

51. Winfield Scott Hancock, Letter to John Earle. 28 January 1844, Autograph File, Houghton Library, Harvard University. As cited in Jordan, 11.

52. J. A. Watrous, *Major General Winfield S. Hancock Memorial Meeting, March 3, 1886*, War Papers Read Before the Commandery of the State of Wisconsin, Military Order of the Loyal Legion of the United States, Volume I (Milwaukee: Burdick, Armitage and Allen, 1891), 300.

53. Statement of William Farrar Smith, *Letters and Addresses*, 1.

54. Statement of Nelson A. Miles, *Letters and Addresses*, 71.

55. Statement of William B. Franklin, *Letters and Addresses*, 14–15.

56. Oliver Otis Howard, "Campaign and Battle of Gettysburg, June and July 1863," *The Atlantic Monthly*, Volume 38, July, 1876, 58.

57. George B. McClellan, *McClellan's Own Story* (New York, 1887), 140. As cited in Tucker, *Hancock the Superb*, 14.

58. Henry H. Bingham, *Memoirs of Hancock by General Henry H. Bingham of Philadelphia* (cited hereafter as Bingham, *Manuscript*) (Cleveland, 1872).

59. Statement of George Meade (son of George Gordon Meade), *Letters and Addresses*, 33.

60. Statement of Charles King, *War Papers: Read before the Commandery of the State of Wisconsin, Military Order of the Loyal Legion of the United States*, Volume I (Milwaukee: Burdick, Armitage & Allen, 1891), 295.

61. Ralph Orson Sturtevant, *Pictorial History Thirteenth Vermont Volunteers War of 1861–1865* (cited hereafter as Sturtevant, *Thirteenth Vermont*) (Vermont Regimental Association, 1910), 319.

62. George Grenville Benedict, *Army Life in Virginia: Letters from the Twelfth Vermont Regiment and Personal Experiences of Volunteer Service in the War of the Union, 1862–1863* (cited hereafter as *Army Life*) (Burlington: Free Press Association, 1895), 183.

63. John Day Smith, *The History of the Nineteenth Regiment of the Maine Volunteer Infantry*

1862–1865 (Minneapolis: The Great Western Printing Company, 1909), 77.

64. Haskell, 9.

65. *Ibid.*, 35.

66. Winfield Scott Hancock, Letter to Peter F. Rothermel, the artist, 31 December 1868, Folder 2, Box 1, Peter F. Rothermel Papers, Pennsylvania Historical and Museum Commission. As cited in Pfanz, *Second Day* (Chapel Hill: The University of North Carolina Press, 1987), 472.

67. Glenn Tucker, "Hancock at Gettysburg," *The Bulletin of the Historical Society of Montgomery County*, Spring, 1963, Volume XIII, no. 4, 280. Jordan, 149–150.

68. *Ibid.*

69. *Ibid.*

70. John W. Barlow, *Major General Winfield S. Hancock Memorial Meeting, March 3, 1886*, War Papers Read before the Commandery of the State of Wisconsin, Military Order of the Loyal Legion of the United States, Volume I (Milwaukee: Burdick, Armitage and Allen, 1891), 304.

71. Statement of William P. Wilson, *Letters and Addresses*, 28–29.

72. Walker, *General Hancock*, 39.

73. *Ibid.*, 39–40.

74. Statement of W. D. W. Miller, *Letters and Addresses*, 31.

75. *Reminiscences*, 92.

76. United States War Department, *The War of the Rebellion: A Compilation of the Official Records of the Union and Confederate Armies*, Volume XXVII, Part I (cited hereafter as *OR*, not to be confused with *OR Correspondence, Etc.*, which contains correspondences as opposed to after–action reports) (Washington: Government Printing Office, 1889), 474.

77. Walker, *General Hancock*, 82.

78. Statement of Harry C. Cushing, *Letters and Addresses*, 41.

Chapter 3

1. Bingham, *Oration*, 11–12.

2. Winfield Scott Hancock, "Gettysburg: Reply to General Howard" (cited hereafter as Hancock, *The Galaxy*) *The Galaxy*, Volume XXII, June, 1876, to January, 1877 (New York: AMS Press Inc.), 821.

3. *OR*, 458.

4. *Ibid.*

5. *Ibid.*, 461.

6. *Ibid.*

7. Hancock, *The Galaxy*, 822.

8. *OR, Correspondence*, 461.

9. *Ibid.*

10. Hancock, *The Galaxy*, 822.

11. *OR, Correspondence*, 461.

12. *OR*, 368.

13. Charles H. Morgan, "Narrative of the Operations of the Second Army Corps. from the time General Hancock assumed command, June 9, 1863 (relieving Major–General D. N. Couch), until the close of the Battle of Gettysburg (cited hereafter as Morgan, *Narrative*)." Appendix A of Almira R. Hancock, *Reminiscences of Winfield Scott Hancock* (New York: Charles L. Webster & Co, 1887), 188.

14. *BP*, 1350. "Report of Lt. Col. Charles H. Morgan," undated.

15. Morgan, *Narrative*, 188.

16. David G. Martin, *Gettysburg July 1* (Conshohoken: Combined Books, 1995), 9. Martin summarizes "The day's conflict involved one–quarter of Meade's army (about 22,000 men) and over one–third of Lee's army (about 27,000 men)… By the numbers of troops engaged, the first day at Gettysburg alone ranks as the twenty–third biggest battle of the war, according to numbers compiled by statistician Thomas L. Livermore."

17. *BP*, 1350. "Report of Lt. Col. Charles H. Morgan," undated.

18. Hancock, *The Galaxy*, 822.

19. *BP*, 1350. "Report of Lt. Col. Charles H. Morgan," undated.

20. *Ibid.*

21. *BP*, 1350. "Report of Lt. Col. Charles H. Morgan," undated.

22. Morgan, *Narrative*, 189.

23. Sidney G. Cooke, "The First Day at Gettysburg," *War Talks in Kansas*, Press of the Franklin Hudson Publishing Company, Kansas City, Missouri 1906 (Wilmington: Broadfoot Publishing Company, 1992), 284.

24. Statement of Gouverneur K. Warren, *Report of the Joint Committee on the Conduct of the War at the Second Session, Thirty–Eighth Congress, Army of the Potomac, General Warren…*, Washington D.C. U.S. Government Printing Office, 1865. As cited in Winfield Scott Hancock, "Gettysburg: Reply to General Howard," *The Galaxy*, Volume XXII, June, 1876, to January, 1877 (cited hereafter as Hancock, *The Galaxy*) (New York: AMS Press Inc.), 828.

25. Carl Schurz, *The Reminiscences of Carl Schurz*, Volume III (cited hereafter as Schurz. *Reminiscences*) (New York: McClure, 1906), 14.

26. Francis Wiggin, "Sixteenth Maine Regiment at Gettysburg," *War Papers, read before the Commandery of the State of Maine, Military Order of the Loyal Legion of the United States*, Volume IV, Portland, Lefavor–Tower Company, 1915 (Wilmington: Broadfoot Publishing Company, 1992), 161–162.

27. Edward N. Whittier, "The Left Attack (Ewell's) at Gettysburg," Ken Bandy and Florence Freeland, 2:757–94, 76 (cited hereafter as Whittier).

28. *OR*, 696–697.

29. Jordan, 105–106.

30. Jordan, 183.

31. Oliver Otis Howard, *The Atlantic Monthly*, Volume XXXVIII (cited hereafter as Howard, *Atlantic Monthly*) (Boston: H.O. Houghton and Company, 1876), 58.

32. Howard, *Atlantic Monthly*, 59.

33. Oliver Otis Howard, *Autobiography of Oliver Otis Howard*, Volume I (New York: Baker and Taylor, 1907), 418.

34. Hancock, *The Galaxy*, 822.

35. Hancock, *The Galaxy*, 824.

For Howard's letter to Meade see endnote 28.

36. Hancock, *The Galaxy*, 824.

37. Charles Howard, "First Day at Gettysburg," *Military Essays and Recollections*, paper read October 1, 1903, 259–260.

38. Eminel Halstead, "Incidents of the First Day at Gettysburg," *Battles and Leaders of the Civil War* (cited hereafter as *Battles and Leaders*) Volume III, Part I, Robert Underwood Johnson and Clarence Clough Beul, eds. (New York: The Century Company, 1887–1888) (Harrisburg: The Archive Society, 1991), 285.

39. *Ibid.*, 13.

40. Extracts From General Doubleday's Monograph, with General Hancock's Autograph Notes Thereon (cited hereafter as "Hancock's Notes"), that "monograph" being Abner Doubleday, *Campaigns of the Civil War: Chancellorsville and Gettysburg* (New York: C. Scribner's Sons, 1882), *Journal of the Military Service Institution of the United States*, Volume XLVIII (New York: Wynkoop Hallenbeck Crawford Co., 1911), 108.

41. *Ibid.*

42. *Ibid.*

Also: Abner Doubleday, *Campaigns of the Civil War: Chancellorsville and Gettysburg* (New York: C. Scribner's Sons, 1882), 151.

43. Hancock, *The Galaxy*, 822–823.

44. Howard, *Atlantic Monthly*, 58–59.

45. *Ibid.*, 59.

46. William Swinton, *Campaigns of the Army of the Potomac* (New York: Charles B. Richardson, 1866), 335.

47. William Swinton, *The Twelve Decisive Battles of the War: A History of the Eastern and Western Campaigns, in Relation to the Actions that Decided their Issue* (New York: Dick & Fitzgerald, Publishers, 1867), 332.

48. J. W. Hoffman, "Field Operations at Gettysburg," paper annotated 1896. Contained in *Military Essays and Recollections of the Pennsylvania Commandery Military Order of the Loyal Legion of the United States*, Volume I, 22 February 1866—May 6, 1903. Compiled by Michael A. Cavanaugh (Wilmington: Broadfoot Publishing Company, 1995), 302.

49. *Ibid.*

50. Eminel (E. P.) Halstead, "The First Day of the Battle of Gettysburg," 5–6.

51. *Ibid.*, 6.

52. J. A. Watrous, "Major General Winfield S. Hancock Memorial Meeting, March 3, 1886," War Papers Read Before the Commandery of the State of Wisconsin, Military Order of the Loyal Legion of the United States, Volume I (Milwaukee: Burdick, Armitage & Allen, 1891), 299.

53. Harry W. Pfanz, *Gettysburg—The First Day* (cited hereafter as Pfanz, *First Day*) (Chapel Hill: The University of North Carolina Press, 2001), 138.

54. *OR*, 702.

55. John Buford, Dispatch to General Meade contained in *Report of the Joint Committee on the Conduct of the War at the Second Session, Thirty–Eighth Congress, Army of the Potomac* (Washington D.C. U.S. Government Printing Office, 1865), LIX.

56. *BP*, 201. Aaron Brainard Jerome, Letter to WSH, 18 October 1865. WSH also includes the entire letter Jerome letter in *The Galaxy* article, page 827.

57. *OR*, 704.

58. Howard, *Atlantic Monthly*, 58.

59. Hancock, *The Galaxy*, 829.

60. Howard, *Atlantic Monthly*, 58.

Also, Oliver Otis Howard, *Autobiography of Oliver Otis Howard*, Volume I (New York: Baker and Taylor, 1907), 418.

61. Hancock, *The Galaxy*, 824.

62. *Ibid.*, 824–825.

63. *Ibid.*, 825.

64. Extracts From General Doubleday's Monograph, with General Hancock's Autograph Notes Thereon (that "monograph" being Abner Doubleday, *Campaigns of the Civil War:*

Chancellorsville and Gettysburg) (New York: C. Scribner's Sons, 1882). *Journal of the Military Service Institution of the United States,* Volume XLVIII (New York: Wynkoop Hallenbeck Crawford Co., 1911), 108.

65. Hancock, *The Galaxy,* 825.
66. *Ibid.*
67. *Ibid.*

Chapter 4

1. Statement of Abner Doubleday, *Letters and Addresses,* 20–21.
2. *Ibid.*
3. *BP,* 1351. "Report of Lt. Col. Charles H. Morgan," undated.
4. Morgan, *Narrative,* 189.
5. Carl Schurz, *The Reminiscences of Carl Schurz,* Volume III (New York: McClure, 1906), 12–13.
6. Abner Doubleday, *Campaigns of the Civil War; Chancellorsville and Gettysburg* (New York: C. Scribner's Sons, 1882), 150.
7. *Ibid.*
8. *Ibid.*
9. Hancock, *The Galaxy,* 825.
10. *OR,* 368.
11. Hancock, *The Galaxy,* 825.
12. *OR,* 368.
13. *BP,* 1351. "Report of Lt. Col. Charles H. Morgan," undated.
14. Henry E. Tremain, *Two Days of War; A Gettysburg Narrative and Other Excursions* (cited hereafter as Tremain) (New York: Bonnell, Silver and Bowers, 1905), 574.
15. Abner Doubleday, *Chancellorsville and Gettysburg* (Charles Scribner's Sons, 1882), 151.
16. Morgan, *Narrative,* 190.
17. *BP,* 1351–1352. "Report of Lt. Col. Charles H. Morgan," undated.
18. Greenlief T. Stevens and Edward N. Whittier, "Stevens' Fifth Maine Battery at the Battle of Gettysburg," *Maine at Gettysburg; Report of Maine Commissioners* (cited hereafter as *Maine at Gettysburg*), Maine Gettysburg Commissioners' Executive Committee (Portland: The Lakeside Press Engravers, Printers and Binders, 1898), 88–89.
19. *Maine at Gettysburg,* 89.
20. Charles S. Wainwright, *A Diary of Battle: The Personal Journals of Charles S. Wainwright 1861–1865,* Allan Nevins, ed. (New York: Harcourt, Brace & World, Inc., 1998), 237.
21. *Ibid.,* 238.
22. *OR,* 368.
23. *Ibid.*

24. *Ibid.*
25. *OR,* 825.
26. Hancock, *The Galaxy,* 827–828.
27. Morgan *Narrative,* 191. The matter of what time things occurred is of some dispute. The accounts by Hancock and his staff set times of some events between thirty and ninety minutes earlier than other accounts of the first day. One should also note that Morgan's source for the time Mitchell set off for Meade's headquarters is not known. That Morgan would have known when Mitchell arrived at his destination is especially questionable, but is not critical to the immediate issue of what was happening on Cemetery Hill and the Gettysburg battlefield.
28. Jordan, 105.
29. Charles Howard to E. Whittlesey, 9 July 1863, Howard Papers. As cited in John A. Carpenter, "General O. O. Howard at Gettysburg." *Civil War History,* Volume 9, No. 3, September 1963. 261.
30. *Congressional Globe,* 38th Congress, 1st Session, 20 January 1864. 257. As cited in John A. Carpenter, "General O. O. Howard at Gettysburg." *Civil War History,* Volume 9, No. 3, September 1963. 261.
31. Abner Doubleday, *Campaigns of the Civil War; Chancellorsville and Gettysburg* (New York: C. Scribner's Sons, 1882), 152.
32. Hancock, *The Galaxy,* 826.
33. Eminel Halstead, "Incidents of the First Day at Gettysburg," *Battles and Leaders,* 285.
34. Oliver Otis Howard, *Autobiography of Oliver Otis Howard* (New York, 1908), 409. As cited in Coddington.
35. *Ibid.,* 409–410.
36. Pfanz, *First Day,* 142.
37. *OR,* 115.
38. *Ibid.*
39. Statement of Meade, George Gordon, from *Report of the Joint Committee on the Conduct of the War at the Second Session Thirty–Eighth Congress* (cited hereafter as *JCCW.*) (Washington: Government Printing Office, 1865), 330.
40. *Ibid.,* 330.
41. *OR, Correspondence,* 466.
42. *OR,* 71–72.
43. *Ibid.,* 72.
44. *OR, Correspondence,* 467.
45. *Ibid.,* 459.
46. *Ibid.,* 458.
47. Charles H. Howard, "First Day at Gettysburg," *Military Essays and Recollections,* IV (Commandery of the State of Illinois, MOLLUS), 258. 1907.

48. Charles Howard to E. Whittlesey, 9 July 1863, Howard Papers. As cited in John A. Carpenter, "General O. O. Howard at Gettysburg," *Civil War History;* Volume 9, No. 3, September 1963, 266.

49. *OR,* 366.

50. Orland Smith. As cited in Hartwell Osborn, *Trials and Triumphs: The Record of the Fifty–Fifth Ohio Volunteer Infantry* *(Chicago: A. C. McLurg & Co., 1904), 97.

51. J. A. Watrous, "Major General Winfield S. Hancock Memorial Meeting, March 3, 1886," War Papers Read Before the Commandery of the State of Wisconsin, Military Order of the Loyal Legion of the United States, Volume I (Milwaukee: Burdick, Armitage & Allen, 1891), 299–300.

52. Carl Schurz, *The Reminiscences of Carl Schurz,* Volume III (New York: McClure, 1906), 15–16.

53. Robert E. Lee, *OR,* Volume XXVII, Part II, 318, 445. As cited in Pfanz, *Gettysburg—Culp's Hill and Cemetery Hill* (Chapel Hill: The University of North Carolina Press, 1993), 72.

54. Winfield Scott Hancock, Letter to Fitzhugh Lee, 17 January 1878. As printed in Fitzhugh Lee, "A Review of the First Two Days' Operations at Gettysburg and a Reply to General Longstreet by General Fitzhugh Lee," *Southern Historical Society Papers,* Volume V, January to June, 1878 (Millwood: Kraus Reprint Co., 1977), 168.

55. *Ibid.*

56. Carl Schurz, *The Reminiscences of Carl Schurz,* Volume III (New York: McClure, 1906), 16–17.

57. *OR,* 368–369.

58. Morgan, *Narrative,* 191.

59. Haskell, 9.

60. Franklin Sawyer, *A Military History of the 8th Regiment Ohio Volunteer Infantry* (Cleveland, 1881), 123.

61. William Kepler, *History of the Fourth Regiment Ohio Volunteer Infantry* (Cleveland: Leader Printing Company, 1886), 124–125.

62. Statement of Winfield Scott Hancock,, from *JCCW,* 405.

63. *Ibid.*

64. *OR,* 115.

65. Morgan, *Narrative,* 194.

66. *BP,* 1353. "Report of Lt. Col. Charles H. Morgan," undated.

Chapter 5

1. Bingham, *Manuscript.*

2. Morgan, *Narrative,* 194.

3. Carl Schurz, *The Reminiscences of Carl Schurz,* Volume III (New York: McClure, 1906), 19–20.

4. John Gibbon, *Personal Recollections of the Civil War* (cited hereafter as Gibbon) (New York: G. P. Putnam's Sons, 1928) (Dayton, OH: Press of Morningside Bookshop, 1978), 133–134.

5. Statement of Winfield Scott Hancock, from *JCCW,* 406.

6. *Ibid.,* 405.

7. Charles E. Davis, Jr., *Three Years in the Army; The Story of the Thirteenth Massachusetts Volunteers from July 16, 1861 to August 1, 1864* (Boston: Estes and Lauriat, 1894), 233.

8. James C. Biddle, "General Meade at Gettysburg," *Annals of the War* (originally published in the Philadelphia Weekly Times) (Philadelphia: The Times Publishing Company, 1879), 211.

9. James Arnold and Roberta Wiener, *Order of Battle; Gettysburg July 2 1863; Union: The Army of the Potomac* (Oxford: Osprey, 2000), 15.

10. *BP,* 1388. John L. Brady, Letter to Bachelder, 24 May 1886. He does not mention casualties at this early stage but his description of the volume of firing suggests the likelihood of fatalities.

11. Henry S. Stevens, *Souvenir of Excursions to the Battlefields By the Society of the 14th Connecticut Regiment and Reunion at Antietam, September, 1891* (Washington: Gibson Brothers, Printers and Bookbinders, 1893), 16. As cited in Elwood W. Christ, *The Struggle for the Bliss Farm at Gettysburg* (cited hereafter as Christ, *Bliss Farm*) (Baltimore: Butternut and Blue, 1994), 5.

12. Christ, *Bliss Farm,* 6.

13. *BP,* 1388. John L. Brady, Letter to Bachelder, 24 May 1886.

14. Jordan, 9.

15. Tucker, 31.

16. Statement from William B. Franklin, *Letters and Addresses,* 13.

17. Tucker, 32.

18. *Ibid.,* 33.

19. *Ibid.*

20. Murray, *Harper's Ferry Cowards.* Page 57 describes the assignment of the 111th and 126th New York to the Second Corps on 24 June 1863. Page 58 places their assignment, along with the Thirty–ninth and 125th New York, as the Third Brigade of the Third Division on 25 June. It also suggests that at the time Hays rose to division commander. Page 43

notes Hays assumed command of the brigade, which then belonged to Major General's Samuel P. Heintzman's 22nd Corps (*Ibid.,* 39).

21. *BP*, 1388. John L. Brady, Letter to Bachelder, 24 May 1886.

22. *Ibid.,* 1389.

23. *Ibid.*

24. Clinton MacDougall, Letter to Gilbert A. Hays (son of Alexander Hays), 29 November 1909, *Life and Letters of Alexander Hays* (cited hereafter as Hays). Edited and arranged with notes and contemporary history by George Thornton Fleming from data compiled by Gilbert Adams Hays (Pittsburgh: 1919), 431.

25. *BP*, 1389–1390. John L. Brady, Letter to Bachelder, 24 May 1886.

26. Christ, *Bliss Farm*, 32–33, 36–37, 39–40.

Chapter 6

1. Statement of Winfield Scott Hancock, from *JCCW*, 406.

2. Pfanz, *Second Day*, 46. William Glenn Robertson, "The Peach Orchard Revisited; Daniel E. Sickles and the Third Corps, July 2, 1863," *The Second Day at Gettysburg; Essays on Confederate and Union Leadership* (cited hereafter as Robertson, "Sickles"), Gary W. Gallagher, ed. (Kent, Ohio: The Kent State University Press, 1993), 34, 36.

3. Robertson, "Sickles," 36.

4. *Ibid.,* 37.

5. *Ibid.*

6. *Ibid.,* 37–38.

7. *Ibid.,* 38.

8. *Ibid.,* 39.

9. *Ibid.*

10. *Ibid.*

11. *Ibid.,* 40.

12. *Ibid.*

13. Walker, *General Hancock*, 125.

14. Francis A. Walker, *Second Army Corps*, 272–273.

15. *Ibid.,* 273.

16. *Ibid.,* 273–274.

17. St. Clair A. Mulholland, "Hancock's Heroism Under Fire; A Graphic Recital of the Stirring Deeds of an Eventful Day," *Annals of the War; Chapters of Unwritten History; The Gettysburg Campaign; The Story of the Second Corps on the March and in Battle* (cited hereafter as Mulholland, *Annals*) (Philadelphia: McLaughlin Brothers, 1880), 7.

18. Statement of Winfield Scott Hancock, from *JCCW*, 406.

19. Henry E. Tremain, *Two Days of War; A Gettysburg Narrative and Other Excursions* (cited hereafter as Tremain) (New York: Bonnell, Silver and Bowers, 1905), 53.

20. Tremain, 53.

21. Statement of Winfield Scott Hancock, from *JCCW*, 406. Mulholland, *Annals*, 7.

22. *OR*, 482.

23. *OR*, 531.

24. Tremain, 37.

25. Kathleen G. Harrison, *Cultural Landscape Report Emmitsburg Road Ridge* (cited hereafter as Harrison), Volume II, Part I, July 2004. Gettysburg National Military Park, 10.

26. Tremain, 129.

27. *OR*, 552.

28. *OR*, 556.

29. Tremain, 53.

30. *Ibid.,* 37.

31. *OR*, 570–571.

32. *Ibid.*

33. *Ibid.*

34. *Ibid.*

35. *Ibid.*

36. *Ibid.*

37. *Ibid.*

38. *Ibid.*

39. *Ibid.*

40. Harrison, 12.

41. *OR*, 482–483.

42. *BP*, 1355. "Report of Lt. Col. Charles H. Morgan," undated.

43. Statement of Andrew A. Humphreys, from *JCCW*, 391.

44. *OR*, 531.

45. Statement of Andrew A. Humphreys, from *JCCW*, 390.

46. *OR*, 532.

47. *Ibid.*

48. *Ibid.*

49. *Ibid.*

50. Haskell, 21.

51. *BP*, 1354. "Report of Lt. Col. Charles H. Morgan," undated.

52. *OR*, 532.

53. *Ibid.*

Chapter 7

1. Tremain, 63.

2. Tremain, 59–60.

3. *Ibid.,* 61–62.

4. James C. Biddle, "General Meade at Gettysburg," *Annals of the War* (Originally published in the Philadelphia Weekly Times) (Philadelphia: The Times Publishing Company, 1879), 211.

5. Tremain, 63.

6. *Ibid.*, 64–65.

7. Haskell, 24.

8. *OR*, 369.

9. Mulholland, *Annals*, 8.

10. *Ibid.*

11. *Ibid.*

12. *BP*, 2002. William Corby to Bachelder, 4 January 1879.

13. Bingham, *Manuscript.*

14. *Ibid.*

15. *OR*, 379. Caldwell's official report, in a pair of strange mistakes, names the "Second" Corps instead of the "Third Corps": "Early in the afternoon the Second Corps, which had moved forward some distance toward the Emmitsburg road, engaged the enemy, and I was ordered to its support. I had moved but part of the distance required, when a column of the Fifth Corps, coming to the assistance of the Second, and by order I resumed my former position.

16. *OR*, 379.

17. *Ibid.*

18. *Ibid.*

19. *Ibid.*, 379–380.

20. Morgan, *Narrative*, 202–203.

21. *Ibid.*, 203–204.

22. *OR*, 380.

23. *Ibid.*

24. Morgan, *Narrative*, 202.

Chapter 8

1. Haskell, 24.

2. History Committee, *History of the Nineteenth Regiment Massachusetts Volunteer Infantry, 1861–1865* (cited hereafter as *Nineteenth Massachusetts*) (Massachusetts: The Salem Press Company, 1906), 229–230.

3. *OR*, 370.

4. *OR*, 416–417.

5. John Day Smith, *The History of the Nineteenth Regiment of Maine Volunteer Infantry* (cited hereafter as "Smith") (Minneapolis: Great Western Printing Company, 1909), 70.

6. Haskell, 24.

7. History Committee, *History of the Nineteenth Regiment Massachusetts Volunteer Infantry, 1861–1865* (Salem: The Salem Press Company, 1906), 229–230.

8. Haskell, 24.

9. *BP*, 1355. "Report of Lt. Col. Charles H. Morgan," undated.

10. *Ibid.*

11. Haskell, 22.

12. John L. Rhodes, *The History of Battery B, First Regiment Rhode Island Light Artillery, in the War to Preserve the Union 1862–1865* (Providence: Snow and Farnham, Printers, 1894), 200–201.

13. *Ibid.*, 201.

14. Minnesota, Board of Commissioners, *Minnesota in the Civil and Indian Wars, 1861–1865*, Volume II, 2nd ed. (St. Paul: The Pioneer Press Company, 1899), 34.

15. *Ibid.*, 35.

16. *Ibid.*

17. John Quinn Imholte, *The First Volunteers, History of the First Minnesota Volunteer Regiment, 1861–1865* (Minneapolis: Ross & Haines, Inc., 1963), 116.

18. *OR*, 880.

19. *Ibid.*

20. Smith, 69–70.

21. Silas Adams, "The Nineteenth Maine at Gettysburg (cited hereafter as "Adams"). Military Order of the Loyal Legions of the United States, Maine Commandery, War Papers Read Before the Commandery of the State of Maine, Military Order of the Loyal Legion of the United States, Volume IV (Portland: Lefavor–Tower Company, 1915), 252.

22. *Ibid.*, 252–253.

23. *BP*, 1136. WSH to Bachelder, 7 November 1885.

24. *Ibid.*, 1651.

25. Smith, 70.

26. Haskell, 25–26.

27. *Ibid.*, 26.

28. Statement of Winfield Scott Hancock, from *JCCW*, 407.

29. Gibbon, 137.

30. *OR*, 370.

31. Murray, *Harper's Ferry Cowards*, 73.

32. *OR*, 533.

33. *OR*, 417.

Chapter 9

1. Mulholland, *Annals*, 11.

2. Adams, 252.

3. Murray, *Harper's Ferry Coward,*. 74.

4. *OR*, 370.

5. *Ibid.*, 371.

6. *OR*, 474–475.

7. *OR*, 474.

8. *OR*, 474. It is not clear whether the regiment was MacDougall's or the 1st Minnesota.

9. Pfanz, *Second Day*, 407.

10. John Bigelow, *The Peach Orchard; Gettysburg; July 2, 1863* (Minneapolis: Kimball–Storer Company, 1910), 24.

11. *OR*, 315–316.

12. Morgan, *Narrative*, 198.

13. *OR*, 371.

14. B,. 1135. Hancock to Bachelder, 7 November 1885.

15. Francis A. Walker, *Second Army Corps*, 283.

16. *Ibid.*

17. Jasper N. Searles, "The First Minnesota Infantry, U.S. Volunteers." Address given April 4, 1888. *Glimpses of the Nation's Struggle*, Second Series, Minnesota Commandery of the Military Order of the Loyal Legion of the United States, Chaplain D.D. Edward D. Neill, ed. (St. Paul: St. Paul Book and Stationery Company, 1890) (Wilmington: Broadfoot Publishing Company, 1992), 105.

18. William Lochren, "Narrative of the First Regiment," *Minnesota in the Civil and Indian Wars, 1861–1865* (St. Paul: Board of Minnesota Civil and Indian Wars, 1891), 35.

19. *Ibid.*, 35–36.

20. *O.R.* 371.

21. Cadmus M. Wilcox, "General C. M. Wilcox on the Battle of Gettysburg," *Southern Historical Society Papers*, Volume VI (Richmond: Southern Historical Society, 1878) (Millwood: Kraus Reprint Company, 1977), 99.

22. *Ibid.*

23. Wilcox, *OR*, Part II (Part II of Volume XXVII contains Confederate as well as Union official reports of the Gettysburg Campaign. Thus, "Part II" differentiates herein the abridged references to Confederate official reports), 618.

24. MacDougall, *OR*, 474–475.

25. Charles Muller, *History Written by Charles Muller of Company A, First Minnesota Regiment of the Civil War*, unpublished manuscript. Minnesota Historical Society. 1921. As cited in John Quinn Imholte, *History of the First Minnesota Volunteer Regiment 1861–1865* (cited hereafter as *Imholte*) (Minneapolis: Ross & Haines Inc., 1963), 119–120.

26. Alfred P. Carpenter, Letter (copy) (Minnesota Historical Society: 1863). As cited in Imholte, 120.

27. Imholte, 113.

28. *Ibid.*, 116.

29. *Ibid.*, 125.

30. Winfield Scott Hancock, Letter to Francis Amasa Walker, 5 November 1885, Civil War Museum of Philadelphia.

31. *BP*, 1134. Hancock to Bachelder, 7 November 1885.

32. *OR*, 880.

33. Winfield Scott Hancock, Letter to Francis Amasa Walker, 5 November 1885, Civil War Museum of Philadelphia.

34. George H. Scott, "Vermont at Gettysburgh; An Address Delivered before the Society, July 6th, 1870," *Proceedings of the Vermont Historical Society*, 1930, Vermont Historical Society (cited hereafter as "Vermont at Gettysburgh") (Rutland: The Tuttle Company, Vermont), 62–64.

35. *OR*, 351.

36. *Ibid.*, 351–352.

37. *Ibid.*, 352.

38. Scott, "Vermont at Gettysburgh," 64.

39. *OR*, 352.

40. *Ibid.* Weir's official report states that he lost only three guns.

41. Scott, "Vermont at Gettysburgh," 64.

42. *Ibid.*, 65.

43. *Ibid.*

44. *Ibid.*

45. *Ibid.*

46. *Ibid.*

47. *Ibid.*, 65–66.

48. *OR*, 870.

49. *Ibid.*, 870–871.

50. Adams, 253.

51. *Ibid.*, 254.

52. *Ibid.*

53. *Ibid.*

54. *Ibid.*

55. *Ibid.*, 255.

56. *Ibid.*

57. *Ibid.*, 256.

58. *Ibid.*

59. *Ibid.*, 257.

60. *Ibid.*

61. *Ibid.*, 258.

62. Smith, 73.

63. Gibbon, 138.

64. *Ibid.* Brigadier General Henry Lockwood commanded the 2nd Brigade, 1st Division, Twelfth Corps.

65. *Ibid.*, 137–138.

66. *OR*, Part II, 618.

67. *Ibid.*, 631–632.

68. *OR*, Part II, 623–624.

69. *Ibid.*, 624.

70. *OR*, Part II, 633.

71. *Ibid.*, 633–634.

72. *Ibid.*, 634.

73. *Ibid.*, 621.

74. *Ibid.*

75. Pfanz, *Second Day*, 386.

76. *Ibid.*, 425.

77. Clinton MacDougall to Charles Richardson, Charles A. Richardson Papers (Canadaigua, New York: Ontario Historical Society) Bound copy in Gettysburg National Military Park Library. As cited in Eric A. Campbell, "'Remember Harper's Ferry!' The Degradation, Humiliation, and Redemption of Col. George L. Willard's Brigade"; Part 2, *Gettysburg Magazine*, Issue No. 8, 1 January 1993. 97.

78. *Ibid.,* 110.

79. Scott, "Vermont at Gettysburgh," 66.

80. *OR,* 372.

Chapter 10

1. Gibbon, 138.
2. Howard, *Autobiography,* 429.
3. Schurz, *Reminiscences,* 24.
4. Whittier, 87–88.
5. *Ibid.,* 85.
6. *Ibid.,* 85–86.
7. *Maine at Gettysburg,* 98.
8. Whittier, 88.
9. *Ibid.,* 88–89.
10. *Ibid.,* 89.
11. *Ibid.*
12. *Ibid.*
13. *Ibid.,* 90.
14. *Ibid.*
15. *Ibid.*
16. William Kepler, Ph.D., *History of the Fourth Regiment Ohio Volunteer Infantry in the War for the Union* (cited hereafter as Kepler) (Cleveland: Leader Printing Company, 1886), 128–129.
17. *OR,* 457.
18. Kepler, 129.
19. Schurz, *Reminiscences,* 25.
20. William Simmers and Paul Bachschmid, *The Volunteer's Manual, or Ten Months with the One Hundred and Fifty–third Pennsylvania Volunteers* (Easton: D. H. Neimann, 1863), 30. As cited in Pfanz, Harry W. *Gettysburg—Culp's Hill and Cemetery Hill* (Chapel Hill: The University of North Carolina Press, 1993), 269.
21. *OR,* 457.
22. Kepler, 129.
23. William Houghton, *Charge of Carroll's Brigade,* The "Cannonier" (no further specifics found). As cited in George H. Washburn, *Military History and Record of the 108th Regiment New York Volunteers from 1862 to 1894* (cited hereafter as Washburn) (Rochester: 1894), 54.
24. Schurz, *Reminiscences,* 25.
25. *Ibid.*
26. *OR,* 457.

27. Whittier, 91–92.

28. *Ibid.,* 92.

29. The "Cannonier," *Early's Charge at Gettysburg, Second Day* (no further specifics found). As cited in Washburn, 53–54.

30. *BP,* 235. Bruce R. Ricketts to Bachelder, 2 March 1866.

31. *Ibid.*

32. *Ibid.,* 235–236.

33. *Ibid.,* 236.

34. Henry J. Hunt, "The Second Day at Gettysburg," *Battles and Leaders of the Civil War,* Volume III, Part I (New York: The Century Company) (Harrisburg: The Archive Society, 1991), 313.

35. *OR,* 372.

Chapter 11

1. Abner Doubleday, *Campaigns of the Civil War; Chancellorsville and Gettysburg* (cited hereafter as *Chancellorsville and Gettysburg*) (New York: C. Scribner's Sons, 1882), 185.
2. *OR,* 372.
3. *Ibid.*
4. Gibbon, 138.
5. Whittier, 91.
6. Gibbon, 140.
7. Henry Hunt.
8. Gibbon, 140.
9. *Ibid.*
10. *Ibid.*
11. *Ibid.*
12. Statement of Gouverneur K. Warren, from *JCCW,* 379.
13. Gibbon, 140.
14. John Gibbon, "The Council of War on the Second Day," *Battles and Leaders,* 313.
15. *Ibid.,* 314.
16. *Ibid.,* 314.
17. Gibbon, 144.
18. *Ibid.,* 145.
19. *Ibid.*
20. *OR,* 372.
21. Samuel Hurst, *Journal–History of the Seventy–Third Ohio Volunteer Infantry* (Chillicothe: 1866), 72–73.
22. Gibbon, 145.

Chapter 12

1. Richard S. Thompson, "A Scrap of Gettysburg," *Military Essays and Recollections; Papers Read Before the Commandery of the State of Illinois, Military Order of the Loyal Legion of the United States,* Vol. III (cited hereafter as

Thompson) (Chicago: The Dial Press) (Wilmington: Broadfoot Publishing Company, 1992), 101.

2. Morgan, *Narrative*, 207.

3. Sturtevant, *Thirteenth Vermont*, 301.

4. Haskell, 38.

5. *Ibid.*, 40.

6. *Ibid.*, 41.

7. BP, 1394. John L. Brady, Letter to Bachelder, 24 May 1886.

8. *Ibid.*, 1394–95.

9. Bingham, *Manuscript*.

10. William P. Seville, "History of the First Regiment, Delaware Volunteers, From the Commencement of the "Three Months' Service" to the Final Muster–Out at the Close of the Rebellion," *Papers of the Historical Society of Delaware*, Volume 5 (Wilmington: The Historical Society of Delaware, 1884), 84.

11. BP, 1183–1184. Charles A. Hitchcock to Bachelder, 20 January 1886.

12. BP, 1395. John L. Brady, Letter to Bachelder, 24 May 1886.

13. Haskell, 41.

14. *Ibid.*

15. Thompson, 100–101.

16. Haskell, 43.

17. *Ibid.*

18. *Ibid.*, 44.

19. *Ibid.*, 42.

20. Sturtevant, *Thirteenth Vermont*, 289.

21. *Ibid.*, 289–291.

22. Hancock's Notes, 117.

23. Sturtevant, *Thirteenth Vermont*, 294.

24. BP, 868–870. Thomas F. Galwey to Bachelder, 19 May 1882.

25. BP, 1132. Franklin Sawyer to Bachelder, 20 October 1885.

26. *Ibid.*, 1132–1133.

27. The Vermonters were part of the 1st Corps, though temporarily their position was at the left flank of the Second Corps line.

28. Letter of David Shields, Hays, 450–451.

29. *Reminiscences*, 97.

30. Haskell, 45.

31. *Ibid.*, 47.

32. *Ibid.*, 45–46.

33. Morgan, *Narrative*, 207.

Chapter 13

1. Statement of Abner Doubleday, *Letters and Addresses*, 21.

2. *OR*, 373.

3. Statement of Winfield Scott Hancock, From *JCCW*, 410.

4. William P. Haines, *History of the Men of Company F, with Description of the Marches and Battles of the 12th New Jersey Volunteers* (cited hereafter as "Haines") (Mickleton, New Jersey: 1897), 41.

5. Sawyer, 130.

6. George R. Stewart, *Pickett's Charge, a microhistory of the final attack at Gettysburg, July 3, 1863* (cited hereafter as *Pickett's Charge*) (Boston: Houghton Mifflin Company, 1959), 152. Copyright renewed 1987.

7. Henry Hunt, "The Third Day at Gettysburg," *Battles and Leaders*, 372.

8. Gibbon, 149.

9. BP, 1360. "Report of Lt. Col. Charles H. Morgan," undated.

10. Bingham, *Manuscript*.

11. Statement of Abner Doubleday, *Letters and Addresses*, 21.

12. Walker, *General Hancock*, 82.

13. *OR*, 373.

14. BP, 228. Henry Hunt to Bachelder, 6 January 1866.

15. Henry Hunt, General Orders No. 94, 20 June 1862. Records of Headquarters, Artillery Reserve, Army of the Potomac. RG–393. National Archives. As quoted in Edward Longacre, *The Man Behind the Guns, A Biography of General Henry Jackson Hunt, Chief of Artillery, Army of the Potomac* (South Brunswick: A.S. Barnes & Co., 1977), 112. As cited in Eric A. Campbell, "'Full Authority over That Line of Battle…' or 'A Sheer…. Usurpation of Authority': A Brief History and Analysis of the Hunt–Hancock Controversy," *The Third Day—The Fate of a Nation—July 3 1863* (cited hereafter as Campbell, "Hancock–Hunt") (National Park Service, 2010), 244.

16. Henry Hunt, *OR*, Series I, 21: 828. As cited in Campbell, "Hancock–Hunt," 245.

17. *Ibid.*

18. BP, 229. Henry Hunt to Bachelder, 6 January 1866.

19. BP, 1361, "Report of Lt. Col. Charles H. Morgan," undated.

20. Schurz, *Reminiscences*, 28.

21. BP, 425–426. "Account of Brig. General Henry Hunt, Chief of Artillery, Army of the Potomac, with his additions in margins," 20 January 1873. Contains WSH quote.

22. *Ibid.*, 426.

23. BP, 1798. Patrick Hart to Bachelder, 23 February 1891. *Bachelder Papers* editors report adding punctuation to this letter.

24. BP, 170–171. Charles Phillips to Freeman McGilvery, 6 July 1863.

25. *BP*, 229. Henry Hunt to Bachelder, 6 January 1866.

26. *Ibid.*

27. *Ibid.*

28. Francis Amasa Walker, "General Hancock and the Artillery at Gettysburg," *Battles and Leaders*, 386.

29. *Ibid.*

30. *BP*, 432. "Account of Brig. Gen. Henry Hunt, Chief of Artillery, Army of the Potomac, with his additions in margins," 20 January 1873.

31. Statement of Henry J. Hunt, *JCCW*, 448.

32. *Ibid.*, 93.

33. *OR*, Series I, 25(1): 252. As cited in Campbell, "Hancock–Hunt," 247.

34. Statement of Henry J. Hunt, from *JCCW*, 93.

35. *BP*, 426. "Account of Brig. Gen. Henry Hunt, Chief of Artillery, Army of the Potomac, with his additions in margins," 20 January 1873.

36. *Ibid.*

37. Henry Hunt, *Battles & Leaders*, 293.

38. Statement of Henry J. Hunt, from *JCCW*, 448.

39. Letter of David Shields, in Hays, 451–452.

40. Coddington, 510.

41. *Ibid.*

42. *Pickett's Charge*, 149.

43. *Ibid.*, 157. Kent Masterson Brown, *Cushing of Gettysburg, The Story of a Union Artillery Commander* (The University Press of Kentucky, 1993), 251.

Chapter 14

1. James Longstreet, as quoted in Jeffry D. Wert, *General James Longstreet: The Confederacy's Most Controversial Soldier: A Biography* (New York: Simon & Schuster, 1993), 283.

2. *OR*, Part II, 623.

3. Statement of Henry J. Hunt from *JCCW*, 393.

4. Statement of Albion P. Howe from *JCCW*, 314.

5. William P. Haines, *History of the Men of Company F, with description of the Marches and Battles of the 12th New Jersey Volunteers* (cited hereafter as "Haines") (Mickleton: 1897), 41.

6. Thompson, 102.

7. Sturtevant, *Thirteenth Vermont*, 41.

8. Haines, 41.

9. George Grenville Benedict, *Army Life in Virginia; Letters from the Twelfth Vermont Regiment and Personal Experiences of Volunteer Service in the War of the Union, 1862–63* (cited hereafter as *Army Life*) (Burlington: Free Press Association, 1895), 177.

10. *OR*, 373.

11. *Ibid.*

12. Walker, *Second Army Corps*, 294.

13. *BP*, 870. Thomas F. Galwey to Bachelder, 19 May 1882.

14. *BP*, 1132. Franklin Sawyer to Bachelder, 20 October 1885.

15. *Ibid.*, 1132–1133.

16. *Ibid.*

17. Franklin Sawyer, *A Military History of the 8th Ohio Volunteer Infantry* (cited hereafter as "Sawyer") (Cleveland: Fairbanks and Company Printers, 1881), 130–131.

18. *Ibid.*, 131.

19. *BP*, 868, 870. Thomas F. Galwey to Bachelder, 19 May 1882.

20. Hays, 439.

21. *OR*, 373–374.

22. *Ibid.*, 374.

23. Gibbon, 152.

24. *BP*, 19. Alexander S. Webb to his wife, 6 July 1863.

25. Haskell, 61.

26. *Ibid.*

27. *BP*, 1878–1879. "Report of Col. Arthur J. Devereux," undated.

28. *Ibid.*, 1879.

29. *Ibid.*

30. *BP*, 1609. Arthur F. Devereux to Bachelder, 22 July 1889.

31. *OR*, 374.

32. *Ibid.*

33. *Ibid.*

34. Adams, 262.

35. *OR*, 374.

36. Benedict, *Army Life*, 177–178.

37. *Ibid.*, 178–179.

38. Sturtevant, *Thirteenth Vermont*, 311.

39. Sawyer, 132.

40. *BP*, 1133. Franklin Sawyer to Bachelder, 20 October 1885.

41. *BP*, 870. Thomas F. Galwey to Bachelder, 19 May 1882.

42. Benedict, *Army Life*, 180.

43. *Ibid.*, 182–184.

44. Sturtevant, *Thirteenth Vermont*, 319.

45. *BP*, 231. William G. Mitchell to WSH, 10 January 1866.

46. *Ibid.*

47. *Ibid.*, 232.

48. *Ibid.*, 1364. "Report of Lt. Col. Charles H. Morgan," undated.

49. *BP*, 351. Henry H. Bingham to WSH, 5 January 1869.

50. *OR*, 366.

51. Morgan, *Narrative*, 216.

Chapter 15

1. Thomas L. Livermore, *Days and Events, 1860–1866* (cited hereafter as Livermore) (Boston: Houghton Mifflin Company, 1920), 264.

2. Hays, 424.

3. *Ibid.*, 464–465.

4. *Ibid.*, 410.

5. Livermore, 264.

6. *Reminiscence*, 220.

7. *Ibid.*

8. *Ibid.*, 221.

9. George G. Benedict, "The Element of Romance in Military History," *War Paper No. 4*. Vermont Commandery of the Loyal Legion (Burlington: 1893) Reprinted in *Vermont War Papers and Miscellaneous States Papers and Addresses for Military Order of the Loyal Legion of the United States* (Wilmington: Broadfoot Publishing Company, 1994), 73.

10. *Ibid.*, 73–74.

11. *Ibid.*, 75.

12. Sturtevant, *Thirteenth Vermont*, 304–305.

13. *Ibid.*, 319.

14. "Vermont at Gettyburgh," 70–71.

15. Haskell, 69–70.

16. *Reminiscences*, 215.

17. *Ibid.*, 221–222.

18. *BP*, 351, 352. Letter of Henry H. Bingham to WSH, 5 January 1869.

19. *Ibid.*, 351.

Chapter 16

1. Abraham Lincoln to George Meade, 14 July 1863. Excerpt from a rediscovered letter as published by the New York Times, 8 June 2007. Lincoln thought better after writing it and never sent it.

2. Robert Lincoln, quoted in *An Oral History of Abraham Lincoln; John G. Nicolay's Interviews and Essays*, Michael Burlinghame, ed., Board of Trustees (Southern Illinois University, 2006), 88.

3. *Ibid.*

4. Hancock, 408.

5. *Ibid.*

6. *Ibid.*

7. *Ibid.*, 409.

8. William Kepler, *Fourth Regiment Ohio Volunteer Infantry in the War for the Union*

(Cleveland: Leader Printing Company, 1886), 131.

9. Statement of Henry J. Hunt, *JCCW*, 455.

10. Statement of Abner Doubleday and a question by Mr. Chandler of the committee, *JCCW*, 311.

11. Statement of Albion P. Howe, *JCCW*, 314.

12. Statement of Abner Doubleday, *JCCW*, 455.

13. Statement of Andrew A. Humphreys, *JCCW*, 394.

14. Statement of James S. Wadsworth, *JCCW*, 414.

15. Statement of Gouverneur K. Warren, *JCCW*, 378.

16. *OR*, 366.

17. Statement of Winfield Scott Hancock, *JCCW*, 408.

18. Statement of George Gordon Meade, *JCCW*, 333.

19. *Ibid.*

20. Statement of Winfield Scott Hancock, *JCCW*, 409.

21. Doubleday, *Chancellorsville and Gettysburg*, 202–203.

22. Statement of Winfield Scott Hancock, *JCCW*, 408–409.

23. *Ibid.*, 409.

24. Statement of Henry J. Hunt, *JCCW*, 455.

25. *OR*, 61.

26. Statement of George Gordon Meade, *JCCW.* 329.

27. Statement of Gouverneur K. Warren, *JCCW*, 378.

28. Statement of Winfield Scott Hancock, *JCCW*, 409.

Chapter 17

1. Statement of John F. Hartranft, *Letters and Addresses*, 19.

Chapter 18

1. Statement of John F. Hartranft, *Letters and Addresses*, 20.

2. A. M. Gambone, *Hancock at Gettysburg ... and beyond* (cited hereafter as Gambone) (Baltimore: Butternut and Blue, 1997), 168.

3. *Philadelphia Times*, undated clipping. Courtesy Historical Society of Montgomery County. As cited in Gambone, 169.

4. Gambone, 170.

5. *Ibid.*, 170.

6. *Ibid.*

7. David Xavier Junkin, *The Life of Winfield Scott Hancock: Personal, Military, and Political* (cited hereafter as Junkin) (New York: D. Appleton and Company, 1880), 125.

8. Samuel S. Carroll, *Army and Navy Journal*, 20 February 1864, 403. As quoted in John Gibbon, *Personal Recollections of the Civil War* (New York: G.P. Putnam's Sons, 1928) (Dayton, OH: Press of Morningside Bookshop, 1978), 201–202.

9. *Ibid.*, 205.

10. Junkin, 125–126.

11. Jordan, 107.

12. Junkin, 125–126.

13. Walker, *General Hancock*, 152.

14. *Ibid.*, 158. Jordan, 105.

15. Walker, *General Hancock*, 180.

16. *Ibid.*

17. Walker, *Second Army Corps*. 470.

18. Walker, *General Hancock*, 200. Walker had published a nearly identical passage in Walker, *Second Army Corps*, 472–473.

19. *Ibid.*, 201–202.

20. Walker, *Second Army Corps*, 487.

21. *OR*, Series I, Volume XXXVI, Part III, 441.

22. Walker, *Second Army Corps*, 506.

23. *OR*, Series I, Volume XXXVI, Part I, 344.

24. Walker, *General Hancock*, 219.

25. *Ibid.*

26. *Ibid.*

27. *Ibid.*, 222.

28. *OR*, Series I, Volume XXXVI, Part III, 531.

29. *Ibid.*

30. Walker, *General Hancock*, 224.

31. Ulysses S. Grant, *Personal Memoirs of U.S. Grant* (New York: Da Capo Press, Inc., 1982), 444.

32. Walker, *General Hancock*, 227.

33. Walker, *Second Army Corps*, 522.

34. Walker, *General Hancock*, 229.

35. Walker, *General Hancock*, 230.

36. *Ibid.*

37. *Ibid.*, 231.

38. *Ibid.*, 231–233.

39. *OR*, Series I, Volume XXXVI, Part I, 304.

40. *Ibid.*

41. Walker, *General Hancock*, 233–234.

42. *Ibid.*, 234–235.

43. Walker, *Second Army Corps*, 539.

44. *OR*, Series I, Volume XL, Part I, 307.

45. Walker, *Second Army Corps*, 547.

46. Jordan, 152.

47. Walker, *General Hancock*, 262–263. Jordan, 160.

48. *OR*, Series I, Volume XLII, Part I, 227.

49. Charles Morgan, as quoted in Walker, *General Hancock*, 275.

50. *OR*, Series I, Volume XLII, Part II, 486.

51. Jordan, 166.

52. Walker, *General Hancock*, 286. Jordan, 168.

53. *OR*, Series I, Volume XLII, Part I, 236.

54. Walker, *General Hancock*, 288.

55. *Ibid.*, 288–289.

56. *Ibid.*, 290.

57. Jordan, 173, 174.

58. *Ibid.*, 174.

59. Walker, *General Hancock*, 294.

60. Jordan, 174.

61. *Reminiscences*, 107–108.

62. *Ibid.*, 108.

63. Junkin, 274–275.

64. *Reminiscences*, 109.

65. Junkin, 276.

66. *The Statutes at Large, Treaties and Proclamations of the United States of America*, Volume XIV, George P. Sanger, ed. (Boston: Little, Brown, 1868), 354.

67. Walker, *General Hancock*, 296.

68. Junkin, 279. Jordan, 183.

69. Jordan, 183–199.

70. Jordan, 199.

71. Junkin, 294.

72. Jordan, 205.

73. Statement of William Farrar Smith, *Letters and Addresses*, 4.

74. Junkin, 307.

75. *Ibid.*, 307–308.

76. Letter by Winfield Scott Hancock, Junkin, 308.

77. Walker, *General Hancock*, 303.

78. Junkin, 333.

79. Jordan, 229.

80. *Reminiscences*, 144.

81. *Ibid.*, 147.

82. *Ibid.*

83. *Ibid.*, 147–148.

84. *Ibid.*, 149–150.

85. Tucker, 298–299.

86. Winfield Scott Hancock, Letter to Sherman, 28 December 1876. Junkin, 354.

87. *Ibid.*, 358.

88. Jordan, 243–244.

89. Junkin, 371.

90. *Ibid.*, 370–371.

91. Jordan, 249–250.

92. *Ibid.*, 305–306.

93. *Ibid.*, 306.

94. Walker, *General Hancock*, 307–308.
95. *Reminiscences*, 172.
96. Walker, *General Hancock*, 308.
97. *Reminiscences*, 179–180.
98. *Ibid.*, 176–177.
99. *Ibid.*, 178–179.
100. *BP*, 10.
101. *Ibid.*, 11.
102. *Ibid.*, 1949.
103. *Ibid.*
104. *Ibid.*, 1946.
105. Gambone, 197. Jordan, 313–314.
106. Gambone, 198. Jordan, 314.
107. Gambone, 200. Jordan, 314–315.
108. Gambone, 200–201. Jordan, 315.
109. Tucker, 310–311.
110. Jordan, 310–311.

Chapter 19

1. Bingham, *Oration*. 13.
2. Jordan, 252. James B. Fry, "Origin and Progress of the Military Service Institution of the United," *Journal of the Military Service Institution of the United States*, Volume I, 1880, 20–25.
3. Statement of William B. Franklin, *Letters and Addresses*, 14, 15.
4. Statement of William P. Wilson, *Letters and Addresses*, 29.
5. Statement of W. D. W. Miller, *Letters and Addresses*, 32.
6. Statement of Thomas B. Musgrave, *Letters and Addresses*, 63.
7. Statement of Edward L. Molineux, *Letters and Addresses*, 48.
8. Statement of Nelson A. Miles, *Letters and Addresses*, 72.
9. Statement of John P. Nicholson, *Letters and Addresses*, 44.
10. *Ibid.*
11. Statement of John F. Hartranft, *Letters and Addresses*, 19.
12. Statement of William Tecumseh Sherman, *Letters and Addresses*, 10.
13. Statement of Orlando B. Willcox, *Letters and Addresses*, 23.
14. Statement of Daniel E. Sickles, *Letters and Addresses*, 17.
15. Statement of James Grant Wilson, *Letters and Addresses*, 45.
16. Statement of Orlando B. Willcox, *Letters and Addresses*, 21.
17. Statement of Egbert L. Viele, *Letters and Addresses*, 46.
18. Statement of George W. Cullum, *Letters and Addresses*, 24.
19. Statement of William B. Franklin, *Letters and Addresses*, 14.
20. Statement of John B. Gordon, *Letters and Addresses*, 70.
21. Statement of William P. Wilson, *Letters and Addresses*, 28.
22. Statement of Horatio C. King, *Letters and Addresses*, 49.
23. Statement of Nelson A. Miles, *Letters and Addresses*, 71–72.

Bibliography

Adams, Silas. "The Nineteenth Maine at Gettysburg." War Papers Read Before the Commandery of the State of Maine, Military Order of the Loyal Legion of the United States, Volume IV. Military Order of the Loyal Legions of the United States, Maine Commandery. Portland, ME: Lefavor-Tower Company, 1915.

Arnold, James, and Wiener, Roberta. *Order of Battle; Gettysburg July 2 1863; Union: The Army of the Potomac.* Oxford: Osprey, 2000.

Barlow, John W. *Major General Winfield S. Hancock Memorial Meeting, March 3, 1886.* War Papers Read Before the Commandery of the State of Wisconsin, Military Order of the Loyal Legion of the United States, Volume I. Milwaukee: Burdick, Armitage and Allen, 1891.

Benedict, George Grenville. *Army Life in Virginia: Letters from the Twelfth Vermont Regiment and Personal Experiences of Volunteer Service in the War of the Union, 1862–1863.* Burlington, VT: Free Press Association, 1895.

Benedict, George Grenville. "The Element of Romance in Military History." *War Paper No. 4,* Vermont Commandery of the Loyal Legion, Burlington, Vermont, 1893. Reprinted in *Vermont War Papers and Miscellaneous States Papers and Addresses for Military Order of the Loyal Legion of the United States.* Wilmington, NC: Broadfoot Publishing Company, 1994.

Biddle, James C. "General Meade at Gettysburg." *Annals of the War* (originally published in the *Philadelphia Weekly Times*). Philadelphia: The Times Publishing Company, 1879.

Bigelow, John. *The Peach Orchard; Gettysburg; July 2, 1863.* Minneapolis: Kimball—Storer Company, 1910.

Bingham, Henry H. *Memoirs of Hancock by General Henry H. Bingham of Philadelphia,* 1872, manuscript. Copy in the Gettysburg National Military Park library, vertical file #5–45. Originals are in the collection of the Western Reserve Historical Society. Cleveland, Ohio.

Bingham, Henry W. *Oration at the Unveiling of the Equestrian Statue of Major General Winfield Scott Hancock on the Battlefield of Gettysburg, June 5, 1896.* Philadelphia, 1899.

Brown, Kent Masterson. *Cushing of Gettysburg, The Story of a Union Artillery Commander.* University Press of Kentucky, 1993.

Campbell, Eric A. "'Full Authority Over That Line of Battle' ... or 'A Sheer.... Usurpation of Authority': A Brief History and Analysis of the Hunt-Hancock Controversy." *The Third Day—The Fate of a Nation—July 3 1863.* National Park Service, 2010.

Campbell, Eric A. "'Remember Harper's Ferry!' The Degradation, Humiliation, and Redemption of Col. George L. Willard's Brigade"; Part 2. *Gettysburg Magazine,* Issue #8. 1 January 1993.

Carpenter, John A. "General O. O. Howard at Gettysburg." *Civil War History,* Volume 9, No. 3. September 1963.

Century Company. *Battles and Leaders of the Civil War.* Volume III, Parts I and II. New York. Harrisburg, PA: The Archive Society, 1991.

Christ, Elwood W. *The Struggle for the Bliss Farm at Gettysburg.* Baltimore: Butternut and Blue, 1994.

Coddington, Edwin B. *The Gettysburg Campaign; A Study in Command.* Paperback edition. New York: Charles Scribner's Sons, 1984.

Cooke, Sidney G. "The First Day at Gettysburg." *War Talks in Kansas.* Kansas City, MO: Press of the Franklin Hudson Publishing Company, 1906. Wilmington, NC: Broadfoot Publishing Company, 1992. Reprint.

Davis, Charles E. Jr. *Three Years in the Army; The Story of the Thirteenth Massachusetts Volunteers from July 16, 1861 to August 1, 1864*. Boston: Estes and Lauriat, 1894.

Denison, C. W., and Herbert, G. B. *Hancock "The Superb": The Early Life and Public Career of Winfield S. Hancock, Major-General U.S.A.* Cincinnati, OH: Forshee & McMakin, 1880.

Doubleday, Abner. *Campaigns of the Civil War; Chancellorsville and Gettysburg*. New York: C. Scribner's Sons, 1882.

Fleming, George, ed. *Life and Letters of Alexander Hays*. Edited and arranged with notes and contemporary history by from data compiled by Gilbert Adams Hays. Pittsburgh, 1919.

Forney, John W. *Life and Military Career of Winfield Scott Hancock*. Philadelphia: Hubbard Brothers, 1880.

Fox, William F. *Regimental Losses in the American Civil War 1861–1865*. Albany: Albany Publishing Company, 1893.

Fry, James B. "Origin and Progress of the Military Service Institution of the United." *Journal of the Military Service Institution of the United States*, Volume I. 1880.

Gambone, A. M. *Hancock at Gettysburg ... and beyond*. Baltimore: Butternut and Blue, 1997.

Gibbon, John. *Personal Recollections of the Civil War*. New York: G.P. Putnam's Sons, 1928. Dayton, OH: Press of Morningside Bookshop, 1978. Reprint.

Goodrich, Frederick E. *The Life and Public Services of Winfield Scott Hancock, Major-General, U.S.A.* Boston MA: Lee & Shepard, 1880.

Grant, Ulysses S. *Personal Memoirs of U.S. Grant*. New York: Da Capo Press, Inc., 1982. Republication of 1952 Ed.

Haines, William P. *History of the Men of Company F, with Description of the Marches and Battles of the 12th New Jersey Volunteers*. Mickleton, NJ: 1897.

Hancock, Almira R., *Reminiscences of Winfield Scott Hancock*. New York: Charles L. Webster & Co., 1887.

Hancock, Winfield Scott. "Gettysburg; Reply to General Howard." *The Galaxy*, Volume XXII, June, 1876 to January, 1877. New York: AMS Press Inc.

Harrison, Kathleen G. *Cultural Landscape Report Emmitsburg Road Ridge*, Volume II, Part I. July 2004. Gettysburg National Military Park.

Haskell, Frank Aretas. *The Battle of Gettysburg*. A paper published by the Military Order of

the Loyal Legion of the United States, Commandery of the State of Massachusetts, Boston, 1908.

History Committee. *History of the Nineteenth Regiment Massachusetts Volunteer Infantry, 1861–1865*. Salem, MA: The Salem Press Company, 1906.

Hoffman, J. W. "Field Operations at Gettysburg." Paper annotated 1896. Contained in *Military Essays and Recollections of the Pennsylvania Commandery Military Order of the Loyal Legion of the United States*, Volume I. 22 February 1866—May 6, 1903. Compiled by Michael A. Cavanaugh. Wilmington, NC: Broadfoot Publishing Company, 1995.

Howard, Charles H. "First Day at Gettysburg," *Military Essays and Recollections, IV*. Commandery of the State of Illinois, MOLLUS. 258.

Howard, Oliver Otis. "Campaign and Battle of Gettysburg, June and July 1863." *The Atlantic Monthly*, Volume 38. July, 1876.

Hunt, Henry J. "The Second Day at Gettysburg," *Battles and Leaders of the Civil War*, Volume III, Part I. New York: The Century Company. Harrisburg, PA: The Archive Society, 1991. Reprint.

Hurst, Samuel. *Journal-History of the Seventy-Third Ohio Volunteer Infantry*. Chillicothe, OH: 1866.

Imholte, John Quinn. *The First Volunteers, History of the First Minnesota Volunteer Regiment, 1861–1865*. Minneapolis: Ross & Haines, Inc., 1963.

Johnson, Robert Underwood, and Buel, Clarence Clough, eds. *Battles & Leaders of the Civil War*, Volume III, Parts I-II. New York: The Century Company, 1887–1888. Harrisburg, PA: The Archive Society, 1991. Facsimile Reprint Ed.

Jordan, David M. *Winfield Scott Hancock, A Soldier's Life*. Bloomington, IN: Indiana University Press, 1988.

Junkin, David Xavier. *The Life of Winfield Scott Hancock: Personal, Military, and Political*. New York: D. Appleton and Company, 1880.

Kepler, William, Ph.D. *History of the Fourth Regiment Ohio Volunteer Infantry in the War for the Union*. Cleveland, OH: Leader Printing Company, 1886.

Ladd, David L., and Audrey J., eds. *The Bachelder Papers; Gettysburg in Their Own Words*, 3 Volumes. Dayton, OH: Morningside House, Inc., 1995.

Lee, Fitzhugh. "A Review of the First Two Days' Operations at Gettysburg and a Reply to

General Longstreet by General Fitzhugh Lee." *Southern Historical Society Papers*, Volume V, January to June, 1878. Millwood, NY: Kraus Reprint Co., 1977.

Livermore, Thomas L. *Days and Events, 1860–1866*. Boston: Houghton Mifflin, 1920.

Lochren, William. "Narrative of the First Regiment." *Minnesota in the Civil and Indian Wars, 1861–1865*. Board of Minnesota Civil and Indian Wars. St. Paul, 1891.

Martin, David G. *Gettysburg July 1*. Conshohoken, PA: Combined Books, 1995.

Military Service Institution. *Letters and Addresses Contributed at a General Meeting of the Military Service Institution Held at Governor's Island, N.Y.H., February 25, 1886, in Memory of Winfield Scott Hancock*. New York: G. P. Putnam's Sons, 1886.

Minnesota, Board of Commissioners. *Minnesota in the Civil and Indian Wars, 1861–1865*, Volume II, 2d ed. St. Paul: The Pioneer Press Company, 1899.

Mulholland, St. Clair A. "Hancock's Heroism Under Fire; A Graphic Recital of the Stirring Deeds of an Eventful Day." *Annals of the War; Chapters of Unwritten History; The Gettysburg Campaign; The Story of the Second Corps on the March and in Battle*. Philadelphia: McLaughlin Brothers, 1880.

Murray, R. L. *The Redemption of the "Harper's Ferry Cowards": The 111th and 126th New York State Volunteers at Gettysburg*. Wolcott, NY: Benedum Books, 1994.

New York Evening Post. 10 February 1886.

New York Herald. 10 February 1886.

Nicolay, John G. *An Oral History of Abraham Lincoln; John G. Nicolay's Interviews and Essays*, Burlinghame, Michael, ed. Board of Trustees, Southern Illinois University. Paperback Ed. 2006.

Osborn, Hartwell. *Trials and Triumphs: The Record of the Fifty-Fifth Ohio Volunteer Infantry*. Chicago: A. C. McLurg & Company, 1904.

Pfanz, Harry W. *Gettysburg: Culp's Hill and Cemetery Hill*. Chapel Hill: University of North Carolina Press, 1993.

Pfanz, Harry W. *Gettysburg: The Second Day*. Chapel Hill: The University of North Carolina Press, 1987.

Rhodes, John L. *The History of Battery B, First Regiment Rhode Island Light Artillery, in the War to Preserve the Union 1862–1865*. Providence, RI: Snow and Farnham, Printers, 1894.

Robertson, William Glenn. "The Peach

Orchard Revisited; Daniel E. Sickles and the Third Corps, July 2, 1863." *The Second Day at Gettysburg; Essays on Confederate and Union Leadership*. Gary W. Gallagher, ed. Kent, OH: The Kent State University Press, 1993.

Sawyer, Franklin. *A Military History of the 8th Regiment Ohio Volunteer Infantry*. Cleveland, OH: Fairbanks & Co. Printers, 1881.

Schurz, Carl. *The Reminiscences of Carl Schurz*, Volume III. New York: McClure, 1906.

Scott, George H. "Vermont at Gettysburgh; An Address Delivered before the Society, July 6th, 1870." *Proceedings of the Vermont Historical Society*. Vermont Historical Society. Rutland, VT: The Tuttle Company, 1930.

Searles, Jasper N. "The First Minnesota Infantry, U.S. Volunteers." Address given April 4, 1888. *Glimpses of the Nation's Struggle*. Second Series. Minnesota Commandery of the Military Order of the Loyal Legion of the United States. Chaplain Edward D. Neill, D.D., ed. St. Paul: St. Paul Book and Stationery Company, 1890. Wilmington, NC: Broadfoot Publishing Company, 1992. Reprint.

Seville, William P. "History of the First Regiment, Delaware Volunteers, From the Commencement of the "Three Months' Service" to the Final Muster-Out at the Close of the Rebellion." *Papers of the Historical Society of Delaware*, Volume 5. The Historical Society of Delaware. Wilmington, DE: 1884.

Smith, John Day. *The History of the Nineteenth Regiment of the Maine Volunteer Infantry 1862–1865*. Minneapolis: The Great Western Printing Company, 1909.

Stevens, Greenlief T., and Whittier, Edward N. "Stevens' Fifth Maine Battery at the Battle of Gettysburg." *Maine at Gettysburg; Report of Maine Commissioners*. Maine Gettysburg Commissioners' Executive Committee. Portland, ME: The Lakeside Press Engravers, Printers and Binders, 1898.

Stewart, George R. *Pickett's Charge, A microhistory of the final attack at Gettysburg, July 3, 1863*, Boston: Houghton Mifflin, 1959. Copyright renewed 1987.

Sturtevant, Ralph Orson. *Pictorial History Thirteenth Vermont Volunteers War of 1861–1865*. Vermont Regimental Association, 1910.

Styple, William B. ed. *Generals in Bronze, Interviewing the Commanders of the Civil War*. Kearny, NJ: Belle Grove Publishing Company, 2005.

Swinton, William. *Campaigns of the Army of the*

Potomac. New York: Charles B. Richardson, 1866.

Swinton, William. *The Twelve Decisive Battles of the War: A History of the Eastern and Western Campaigns, in Relation to the Actions That Decided Their Issue.* New York: Dick & Fitzgerald, Publishers, 1867.

Thompson, Richard S. "A Scrap of Gettysburg." *Military Essays and Recollections; Papers Read Before the Commandery of the State of Illinois, Military Order of the Loyal Legion of the United States, Vol. III.* Chicago: The Dial Press. Wilmington, NC: Broadfoot Publishing Company, 1992. Reprint.

Tucker, Glenn. "Hancock at Gettysburg." *The Bulletin of the Historical Society of Montgomery County.* Volume XIII, no. 4. Spring, 1963.

Tucker, Glenn. *Hancock the Superb.* Indianapolis, IN: The Bobbs-Merrill Company, Inc., 1960. Dayton, OH: Press of Morningside Bookshop, 1980. Reprint.

United States Congress. *Report of the Joint Committee on the Conduct of the War at the Second Session, Thirty-Eighth Congress.* Washington, D.C.: U.S. Government Printing Office, 1865.

United States War Department. *The War of the Rebellion: A Compilation of the Official Records of the Union and Confederate Armies.* 128 Volumes. Washington, D.C.: Government Printing Office, 1880–1901.

Wainwright, Charles S. *A Diary of Battle; The Personal Journals of Charles S. Wainwright 1861–1865.* Allan Nevins, ed. New York: Harcourt, Brace & World, Inc., 1998.

Walker, Francis A. *Great Commanders: General Hancock.* New York: D. Appleton and Company, 1895.

Walker, Francis A. *Hancock in the War of the Rebellion.* A paper read at a meeting of the New York Commandery of Military Order of the Loyal Legion of the United States, February 4, 1891. Published in "Personal Recollections of the Rebellion." New York Commandery Loyal Legion. 1891.

Walker, Francis A. *History of the Second Army Corps.* New York: Charles Scribner's Sons, 1886.

Washburn, George H. *Military History and Record of the 108th Regiment New York Volunteers from 1862 to 1894.* Rochester, 1894.

Watrous, J. A. *Major General Winfield S. Hancock Memorial Meeting, March 3, 1886.* War Papers Read Before the Commandery of the State of Wisconsin, Military Order of the Loyal Legion of the United States, Volume I. Milwaukee: Burdick, Armitage and Allen, 1891.

Wert, Jeffry D. *General James Longstreet: The Confederacy's Most Controversial Soldier: A Biography.* New York: Simon & Schuster, 1993.

Whittier, Edward N. "The Left Attack (Ewell's) at Gettysburg." *Civil War Papers: Military Order of the Loyal Legion of the United States, Commandery of the State of Massachusetts, Volume I.* Boston, MA: 1900.

Wilcox, Cadmus M. "General C. M. Wilcox on the Battle of Gettysburg." *Southern Historical Society Papers,* Volume VI. Southern Historical Society. Richmond, VA: 1878. Millwood, NY: Kraus Reprint Company, 1977.

Index

Numbers in **bold italics** indicate pages with photographs.